RADICAL CULTURE

RADICAL CULTURE

Discourse, Resistance and Surveillance,
1790–1820

David Worrall

WAYNE STATE UNIVERSITY PRESS
DETROIT

U.S. Edition published by
Wayne State University Press
Detroit, Michigan, 48202

Typeset in 10/12 pt Palatino
by Photoprint, Torquay, Devon
Printed and bound in Great Britain by
BPCC Wheatons Ltd, Exeter

Library of Congress Catalog Card
Number 92–064371

ISBN 0–8143–2452–5

Contents

Contents

List of Figures

List of Figures

Preface

'I suspect however the lower Class have some separate game playing', the Government's spymaster Richard Ford told his deeply covert spy John Moody, alias 'Notary', during the run up to Colonel Despard's abortive *coup d'état* in the autumn of 1802. *Radical Culture* is my once-in-a-lifetime opportunity to try to give something back.

Iain McCalman's *Radical Underworld: Prophets, Revolutionaries and Pornographers in London, 1795–1840* has proved an inspiration and my effort retains more than just a similarity of title with this pioneering work. E.P. Thompson's *The Making of the English Working Class* has proved as formative to me now as it was when I first read it in conjunction with David V. Erdman's *Blake: Prophet Against Empire*. To David Erdman I owe many subtle debts of support and encouragement over many years. Advisers and patient sounding-boards have been colleagues and friends, Morton D. Paley, Marion Lomax and Steve Clark, co-organizer of the 'Historicizing Blake' conference in 1990 which helped me focus on what I was doing. The staff of the British Library and the Public Record Office at Kew have been uniformly civil and helpful. I am grateful to the Public Record Office, the British Library and the British Museum's Department of Prints and Drawings and Department of Coins and Medals for allowing me to make use of their holdings. My greatest thanks are to June who has coped cheerfully with piles of paper in the living room.

Jackie Jones at Harvester Wheatsheaf has been an exemplary editor, from the first glint. All errors are my own. I have retained the idiomatic spelling of the many contemporary manuscripts I have consulted. Where there might be unnecessary confusion, I have included '[*sic*]'. Illegibility, I have signalled by 'xxxx'.

Introduction

'I have nothing to complain of in my treatment except the most material[:] my confinement.' These are the words of Thomas Evans, author, debating club organizer and Spencean activist, recorded by an official who had been sent to Surrey gaol to interview him concerning his complaint about his conditions of confinement under the provisions of the Suspension of Habeas Corpus Bill passed in February 1817. The conditions were reasonably civilized. Evans had books, 'dumb bells for his exercise', pen, ink, paper and a 'Telescope' but at the time of his interview he had been in prison for six months without charge or trial and it would be another six months before he was released without indictment. His son, Thomas John Evans, was also in the same gaol under the same circumstances.[1]

Although the Habeas Corpus Act had been suspended during the wartime conditions of 1794 and 1798, by 1817 England was no longer at war with France and reasons for this peace-time Suspension Bill were considerations of internal rather than external security. The December before there had been a riot or uprising at a Spencean-organized meeting held at Spa Fields, London and the Spenceans were becoming known as the 'Ultra (or Fighting) Radicals', more extreme than reforming radicals like Burdett, Cochrane or Hunt and 'considered as the most determined for carrying the Government by force of Arms of any in London'.[2] It was this fear, subsequently unsubstantiated at James Watson Snr's trial for high treason in June 1817, which precipitated the Suspension Bill. The Suspension removed all civil rights simply by virtue of the power to imprison without trial. The subject, devoid of liberty, was powerless to do anything other than, like Thomas Evans, plead mercy of his captors.

1

Introduction

Although the Suspension Bill did not give the magistracy or judiciary general powers to imprison without trial and though imprisonments under its conditions had to be personally authorized by a member of the Privy Council, for the individual so incarcerated, the Suspension of Habeas Corpus was a suspension of all laws protective of liberty.

This effective removal of civil liberty is the basis of my dialogue and interrogation of what I report here because I take it that this resistance to perceived oppression is the mentality of all of the personalities discussed in these pages. Objectively, the Habeas Corpus Act, in its unsuspended state, gave only poorly defined and difficult to implement protection. Nevertheless, the suspension allowed all those deemed by the Home Office subversive of the State to be put into prison and taken out of political circulation. Thomas Evans was one of those Spenceans who had been associated, in the Government's mind, with the Spa Fields rising. Evans had been imprisoned under the last Suspension in 1798 on quite good evidence (as the Government viewed it) but he had not been found at the scene of any of the crimes against person or property committed during the rowdy night of broken-open gunshops and general mayhem which took place in the vicinity of the Tower on the night of 2 December 1816. Evans was imprisoned in 1817 for activities which were political and not criminal: he was an articulate ideologue. Evans's prison interviewer found him 'a man of strong acute mind' 'who has read Q remember'd a good deal', a man capable of 'very fluent & most elaborate bursts of eloquence'.[3] A Government informer, a 'Mr. Clarke', had already found Evans, a month before Spa Fields, addressing a fifty-strong group in the Nag's Head, Carnaby Market. Evans was there to elaborate 'Spence's System'.

The basic tenets of 'Spence's Plan', which are of fundamental importance to this book, could be encapsulated in the briefest of terms for the least educated. Under 'Spence's Plan' all land was to be owned by the people, administered by the parish, and all rental profits distributed equally to every man, woman and child. This was to be implemented by a revolutionary uprising or *coup d'état*. That was it. There were other refinements, but national land incorporation and rental redistribution was the basis of the Spencean ideology.[4] It was an ideology which brooked no compromise and it had the participation of its culture: at the Nag's Head in early 1817, 'Evans stated &c that the Land was the Peoples right &c, [and] asked every Individual present if they agreed, and each answered Yes upon their Honour'.[5]

Radical Culture is about the ability of Evans to hold that dialogue with the Nag's Head audience. Verbal articulacy and the circulation of a set of revolutionary texts in a political context of laws enacted against seditious assembly and seditious utterance is the main theme of this book. Above anything else, I want to make this radical culture visible, to operate a recovery in the tradition so firmly established by feminist literary history. My book is produced from the thousands of spy and informer reports, seized documents and pamphlets which constituted the Home Office's surveillance of the populace both during the Napoleonic War, when there was the semblance of an excuse for such surveillance, as well as afterwards when there wasn't. My study ends quite artificially in 1820 with the execution of the Cato Street conspirators but nothing stopped there because it was impossible to dismantle a culture. The Spencean land issue gradually transformed itself into an element of the Chartist platform of the 1830s and 1840s. As for the oppressive powers of Government, E.P. Thompson in beginning his account of Cato Street in *The Making of the English Working Class* remarks that 1820 was only the beginning of 'the most sustained campaign of prosecutions in the courts in British history'.[6]

Ireland and Irish metropolitan activism also comprises a scattered but recurrent subject in *Radical Culture*. The cultural trace of the London-based Spenceans, I have too lately come to realize, is Ireland. Out of Ireland came the emphasis on tillage rather than pasture, on small farms rather than agricultural enclosure and, most importantly, on rebellion rather than reform. Behind the duality of the criminal/political underworld of the Spenceans lies the shadowy outline of the cultural and political apparatuses of Irish groups like the Caravats, Shanavests and Whiteboys who were able to direct physical violence towards a local and national political end, to articulate a viable culture and to alternate between politics and criminality.[7] Ireland's French-backed invasions, most notably the well-funded one initiated by Wolfe Tone, only made Ireland more attractive as a model for English revolutionaries.[8]

Radical Culture claims to be a theorized book. Its theoretical structure is not worn upon the sleeve but, instead, has been assimilated, but there are some glaring limitations. I have tried to avoid obvious historical tropes, such as irony, and I have tried not to make my writing gender specific. I have probably been less successful at eliminating melodrama and I have been completely unable to avoid the central problem that much of my text has been produced by those who were doing the surveillance of the culture I report. Police spies like the veteran John Stafford, who was chief clerk at Bow Street, presumably reported what they thought would be useful. On the other hand, informers (or voluntary spies as one might call them) such as John Shegog, the Tower labourer and Whitechapel preacher, may have allowed themselves more autonomy in expressing opinions because they had no civil context to which they might be referred. Balancing out the status of the different types of information is something I have not done. In turn, there is a connected problem of the role of my narrativity: again, this has presented a problem which has seemed to me to be effectively insuperable.

Radical Culture also has a more general claim to make about the artisan ultra-radicals whose experiences form the subject of this book. Taking my lead from developments implicit in Ferdinand de Saussure's *Course in General Linguistics* (1915), none of the discursive activities I comment on are marginal in terms of their place in the language system. Saussure's structuralist inquiries into language in the *Course* suggest that the signs which go to make up *parole* (an act of speech or utterance) can only be taken, ready made, from out of the available *langue* (the available and constituted language). This has important implications for the study of the historical texts studied in *Radical Culture*. It is not strictly necessary to prove the extent or the circulation of any ideology (which I think of as a readable formation of signs as texts), nor is it necessary to show that the performance of linguistic or other sign utterances is connected with other historical events involving human agency. Human agency is already in speech and writing which is already constructed as social. One utterance or *parole*, ideologically marked, proves the availability of the system of *langue* which, in turn, enables it to be infinitely articulated. To repeat, there are no discursively marginal figures in *Radical Culture*.

According to the implications of Saussure's descriptions, it would be incredible for the syntax of any particular *parole* to be unique. Because of Saussure's complementary insight that all signs are social, language cannot be modified or manufactured by any single human agent. Repeatability is inherent in articulation. No articulation can be marginalized linguistically because the 'marginal' *parole* is always an articulation already fully within the boundaries of the existing *langue*. To people like myself trained in English literary history, this point is an important one to establish because the traditional canon of literary Romanticism (six male poets plus Jane Austen) has been remarkably restrictive in its selection of the texts it has chosen to study. My crude interpretation of Saussure's structural linguistics is of some import-ance because I consistently examine, narrate and make visible discourse which may, at first, be considered marginal to the dominant cultural formations of the time. The ideology of Romanti-cism and its refined metaphysics, transmitted via the literary institution of canonical texts, was not intrinsically more valuable at the moment of its original historical production than any others less socially privileged. By insisting on a theorized position for their discursive activities, I hope to have pre-empted their marginalization.

However, although all areas of a culture employ signs, some signs are more pervasive and empowered than others. What *Radical Culture* sets out to show is the viability of the discursive systems which carried the Spencean ultra-radical ideology. Every ultra-radical utterance is already fully constituted elsewhere within the culture of its specific language system: there are no soliloquies. The ultra-radicals preferred speech to writing because the oral mode of textuality was less susceptible to scrutiny by the Government's surveillance system. This surveillance was reasonably systematic. Perhaps the case of the canonical poet Percy B. Shelley exemplifies the operation of surveillance and makes a context for my attitude to the institution of literary Romanticism, which is my lesser concern.

In 1812, during the war against the French, Shelley twice came to the attention of the Home Office.[9] His case typifies many others. The first incident was when a package of Shelley's *Declaration of Rights* and some private letters on discontent in Ireland were opened after having loitered too long near the Post Office in Holyhead, Anglesea. The second incident came when Shelley's servant, Dan Healey, was imprisoned for six months in Barnstaple, Devon, for bill-sticking the *Declaration of Rights* and 'The Devil's Walk' (Shelley's getting somebody else to bill-stick fits in with Spencean practices). The authorities in Barnstaple reported to the Home Office general suspicions of Shelley's radical activism. Both Lord Sidmouth, Secretary of State for the Home Office, and 'Mr. Beckett' the Under-Secretary who co-ordinated the surveillance of the Spa Fields meeting in 1816, advised the Barnstaple authorities before Shelley was lost to sight when he removed to Wales. At this stage in his career, Shelley was a person largely unknown to those beyond his immediate circle of family and friends. In other words, Shelley's brief moment in the glare of the Home Department's surveillance and intelligence gathering system makes him completely typical. Shelley, like E.J. Blandford, Allen Davenport and William Blake, was the subject of a system which found it difficult to discriminate between the different types of perceived threat they posed. Although Home Office intelligence gathering was fairly haphazard, its information backbone lay with local authorities, loyal zealots and a willingness to forward information as a matter of public duty, a busybodying diminishment of the civic ideal based upon alarmist and hearsay evidence. Shelley's bottle containing the *Declaration of Rights* fished out of the sea off Milford Haven (a fragment of a torn letter addressed to him being enough to identify him) is an example of the conscientious good fortune which characterized the Home Office's erratic surveillance.[10] However, the system was effective enough to transmit much intelligence information between provincial devolved authority and the centralized power, ensuring a more effective national surveillance than might be thought possible. Percy Shelley in 1812 was of less importance to the authorities than Preston, Blandford, Evans and Thistlewood were to become in the post-war years, but he still fell subject to similar aspects of the Government's scrutiny.

Meanwhile, at the sharp end of the law, the magistrates who made judgements about seditious activity were also inextricably involved in duties which extended beyond the judicial. Magistrates contributed to national surveillance and took an inescapably political role when they forwarded information about seditious activity to the Home Office in the course of applying for central funding for prosecutions (although no Home Office response to the allegations made against William Blake has so far come to light). Magistrates also sometimes combined the judicial/political with the spiritual when they doubled as local clergymen. William Hone's much reprinted satirical chapbook, *The Political House That Jack Built*, pictured 'The Clerical Magistrate', 'the State's Agent' who is a Janus-figure of a cleric back-to-back with a magistrate holding leg-irons, cat-o'-nine-tails and a gallows.[11] It is little wonder that anti-clericalism was so buoyant in radical circles. If clerical-magistrates were not enough, there was always the store of *ex officio* information to fall back upon.

Although informations *ex officio* were not used often, during the Suspension of Habeas Corpus the Home Office was busily taking down anonymous depositions which it might deploy at its convenience. In April 1817, 'A.A.' declared 'I further make oath that [?]W.R.L. repeatedly told me that the object of the Spenceans was to obtain the possession of the Land by violence'.[12] *Ex officio* informations, Suspensions of Habeas Corpus and routine spying during peace-time represent the nadir of the civic ideal. For the vast majority of the people who populated the taverns and conspiratorial meetings followed by spies and informers, there is no other record left than these secret narratives of 'Satans Watch-fiends', as William Blake called them.

Taken individually, the Spenceans may appear insignificant figures, people whose dogged articulacy and textual cat-and-mouse with the authorities have exerted little influence on our own culture. Even in Thompson's innovative account of them, they are edged off the agenda of industrialized labour organization presented in *The Making of the English Working Class*. Collectively, and in their enormous variety and quantity of discursive activity, their absent role in the outcome of modern English history is profound. Instead of an industrial economy, we could have had an agrarian society, even a 'green' one in the late-twentieth-century sense of the word. Instead of nineteenth-century imperialism, there might have been a self-sufficient and equable nation decentralized into parishes, perhaps even into a welfare state, on a Paineite model, whose clock could not be turned back by successive trimming and cutting. It did not have to be the way it is now.

Britain 1790–1820 was a spy culture. Even the surveillers were surveilled. On 28 November 1819 the informer 'B.C.' wrote to the Home Office with a routine piece of intelligence about the financing of communication between elements of the near-national revolutionary party:

> The person mentioned in former reports as *Benton* of Queens Sq. furnishing money at diferent times to Thiselwood is the noted *Jeremy Bentham* of Penitentiary celebrity he furnished money to send Walker back to Manchester last Week.[13]

Jeremy Bentham funded the leader of the Cato Street conspirators who had the intention of murdering the Cabinet. Occasionally desperate for revolutionary change in those post-Peterloo months, the inventor of the Panopticon had already been fixed in the Government's panoptic gaze.

CHAPTER ONE

Sedition and Articulacy in the 1790s

THOMAS SPENCE'S ARREST, 1792

Shortly before nine o'clock on the morning of Thursday 6 December 1792 the future radical bookseller William Hone was passing through Chancery Lane en route to 'a situation' when he came across Thomas Spence opening the shutters of his bookstall. Two Bow Street runners, prototypes for the capital's police force, appeared. One of them bought a book entitled *The Rights of Man*. The officer of the law was not, however, a disinterested student of post-Revolutionary British radical polemics. Hone knew that Spence clinched his sales with 'strong expressions of hate to the powers that were, & prophecies of what would happen to the whole race of "Land-lords" ' and the commotion to which Hone was the sole witness revealed that this was no ordinary book sale but Thomas Spence being 'pounced upon'.

Hone saw Spence remonstrate 'in dispute' with the runners who, 'With their usual ceremony', Spence retorted, marched him off to Hatton Garden magistrates. Spence's arrest happened some six months after the first Royal Proclamation against Seditious Writings and Publications (21 May 1792) and five days after a second Royal Proclamation had reinforced the first (1 December 1792). The staunching of Paine's *Rights of Man*, Part 2, was the principal object of the Royal Proclamation and it was Paine's book the Bow Street runner thought he had purchased.[1]

Over in Hatton Garden the magistrate perused the title page more closely. Something not quite right (the pamphlet perhaps a little slim?). Case dismissed! Embarrassingly, the Bow Street runner had purchased, not Paine's *Rights of Man*, but *The Rights of Man as Exhibited in a Lecture Read at the Philosophical Society in Newcastle*, author Thomas Spence. Finding 'no statute to justify him in it', the magistrate could offer no charge. Now it was Spence's turn. Spence 'told him in his defence that he might as well commit every one who sold Gulliver's Travels, More's Eutopia, Locke on Government, Puffendorf on the Law of Nature, &c. &c. all of which treated the subject of government in a manner vastly opposite to the British system'. Spence then went back to his bookstall.[2]

Four days later, Monday 10 December 1792, between two and three o'clock in the afternoon, two more Bow Street runners arrived. After first making sure they had purchased the right *Rights of Man*, Part 2, 'they obliged him to put up the shutters of his stall and hustled him into a hackney coach which they ordered to be driven to Bow Street'. As redoubtable as ever, Spence 'remonstrated with the prostituted ruffians' as they drove along and 'modestly asked them whether he was to consider himself in Spain, Turkey, Algiers or England?' Had he been 'enchanted to one of the most despotic spots in the universe'? 'Shall we wonder if the complaints of individuals . . . should drive them to acts of desperation', he added.

The magistrate, as it happened, was 'at dinner' and Spence was taken to a nearby public house to wait until the magistrate 'had finished his repast'. Meanwhile, the runners 'searched Mr. Spence's pockets' and looked through his pocketbook which 'contained extracts from Locke, Puffendorf, Swift, Pope, and even the 25th chapter of the book of Leviticus, all of which . . . may, according to the present system of proceedings, be equally termed libellous'. Remarkably, while Spence was being held in this custody, a person 'assuming the air of a gentleman' came into the room and 'seized Mr Spence by the throat, and had not fear prevented, would willingly have strangled him'.

His 'repast' digested, the beak returned. 'After the usual technical formula Mr Spence requested his worship to inform him by what authority his journeymen were justified in their proceedings?' The magistrate replied by adverting to 'the royal proclamations [on sedition] and . . . the opinion of the Grand Jury'. Spence said that he was 'led to doubt either the validity of indefinite proclamations or the legality of the opinion of the Grand Jury in justification of arbitrary proceedings previous to a public trial'. At this point the 'mercenary attendants' (i.e. the Bow Street runners) subjected Spence to such 'threats and violent pushes that even the American Indians would have thought a disgrace to their savage manners'.

After committal by the Bow Street magistrate to Clerkenwell prison, the runners ('will it be credited?') had a further line of intimidation: Spence was to choose either to 'submit to pay the hire of a coach to Clerkenwell', or to be led through the streets 'heavy ironed' (the irons were brought out for the purpose). Eventually, the runners relented and 'without those unnecessary implements', Spence arrived at the gaol at about 11 p.m. Some thirty hours later, Spence was released on bail. On returning to his bookstall in Chancery Lane, he found three handbills mischievously pasted to the shutters stating 'That the owner was confined in gaol for selling seditious books'.

The story was not quite over yet. Three days later, Thursday 13 December 1792, on the day of the state opening of Parliament (its opening having been brought forward because of the urgency of those seditious times):

A gentleman, or [one who] aimed to be thought so, came to Mr Spence's stall and, seeing a young man with the first part of Paine's Rights of Man in his hand . . . seized the book and in a curious (alias Grub Street) dialect, abused Mr Spence, hustled him about, tore his shirt and dragged him to an adjoining shop where, joined by more of his brutal fraternity, he robbed the poor man of two other books. One of the villains hastened to the Public Office to fetch some runners, while the others guarded the persecuted man, uttering violent threats, savage menaces, &c. &c. The spectators, however, to their honour be it mentioned, observing the lengths the ruffians would carry their infamous conduct, calmly interfered and rescued the prisoner from the hands of the most diabolical and lawless banditti that ever threatened the peace of the metropolis. Perhaps these were some of the immaculate members of a certain inquisitorial society; at least they must be sanctioned by a dark and mysterious group not less diabolical than themselves.

Exactly eight days later, 18 December 1792, Thomas Paine was outlawed in his absence and on Christmas Eve, 24 December 1792, Thomas Spence received notice from his landlord terminating his lease of the stall. By March 1793 he had set up another stall, determinedly called 'The Hive of Liberty'.

The above account is more than just 'thick description'. It conveys something of the agency of those involved. The day-to-day details are chronologically complex and fast moving: there are various stories here of political, physical and commercial intimidation as well as the use of fairly arbitrary powers of arrest. This is what it meant to be a radical writer in the England of the 1790s.

Far beneath the writings of the 'literati', a long struggle was taking place to occupy representational niches which circumvented the law or stayed one step ahead of it. Thomas Spence was the founder of a radical English ideology which survived organized Government repression all the way through and beyond the long Napoleonic War, an ideology robust enough to be carried into a second generation. The principal discourse of the Spenceans was speech, their main immediate political aim was the reorganization of the ownership of land and this was to be achieved by *coup d'état* or popular insurrection.

What is at issue, quite apart from any Spencean ideology, is the very means and conditions under which texts circulate. In London in the early 1790s and for the next thirty years, the act of writing and speaking was squeezed, shaped and misshaped by the immediate agency of the State. Outlaw discourses, oral or written, could originate the operation of other powerful sets of discourses. The discourses of low culture, which were produced and consumed within those who were economically and socially marginal, had a low investment in capital and therefore a low ability to capitalize its discourses by protective laws, were thoroughly scrutinized by the State. Trials, judicial judgements, sentences, fines all became the apparatus Spence and his successors had to negotiate.

The pressure was continuous. Standing one's ground, acting under the immediate agency of the self is a characteristic of the period which is something beyond the self-dramatization which has been called 'the characteristic vice of the English Jacobins'.[3] Think of Spence roughed up, isolated and alone, arguing his case to the magistrate after a dark night in His Majesty's prison, Clerkenwell.

Texts do not circulate freely. Francis Place, collecting materials for a biography of Spence, kept a newspaper cutting from 16 February 1793 which refers to Spence 'the Poor Pamphleteer' once again before the bar at Hick's Hall under indictment for having sold 'The Second Part of Paine's Rights of Man', whereupon 'the different passages of the Book assigned as Libellous in the Information were read'. As the offending passages were read out, Spence's counsel (he seems not to have been defending himself) discovered 'a variance' in the Record of indictment. Paine's 'resist' had been mistranscribed as 'exist'. 'After some resistance', quipped the journalist, 'the Solicitor General allowed the variance to be fatal, and that he could not support the Indictment': Spence was acquitted on this technicality.[4]

Punishments for peddling sedition could be severe. Spence had the dubious benefit of being in at the beginning of the Government's clampdown as it progressed from late 1792. By the beginning of 1794, sedition had become a crime which, to those at the time, seemed to signal draconian sentences. Probably the most notorious case was that of William Skirving, Maurice Margarot and Joseph Gerrald in Scotland for having seditiously called for the organization of a British Convention. Gerrald had written two pamphlets: *A Convention the only means of saving us from Ruin, in a Letter addressed to the People of England* and *Address of the British Convention assembled at Edinburgh, November 19, 1793 to the People of Great Britain* (1793). The spy 'J.B.' was posted to the Edinburgh Convention and reported that United Irishmen were present. Gerrald, Margarot and Skirving were arrested in Edinburgh in December 1793. Remarkably, Gerrald was released on bail. He returned to London where he attended a London Corresponding Society anniversary dinner at the Globe Tavern, Fleet Street on 20 January 1794 and gave a speech of tribute to Maurice Margarot who, in the second week of January, had received a fourteen-year sentence of transportation to Australia from the Scottish court. Gerrald faced the prospect of returning to Scotland to stand trial, which he did.

Gerrald was a trained lawyer who had practised in Pennsylvania. Nevertheless, the Scottish courtroom was a school of hard knocks. Even before the reading of the indictment, Gerrald objected that Lord Justice Clerk Robert McQueen had compromised the fairness of the trial (Gerrald put it more tactfully) by having already reached a personal decision on what the outcome should be. 'His lordship has deviated from the strict line of his duty, in prejudicing the cause' claimed Gerrald because he had discussed his case in a private house where McQueen had said that 'the Members of the British Convention deserved transportation for fourteen years, and even public whipping'.[5] McQueen vacated the Chair while Lords Henderland and Eskgrove gave their views. Although it had scarcely begun, the trial was quickly turning nasty:

> *Lord Eskgrove*: My lord, to say that this is prejudicating him, because he spoke of a punishment with one exception (a corporal punishment) which had been inflicted upon persons who had before been convicted, is carrying the objection beyond all degree of reason; and I can ascribe it to nothing but malevolence and – desperation.

> *Mr. Gerrald*: My lord, I come here not to be the object of personal abuse, but to meet the justice of my country: had I been actuated by such motives, I am sure I should never have returned to this country.

At this point Joseph Gerrald must surely have reflected exactly how easy it would have been to skip bail and disappear to America. The exchange proceeded:

> *Lord Henderland*: I desire you will behave as becomes a man before this
> High Court; I will not suffer this Court to be insulted.
>
> *Mr. Gerrald*: My lord, far be it from me to insult this Court –
>
> *Lord Henderland*: Be silent, sir.
>
> *Mr. Gerrald*: My lord –
>
> *Lord Henderland*: I desire you will be silent, sir.[6]

This necessity to stand up for oneself alone and in hostile and unjust
circumstances was a lesson well heeded by Spence. English law could
hardly be expected to be fairer or freer than Scottish.

There was worse to follow. In McQueen's summing up, the
prejudice Gerrald had correctly identified at the beginning of the trial
surfaced again when McQueen made a supposition:

> *Lord Chief Clerk*: When you see Mr. Gerrald taking a very active part,
> and making speeches such as you have heard today, I look upon him as
> a very dangerous member of society, for I dare say, he has eloquence
> enough to persuade the people to rise in arms.

There had been no suggestion that the delegates to the Edinburgh
Convention were armed or else, one may be sure, the trial would
have indicted the defendants for high treason rather than for
sedition. Gerrald's protests still read vividly:

> *Mr. Gerrald*: Oh my lord! – My lord, this is a very improper way of
> addressing a jury, it is descending to personal abuse. – God forbid that
> my eloquence should ever be made use of for such a purpose.

Lord Chief Clerk McQueen's reply was a vicious fudging:

> *Lord Chief Clerk*: Mr. Gerrald, I don't say that you did so, but that you
> had the abilities to do it. Gentlemen, he has no relation, nor the least
> property in the country, but he comes here to disturb the peace of the
> country, as a delegate from a society in England to raise sedition . . .[7]

Clearly, Gerrald's 'eloquence enough' verged on being his epitaph as
McQueen rummaged at Gerrald's 'abilities' 'to persuade the people to
rise in arms' as he floundered to find a point of unlawfulness.
Gerrald's sentence was the same as Margarot's and Skirving's:
fourteen years' transportation. Skirving and Gerrald died in 1796
shortly after reaching Botany Bay. E.P. Thompson's verdict on the
trial puts it in its context of significance: 'By sacrificing themselves,
they helped to save England from a White Terror'.[8]

14

To what extent the English radical intelligentsia appreciated Gerrald's or Margarot's political position it is difficult to say. Both may have tended more towards the revolutionary wing than was appreciated by the middle-class English literati. Margarot survived and returned to England where, remarkably, he re-entered ultra-radical politics where he had his movements reported to the Home Office by an informer. This kind of very long-term political commitment is what distinguishes artisan radicalism from the short-lived radicalism of middle-class writers like Southey, Coleridge or Wordsworth.

What happened is this. In January 1813, according to the informer Arthur Kidder, Margarot was believed to be involved in an abortive attempt to accompany the future Cato Street conspirator Arthur Thistlewood on a trip to France to persuade Napoleon to invade England. Kidder, who said that he hoped to convince the authorities that 'the democrats are the dupes of Bonapartes gasconades', related that 'At this moment Margarot is raising money for the purpose of going to France'. Thomas Hardy, the 1794 treason trial defendant, 'was to indorse the bill but Margarot observed that it would be prudent for many reasons that Hardy's name should not appear in the business'. There is some doubt about Kidder's motives but, according to his testimony, Margarot believed he could negotiate 'terms' with Napoleon which would be 'for the public cause, for the cause of truth &c. &c.'. These would involve such traditional radical and Spencean goals as 'The revival of the old Saxon laws – The confiscation & Sale of all the great estates . . .' The Home Office found Kidder credible and, with the benefit of hindsight, Thistlewood's intentions appear authentically reported.[9]

Coleridge's reflections on Gerrald, Margarot and the earlier sedition victims Thomas Fysshe Palmer and Thomas Muir in his *Moral and Political Lecture* of 1795 certainly seems to get, at least, Gerrald wrong:

> . . . men who have encouraged the sympathetic passions till they have become irresistable [*sic*] habits . . . Accustomed to regard all the affairs of man as a process, they never hurry and they never pause . . . Calmness and energy mark all their actions, benevolence is the silken thread that runs through the pearl chain of all their virtues.[10]

Coleridge's position is a development of the human perfectibility theory of Godwin's *Political Justice*, but his attribution of 'Calmness' threaded with 'benevolence' seems wide of the mark with respect to Gerrald's thoughts on such virtues.

Around 1792, when optimism about the positive possibilities of the French Revolution were mostly unsullied by British bellicosity and liberal qualms about regicide, Gerrald had written an 'Ode to Moderation' which manifestly rejects the notions of progressive perfectibility which were currently being given serious consideration and development by Godwin and Coleridge. Gerrald's poem seems to have been written during the confused deterioration of the continuing French Revolution but his answer is more, not less, revolutionary fervour. In Gerrald's ode, moderation is a 'HYPOCRITE!':

> 'Tis true, seductive is thy mild discourse,
> With dainty terms of soft benevolence,
> And honied phrases fill'd, abjuring force,
> Trusting to time, and to progressive sense,
> Thus the wild jargons of submissive peace,
> Of calm endurance, petrify the heart,
> Check the bold tear of manhood ere it start,
> And bid the holy animation cease,
> By due and slow degrees, by sober zeal,
> Profess to rectify the public weal,
> Which, by confusing parts, confound the whole,
> Disorganize the will, and dislocate the soul.

Moderation's 'seductive' and 'mild discourse' of 'soft benevolence' and 'calm endurance' serves only to 'petrify the heart' into 'submissive peace'. What is noticeable here is that Gerrald is rejecting the eighteenth century's discourse of sensibility precisely because he recognizes that it is simply a discourse; a 'mild discourse' of 'dainty terms', 'honied phrases' and 'wild' untamed 'jargons'. Although Gerrald's poem looks towards a Romanticized sensibility valorizing the 'bold tear of manhood' and 'holy animation' unchecked by moderation, the poem firmly defines the political corollaries of its poetics of behaviour. Progress to 'rectify the public weal' by 'due and slow degrees', Gerrald continues, lets 'tyrants triumph with their wrath BENIGN':

> At thy approach, true principle decays,
> Cabals succeed, with reasonings most abstruse;
> Of Gothic governments the placid praise,
> Of tender words and savage deeds profuse.
> UNHAPPY FRANCE! I see thy laurels die,
> I see thy fading glories dimly shine,
> The tyrants triumph with their wrath BENIGN.
> The MODERATE wrath of boundless cruelty,
> The bold terrific energy is past,

16

And peace and tyranny return at last,
The star of vict'ry rose – when at the sight,
PALE MODERATION SHRIEK'D, AND ALL AGAIN WAS NIGHT.

'On Moderation' is a significant poem.

Gerrald decisively rejects the Enlightenment's discourse of rational progress through moderation: 'MODERATION' brings 'NIGHT', says Gerrald. The antidote is 'true principle' coupled to 'bold terrific energy'. Gerrald's poem is an effective deconstruction of moderation where 'tyrants' are 'BENIGN' and at the 'MODERATE' centre is 'boundless cruelty'. Moderation has to be rejected because it is contaminated by the extremes it attempts to avoid ('due and slow degrees' or else 'bold terrific energy'). To reject moderation is to opt for one of the two extreme binaries and Gerrald is unlikely to be recommending political passivity. Amongst the 'Ultras', the physical force artisans, it was Gerrald's martyrdom and revolutionary views which prevailed when 'On Moderation' was reprinted in *Sherwin's Political Register* in 1818.[11] At that time it spoke for a long insurrectionary tradition from Colonel Despard through the Luddites, the Spa Fields riot and the Pentrich rising. Had he survived his sentence, Gerrald might have become one of the true 'Fighting Radicals' who, like Margarot on his safe return to England, immediately flung themselves into promoting the radical cause against the backdrop of an England which had been imperially successful but whose economy, as it affected the poor, was at breaking point.

'MR. REEVES'S REPORT ON SEDITION &c.' [1794] AND SPENCE'S PAMPHLETS

Sedition was an offence which always wounded its victims and although Clive Emsley has commented on the inconsistency of sentencing for sedition in the 1790s, Spence was hit hard.[12] While confined in Shrewsbury gaol for his pamphlet *The Restorer of Society*, on 20 November 1801 Spence wrote a touching letter to Jonathan Panther, a Jacobin and Oxford Street coachmaker, on the back of a corrected proof title page of his own *The Pronouncing and Foreigners' Bible* (which was 'likewise [peculiarly MS] calculated to render English universal'). The letter catches him in uncharacteristic despondency:

> Though there may be Merit in Suffering publicly there can be none in
> private Suffering it can answer no Purpose whatever but is quite

thrown away and lost. I have therefore written to two or three Friends informing them of my Case but have received no Answer. My Case Sir is briefly that I have long been reduced to the bare Gaol Allowance which is a small Loaf of Bread and an Ounce of Butter per day.

A postscript adds 'I am very well in Health thank God though thin in Person. Please remember me to all enquiring Friends'.[13] Spence's apparent neglect by his radical colleagues may say a lot about the depredations of the Napoleonic War and the attrition of Government repression. A letter concerning a passport applied for by 'Jo—— P—— the C—— M—— in Oxford Road', identified by spymaster Richard Ford in a letter to the deep spy 'Notary' one month after Spence's letter, shows how far this radical culture was under deadly surveillance.[14]

For every way in which Spence withstood or fell victim to the Crown's prosecutions, there were other less visible forces at work beneath the surface. Laws against sedition, treasonable practices, the seduction of the soldiery, the occasional Suspension of Habeas Corpus were all supported by a reasonably systematic network of spies and informers. Although Government surveillance was never complete (the Luddites, for example, had developed their organized attacks in a manner which was resistant to penetration by spies), the Home Office usually had a spy buried in the organizational committees of the radical movement.

Clive Emsley has noted that the 1790s saw a sixfold increase in expenditure for the Home Office's secret service. Some of this was in response to the war against France but a proportion of it was detailed for internal intelligence work.[15] In the early 1790s the Government was a letterbox for the sinister 'Association for Preserving Liberty and Property against Republicans and Levellers' headed by John Reeves. The Association seems to have been fairly thoroughly infiltrated into society. Association sympathizers turned up to speak up for King and Constitution at metropolitan debating clubs like the one at Panton Street (see below p. 35), while Jane Austen's fictional General Tilney might be glimpsed as a covert Associationist, 'poring over' 'many pamphlets' in his surveillance, real or imaginary, of 'the affairs of the nation'.[16] Reeves had no official post in Government, but he was an influential informant at a time when the Government's intelligence was only beginning its period of expansion.[17] Reeves seems to have orchestrated the informations spurring Bow Street runners to visit Spence's Chancery Lane bookstall in 1792. Two years later, he was again addressing himself directly to the Home Office. Of particular significance (because it is tipped into documentation prepared by the Crown for the great treason trials of 1794) is 'Mr. Reeves's Report on Sedition &c.' of 29 April 1794.[18]

The 'Report on Sedition &c.' is pretty comprehensive: 'But there are . . . two other Engines that are constantly kept at work by the Members of this Society [the London Corresponding Society]. One is the Lectures of Mr Thelwall, the other is, the printing of seditious Pamphlets at a small price'. Reeves considered pamphleteering more dangerous than John Thelwall's lectures 'because what is in print may be bought by any body, and speaks for itself'. Reeves might have added that 'print' could also be repressed by legislation covering production, sale and distribution: speech, much more difficult to prosecute, was to become a dominant form for the sort of extreme radicalism Reeves most feared. Nevertheless, while John Thelwall is of importance in charting the development of middle-class responses to internal repression, this time Reeves was making a precise connection between bookselling and armed revolution.

A significant part of the prosecution's argument during the 1794 treason trials was that the London Corresponding Society (LCS) was an armed organization committed to the forcible overthrow of Government. It is difficult now, just as it was then for the contemporary juries, to know how far to credit reports of organized armed English radicalism but Reeves's report was the evident basis for the prosecution: 'It is . . . established upon the evidence of a person, who was enrolled for the express purpose of making the discovery'. That is, a spy has been planted and has found 'that persons are exercised and trained at the house of a very active manager'. The spy was Frederick Pollydore Nodder, an engraver and botanical painter. The 'very able manager' was Thomas Spence: 'It appears that People are trained at Mr Spence's a seditious Pamphlet seller in little Turn Stile, and at one or two houses in the Borough. For testimony of this, reference may be had to the Letters of Mr Nodder who was an eye witness and party'. The connection between Spence's bookshop 'The Hive of Liberty' 8, Little Turn Stile, reportedly being used as a place for training to insurrectionary arms, and Spence's selling of inexpensive political tracts was enough to have him arrested for high treason. For Reeves, sedition and armed treason were two sides of the same coin.

Seditious libel was rife because it was cheap: 'The people', Reeves thundered, 'have carried to the utmost extent the abuse that may be made of the Press. They print the most licentious libels against every branch of the established government'. What was worse, this was done 'in small pamphlets that sell for two pence, for one penny and for a half penny'. Worse still: '– and they are sold cheaper in the gross to persons who give them away'. This is a case of the kettle calling the pot black because the same tactics of cheap or giveaway right-wing tracts was a tactic extensively employed by Reeves's Association, aided by the co-operative authorship of Hannah More.

It was Thomas Spence's bookshop, however, which provided the link between 'disseminating seditious publications' and armed rebellion. Reeves's report was pretty devastating: 'Another shop is Spence's in Little Turnstile where a periodical work entitled Pigs' Meat is published. This man lives in the dirtiest poverty, but his shop is decorated with Lines in prose and verse, expressing a determination to carry on his traffic in spite of Laws and Magistrates. This is one of the Houses where they train to Arms'.

Reeves added an important cautionary note to his account: 'But it should be recollected that the persons who have given much of this information, are so circumstanced that they could not be brought forward as witnesses without exposing their lives to the resentment of a great body of persons'. The recourse to violence is a consistent undertone in most of the radical discourse examined in this book.

Beginning on Monday 12 May 1794, thirteen days after Reeves's report was written, and as a part of a wider move against the supposed formation of a National Convention of the people, Thomas Hardy and other leading members of the LCS were arrested.[19] Not listed by Goodwin but also arrested around this time was Thomas Spence.[20] Spence's name has been largely left out of recent historical accounts of the trial events which have concentrated on the persecution of the members of the increasingly middle-class LCS.

On 18 May 1794, Pitt's bill temporarily suspending Habeas Corpus passed its third reading. On 22 May it passed the House of Lords. On the same day that the bill was before the Lords, Frederick Pollydore Nodder was spilling the beans at a formal Privy Council hearing in front of Home Secretary Henry Dundas. What Nodder ('He says he is Botanic painter to Her Majesty') talked about was the Lambeth Loyal Association, an organization belied by its name because it purposely mimicked the many associations of loyalists which had sprung up to defend King and Country against the enemy without and within.

Spence's house was the Eldorado of Reeves's campaign, the place where 'persons were secretly trained to the use of Arms, and military Exercises'. Nodder may well have been Reeves's spy rather than the Home Office's. He lost no time in confirming all the Privy Council wished to hear in order to proceed confidently with its case against the LCS members. Spence was in Division 12 of the London

Corresponding Society. Spence's house was used for drilling. Nodder told how, in the words of the précis made by the Privy Council's secretary, he had gone to Spence's house where he 'Went up to two pair of stairs front Room – found there an old rusty Musket and a Broomstick or two . . . They exercised with the Musket and the Sticks – Williams [a gun engraver] exercised them'. The weaponry of an 'old rusty Musket and a Broomstick or two' is, of course, hilarious comic operetta in the context of the 1794 high treason trials and the State prisoners languishing in the Tower. 'Sticks', however, might easily transmogrify into pikes.[21]

The prosecution at the trials could secure no direct link between the LCS and the Lambeth Loyal Association other than the coincidence of Thomas Spence being a confirmed member of the one and allowing his house to be used for the other. Nevertheless, seen within the later context of the Nore mutinies, the Despard plot, the Spa Fields and Pentrich risings and the Cato Street conspiracy, it is significant that the ability to manifest English radicalism in an organized armed form was present right at the beginning of the post-French Revolutionary period. In Reeves's own words, spies did indeed risk 'exposing their lives to the resentment of a great body of persons'.

Nodder's account shows that the Lambeth Loyal took the precaution of ensuring that 'A Curtain was put against two Windows' and regularly changing their rendezvous.[22] Nodder's spying colleague, George Sanders, claimed that 'He regularly attended Spence's twice a week – they were regularly trained' and they made hints about 'dispatching Mr. Pitt' as he went over Putney Bridge.[23]

This poorly planned hotchpotch of swiftly changing venues, indifferent arms and hopes of assassination sounds very much like the tactics of those who grouped around Thomas Preston, James Watson Snr and Arthur Thistlewood in the aftermath of the Spa Fields rising of December 1816. Not surprisingly, when interrogated, they told highly edited stories. The leader of the Lambeth Loyal was Philip Franklow who claimed before the Privy Council that he was 'the only person in Lambeth who was of this association'. This is perfectly possible but Lambeth, as well as being the district where Despard was arrested in 1802, figures frequently as a place of ultra-radical activity throughout the period.

The next day, 23 May 1794, Spence was brought before the Privy Council (which on this occasion included Prime Minister Pitt as well as Dundas). Spence was not very helpful. Just as he had done in front of many a magistrate before, he gave his opinion in a manner which even the secretary's précis reveals as blunt and decisive: 'Spence said the plot for the Reform of Parliament will go on, notwithstanding all this Examination of persons and seizing of papers'. Furthermore, 'He said, if the Burthens and Greivances [sic] were not attended to, they must look to the Consequences'. Finally, no doubt to the considerable consternation of the Prime Minister and Home Secretary, Spence stymied the examination when 'He declared he would answer no Questions'. Twenty-five years later, Spence's follower Thomas Preston would be similarly blunt in his correspondence with the then Home Secretary.[24]

The treason trials of 1794 went on apace. On 6 October 1794 a True Bill of High Treason was returned against twelve of the accused.[25] The whole panoply of middle-class liberalism swung into action: the future Lord Chancellor, Thomas Erskine, was engaged as defence council; William Godwin wrote his timely and influential *Cursory Strictures on the charge delivered by Lord Chief Justice Eyre to the Grand Jury, Oct. 2, 1794.*

Meanwhile, Thomas Spence had been in prison since his Privy Council hearing in May. Because of the Suspension of Habeas Corpus he was as yet uncharged. On 25 October 1794, the day that the twelve prisoners were formally arraigned at the Old Bailey, Thomas Spence's first hearing came up in the same sessions and a True Bill of High Treason was found against him and the case adjourned.[26] Hardy was the first to be tried and by 6 November the verdict of 'Not Guilty' had been announced. By 5 December the last trial, that of John Thelwall, had finished with the announcement of a similar verdict. By 18 December all twelve had been discharged. Spence was released on 22 December 1794, *noli prosequi*. Beyond any doubt, had the trials of Hardy and the others been successful, Thomas Spence would have been tried for high treason.

After high treason, high spirits. But what happened to Spence? When John Reeves reported on sedition he also popped in with it an issue of Spence's periodical *Pigs' Meat: or, Lessons for the Swinish Multitude. Published in Weekly Penny Numbers. Collected by the Poor Man's Advocate (an old Veteran in the Cause of Freedom) in the Course of his Reading for more than Twenty Years*. The title was, of course, one of the many radical ripostes to Edmund Burke's description of the people as the 'swinish multitude' in his *Reflections on the Revolution in France* (1791). Daniel Isaac Eaton's *Hogs' Wash* was another (which Reeves also enclosed to the Home Office) and Spence had sought to advertise his new publication even while he was in Newgate, 'High Treason Side'.

According to a remarkable letter by Spence in *The Morning Post*, 18 December 1794 and dated the day before, it had been his arrest on 17

May which had stopped an advertisement being entered for the second volume of *Pigs' Meat*. Spence pointed out that that was also 'the day on which the Commons passed the Suspension of the Habeas Corpus Act' and that, 'terror being the order of the day', *The Morning Post* had 'declined inserting my advertisement'. This sprightly letter with its swift account of how he was 'dragged to the Secretary of State's office' but 'to the honour of the Government, remain untried' was an excellent announcement of how Spence had 'essayed once more' into the world of the pamphleteer.

Spence had begun publication of *Pigs' Meat* (or, *Pig's Meat*) in 1793 and it did much to confound Reeves's Association by aiming always to sell his own writings cheaply so that they were affordable by that underclass which existed beneath the level of the relatively bourgeois London Corresponding Society. *Pigs' Meat*'s seditious qualities were quickly noted because, by the end of 1793, *Pigs' Meat* began to figure in Spence's inveterate court appearances. December 1793 found him arrested on three indictments for the sale of Paine's *Rights of Man*, Part 2 but also of *Pigs' Meat*. He was acquitted on all three counts.

The format, structure and content of *Pigs' Meat* are important. It is somewhere between being a partwork (the story of 'The Rise and Fall of Masaniello' was carried across several issues) and a political journal. *Pigs' Meat* had the resources to include at least one coloured print (a frontispiece to the Masaniello story), as well as political prose and verse by Spence usually promoting his Plan for the parochial ownership of land.[27] But there were also lots of short excerpts from such diverse rationalist and political theorists as Locke, Volney, Joel Barlow, Harrington, and Voltaire. This excerpting stood a better chance of reaching the lower artisan audience he sought. With *Pigs' Meat* people did not need to buy Voltaire, Locke or Volney even in abridged versions. Spence found the important bits for his readers, fulfilling the claim of *Pigs' Meat*'s subtitle *Collected by the Poor Man's Advocate . . . in the Course of his Reading for more than Twenty Years*. *Pigs' Meat* under Spence's control could go back to seventeenth-century Harrington or be right up to date with Joel Barlow. By these means Spence was able to evolve a journal without a centre, one in which excerpts could contest with each other for authority and even challenge, in a running dialogue, *Pigs' Meat*'s would-be persecutors.

For example, in *Pigs' Meat* he printed a short piece called 'Examples of Safe Printing' which was subtitled and introduced as 'To prevent misrepresentation in these prosecuting times, it seems necessary to *publish* every thing relating to tyranny and Oppression, though only among the brutes, in the most guarded manner. The following are meant as Specimens: –'. He then chose an extract from 'Spencer's' [*sic*]

Faerie Queene (a visible pun on Spence even if a common eighteenth-century spelling) which reveals very clearly how an Elizabethan canonical text could be grafted to the political causes of the 1790s:

> That tyger, or that other salvage wight
> Is so exceeding furious and fell,
> As WRONG,
> (*Not meaning our most gracious sovereign Lord the King, or the Government of the country*)
> when it has arm'd himself with might;
> Not fit 'mong men that do with reason mell
> But 'mong wild beasts and salvage woods to dwell;
> Where still the stronger
> (*Not meaning the Great Men of the country*)
> doth the weak devour,
> And they that most in boldness doe excell,
> And draded most, and feared by their powre.
>
> SPENCER[28]

This tactic of establishing intentional meaning by the elaborate use of the ironical reader (so that texts mean what they are said not to mean) received further elaboration when he published a purported *Spence's Recantation of The End of Oppression* as a sequel to his own *The End of Oppression* (1795). We are not meant to believe the supposed 'Recantation'. This use of an ironic dialogue with readers could become quite sophisticated and because Spence seemed to have owned the means of production (apart from the printing) and the means of sale (sometimes from a 'Baker's close barrow' as William Hone recollected it).[29]

On the title page of *A Fragment of Ancient Prophecy*, which appeared in 1796, Spence printed a whole letter which we are to understand he received from an irate purchaser of *The End of Oppression*:

> May 17, 1796
> Mr. Spence – I bought at your shop a few days back a book intitled 'The End of Oppression', which I conceive to be the basest book that was ever printed, and as a fellow citizen, I advise you to stop the sale of it, or otherwise, I hope your book will be publicly burnt, and yourself hanged, for you richly deserve it. – A DEMOCRAT

As well as being excellent advertising for his own radicalism, the humour of a Jacobin 'fellow citizen' calling for book-burning and author-hanging is not to be missed when signed off with the finishing flourish of 'A DEMOCRAT'. While such humour is obvious, Spence seems to have claimed himself to be more radical than contemporaries who were themselves considered to be fairly ultra.

When the leading members of the LCS were released from prison in December 1794, a series of celebratory dinners and some amount of financial help from sympathizers were awarded. Hardy and Thelwall had their defence costs met and there were other private acts of generosity for the defendants, all co-ordinated by Francis Place.[30] The principal event was a public dinner at the Crown and Anchor Tavern, Strand, on 4 February 1795 which was attended by 1300 'respectable citizens' with (ex-London Revolutionary Society member) the 3rd Earl of Stanhope as the principal guest. Although he was a member of the LCS, Spence's hardships and imprisonment appear to have been ignored amidst all this bourgeois hurraying.

He exposed his own neglect and the conspicuous consumption of radical-chic celebrity dinners in a *Pigs' Meat* poem 'On the late Barren Patriotic Meetings; particularly that on the 4th of February 1795' dated four days after that event:

> The Stanhopites, deficient no wise
> To celebrate their recent vict'ries,
> By hundreds meet to drink and feed,
> To show themselves of the true breed;
> That Burke then named in his ire,
> Who for to feed would dig in mire;
> But nought afford to give relief
> To patr'ot woe, patr'ot grief.

What the verse discloses is Spence's perception of the distance between what he calls 'the Stanhopites' with 'their . . . vict'ries' and his own position. The 3rd Earl of Stanhope may have attracted Spence's satire as an example of a fair-weather radical because of his resignation from the London Revolutionary Society.[31] In view of the radicals' post-war distrust of 'great men', it may be that Spence found the set-up all too cosy, especially if he felt his own hardships had been ignored. Hence, the crew of the LCS are the 'true breed' of troughing swine who must be distinguished from radical 'men'. 1795 was to prove a year of unusual hardship for many of the population and Spence may be counted as one of the earliest objectors to such lavish consumption:

> Farewell, ye gorging parties, then,
> Go feed like swine, ye are not men;
> Whate'er your parties you may call,
> You're all alike, so damn you all.

In accessible doggerel like this, Spence was distancing himself from the Whigs, betrayers of the people who had factionalized the possibilities of radical populism.

Spence's political token coinage was another way in which he could occupy and exploit novel modes of representation. Never one to miss a trick to get his idea publicized, Spence used to throw his coins out of his shop window in order to attract attention. At his funeral in 1814, his token coins were distributed amongst mourners. What was their attraction? Coins and medallions, as well as being in vogue amongst collectors, could carry an abbreviated political message of Spence's own choosing illuminated by a visual image.[32] Because the motto and image are in such simple and compact conjunction, they handily breached the boundary between the literate and illiterate and it is noticeable that it was exactly this audience Spence reached if the later example of the notable Spencean Robert Wedderburn is anything to go by.[33]

Spence's coins are extremely durable and have survived in scores, whereas copies of *Pigs' Meat* are scare. There is something fascinating about carrying around a pocketful of sub/ersive messages although it is not clear to what extent Spence may have thought he was, symbolically at least, subverting legal currency. The very basis of Spence's land plan was an economic as well as a political argument, indeed Spence's plan was nothing if it was not a scheme to provide more food under fairer conditions.[34] Most tellingly of all, the planned Bartholomew Fair insurrection of 1817 envisaged that the 'numerous Mob' would strike at the heart of the country's financial system when it assembled to 'go to the Bank, and blow open the Gates, and destroy the Books'.[35] The subversion of currency was an initial measure Spence must have found attractive.

While Spence mostly manufactured his own token coinage (by farming out die-making) rather than defacing coins of the realm, the legal tender which he overstamped carry vivid messages such as 'SPENCE'S PLAN+++YOU ROGUES!' (on a halfpenny) and 'NO NO LANDLORDS YOU FOOLS SPENCE'S PLAN FOR EVER' (on a shilling). While the sum total effect of publicizing 'SPENCE'S PLAN' on coins re-entering circulation may have been negligible, the discursive implications are more far-reaching. By occupying the site of the authorized, legitimated currency, Spence was showing a revolutionary willingness to take over the sites of the dominant discourse of king and coin. That it happened on only penny or halfpenny pieces is unimportant. What is significant is that the site of Spence's discursive utterances is here superimposed on that most authorized of dominant discourse, the discourse of money. Spence

26

Figure 1.1 Thomas Spence, political token, 'IF LORDS ALL MANKIND ARE / THEN THEY Y^E RENTS SHOULD SHARE / PIGS MEAT' *c.* 1794. (Courtesy of the British Museum: Department of Coins and Medals)

Figure 1.2 Thomas Spence, political token with portrait bust, engraved by 'JAMES' and inscribed, 'T. SPENCE + 7 MONTHS IMPRISOND FOR HIGH TREASON / 1794' [the last digit reversed]. (Courtesy of the British Museum: Department of Coins and Medals)

was adept at occupying sites of the dominant discourse which had become ramshackle or poorly defined or which could be used subversively. One example would be Spence's printing of the whole of the provenly seditious *The Restorer of Society* in his published account of the trial at which he had read out the pamphlet's entire contents. Another example would be the later Spenceans' use of legitimately licensed seditious 'Chapels'. For many years in the eighteenth century there was a shortage of coin: hence the necessity for some employers to manufacture the token coinage which Spence imitated for political ends. Spence was mimicking, manipulating and taking advantage of the State's inability to provide its own currency by producing its parody.[36]

In the aftermath of the 1794 treason trials, and his own neglect, Spence used political tokens to publicize his political message. This was a fairly successful venture for Spence and he went into it to the extent of publishing *The Coin-Collector's Companion; being a Descriptive Alphabetical List of the Modern Provincial Political, and Other Copper Coins* (1795). One of the first must have been '+T*SPENCE+7 MONTHS IMPRISOND FOR HIGH TREASON+ / 1794' which highlighted his predicament. While the tiny caricature of Pitt's head on a pole on the token 'TREE OF LIBERTY' may have been too small and crude to attract notice, Spence could use *The Coin Collector's Companion* to make the sharper ironic comment that this was 'the head of the protector of men's liberties upon a pole in glory, and the people dancing round it'.[37] Similarly, 'AFTER THE REVOLUTION' with its picture of three men dancing and a fourth feasting below a (liberty?) tree is accompanied in *The Coin Collector's Companion* by a comment that this is 'a prospect of happiness and plenty', an essential image of carnival festivity.

The token coins could also promote the radical authors excerpted in *Pigs' Meat*. 'WE ALSO ARE THE PEOPLE / 1796' is a phrase from the fifteenth chapter of Volney's *Ruins of Empire*, a work Spence had excerpted in *Pigs' Meat*: '*People*: Soldiers, our blood flows in your veins! will you strike your brothers? If the people be destroyed, who will maintain the army? And the soldiers, grounding their arms, said to their chiefs: – We are a part of the people; we whom you call upon to fight against them'.[38] The political significance of this token coin is considerable because attempts to show the identity of cause between the radicals and the armed forces were fundamental to metropolitan ultra-radicalism. The coin's date of 1796 shows how radical propaganda reflected unrest in the armed forces which was manifested the next year at the Spithead and Nore mutinies where the LCS were active. The immediate result was the introduction of legislation to make the sort of 'seduction' of the armed forces visualized on Spence's coin a capital offence.[39]

Physical force as a civic duty uniting citizen and soldiery is also pictured in the political token 'WHO KNOW THEIR RIGHTS AND KNOWING DARE MAINTAIN / 1795'. The design shows three armed soldiers in contemporary uniform. The token's text is extracted from Sir William Jones's 'Ode in Imitation of Alcaeus' which was also quoted in *Pigs' Meat*.[40] Sir William Jones's ode asks 'What constitutes a State?':

> – MEN, high-minded MEN,
> With pow'rs as far above dull brutes endured
> In frost, brake, or den,
> As beasts excel cold rocks and brambles rude;
> Men, who their duties know
> BUT KNOW THEIR RIGHTS, AND, KNOWING, DARE MAINTAIN,
> Prevent the long-aimed blow,
> And crush the tyrant while they rend the chain:
> These constitute the State.

The straightforward egalitarian reading given by Spence to 'Men' enables it to convey the spirit of Paine and give rebuke to Burke's epithet of the 'swinish multitude' since, in Jones's poem, men have 'pow'rs as far above dull brutes' as 'beasts excel cold rocks and brambles rudes'.[41] The maintaining of rights necessitates the crushing of tyrants. Such 'duties' are essential to the existence of the state.

'WHO KNOW THEIR RIGHTS AND KNOWING DARE MAINTAIN / 1795', dated the year following Spence's release from prison, demonstrates Spence's commitment to physical force. It adds a further dimension to his links with the Lambeth Loyal Association. Spence's advocacy of physical force places him in the mainstream of ultra-radical politics and it can be dated back to 1795 with certainty and probably further back to 1794 or even 1793 if the testimony of the spy Frederick Pollydore Nodder is accepted. Later Spenceans, speaking at Hopkins Street Chapel after Peterloo, strongly insisted on the legitimacy of citizens to bear arms and to have military training: 'Every person about was allowed to Learn the use of arms and further . . . the Marster of the house had a right to stop so much Money out of there wages to Learn them the use of arms either in public or private'.[42]

Spence's advocacy of physical force seems to have been shared by his earliest followers. What is implicit in the 'WE ALSO ARE THE PEOPLE / 1796' and 'WHO KNOW THEIR RIGHTS AND KNOWING DARE MAINTAIN / 1795' coins becomes explicit when one looks at another of Spence's coins and how it uncovers the history of radical politics. 'ENGLAND*IRELAND*SCOTLAND / 1796' shows the three nations symbolized by a harp, crowned, with two thistles. The coin's obverse was a 'UNITED TOKEN': a head radiating light and perhaps made to resemble an Irish halfpenny.[43] To trace the background of these coins is to observe 1790s ultra-radicalism at its most extreme and dangerous.

Throughout the 1790s there were attempts to create and combine nationally based revolutionary groups. Their history is complicated and shadowy but, briefly, a cell of United Irishmen (spawned from the anti-colonial United Irishmen in Ireland) surfaced in London in mid-1796 to be linked with semi-autonomous organizations of United Scotsmen and United Englishmen early in 1797, modelled on the United Irishmen. What was of particular importance about the United Irishmen was their complete dedication to joint operations with the French in promoting a French invasion of England which Marianne Elliot's biography of Wolfe Tone has shown to have been a well-armed, well-funded (if ill-fated) expedition.[44]

The most direct link between the various United movements and Spence is via Thomas Evans. Evans was Spence's chief promoter in the years towards the end of the Napoleonic War. He was also the last secretary of the LCS before it disbanded in 1798 but by that time he had also begun to organize a divisional group in London called the United Britons. The United Britons changed their name to the United Englishmen. In 1798 Evans was assisting the United Irishmen emissary James O'Coigley. On 18 and 19 April 1798 the Government decided to act in order to eliminate the United threat and O'Coigley and Evans were arrested and a copy of an oath for the United Englishmen was found in Evans's pocket. The Government's putting together of Evans and O'Coigley indicates the association they were preparing to make between Spencean radicalism and Irish insurrection. A clinching factor between the two movements is Spence's own temporary arrest on 19 April during the Suspension of Habeas Corpus.[45] Looking towards the future of metropolitan revolutionary organization, this was the same sweep of arrests which took in Colonel Despard. O'Coigley was hanged for high treason in 1798 and Despard in 1803. Evans and Spence were in the thick of it.[46]

The coupling of 'ENGLAND*IRELAND*SCOTLAND / 1796' and 'UNITED TOKEN' as the obverse and reverse of one of Spence's political tokens finds his sympathies tending towards the most extreme physical force revolutionary models. The brevity of the token's wording ensured its freedom from sedition hunters. A 'UNITED' 'ENGLAND*IRELAND*SCOTLAND' might mean nothing more than the patriotic unity of the three nations pulling together against the French. What counts is the context within which a united England, Ireland and Scotland is to be constructed. This token is an artefact fully revealing the contestation of the ownership of the national identity. The dominant, English and London-based Government was already contending with the (French-derived) 'National' convention promoted by Gerrald, Margarot and Skirving. A spy report on the Thistlewood group at the end of 1817 finds the Spencean radicals envisaging a 'Proclamation . . . to the following Purport – Liberty, Equality, Humanity and Emancipation from Slavery, and Oppression' together with a version of the Spencean ideology of land ownership: 'The Church and Crown Lands are to be considered as vested in the People'. 'A Convention is to be chosen', and 'the Lords, and Commons, and all Aristocrats are to be executed' but also 'there is to be no Distinction of Countries, or Counties, but the People are to be distinguished as Northern Britons, Western Britons, &c. &c.'[47] This unity of Britons, decentralized into parochial units and enjoying a new post-revolutionary national freedom, shows how the language of patriotism could be occupied by radicalism and turned to vastly different effect.

Spence repeated his parochial land reform plans so frequently that a lot of other political considerations are subservient to it. For example, *The Rights of Infants*, written at the end of 1796, seems to portray a place for women in the system of corporate ownership of land. However, reading carefully through what Spence does and does not say reveals a fairly anti-progressive picture within a revolutionary setting: landlordism is overthrown with the help of women but Spence says nothing else about their economic position. While Spence envisages that the 'overplus', the surplus of his land plan, would be shared out exactly equally 'whether male or female; married or single; legitimate or illegitimate; from a day old to the extremest age', Spence also details that this would be paid to a traditional patriarchal family ('to the head of every family a full and equal share for every name under *his* roof').[48]

The active political position Spence outlines for women is one in which they are confined to the role of being immediate agents of revolution. *The Rights of Infants*, an eye-catching title in the idiom of satiric responses to Paine and Mary Wollstonecraft, is a dialogue between a presumably male figure called 'Aristocracy' and a character called 'Woman'. 'Woman' does nearly all of the talking but most of what she says turns out to be a repetition of Spence's land plan. On the one hand there is a vision of feminine radical action:

> We have found our husbands, to their indelible shame, woefully negligent and deficient about their own rights, as well as those of their wives and infants, we women, mean to take up the business ourselves, and let us see if any of our husbands dare hinder us . . . you will find

the business much more seriously and effectually managed in our hands than ever it has been yet.[49]

However, in the same way as revolutionary women always have husbands (according to Spence), they are similarly always envisaged as returned to Nature and the care of infants. In the next sentence, Spence writes that 'nature has implanted into the breasts of all mothers the most pure and unequivocal concern for their young'.[50]

Spence was, at best, an opportunist feminist, someone who perhaps drew a quick political lesson from events like the women's march on Versailles in 1789, but the tactics of having women in the vanguard of a *coup d'état* was a piece of practical revolutionary politics that the Spenceans well understood.[51] Spence saw a correlation between male domestic apathy and male political apathy:

Woman: Yes, Molochs! Our sex were defenders of rights from the beginning. And though men, like other he-brutes, sink calmly into apathy respecting their offspring, you shall find nature, as it never was, so it never shall be extinguished in us. You shall find that we not only know our rights, but have spirit to assert them to the downfall of you and all tyrants. And since it is so that the men, like he-asses, suffer themselves to be laden with as many pair of panyers [panniers] of rents, tythes, &c. as your tender consciences please to lay upon them, we, even we, the females, will vindicate the rights of the species and throw you and all your panyers in the dirt.[52]

Here, while Spence constructs female resilience and independence as 'nature', he does so with the equal provision that the political articulation of 'rights' is natural in much the same way as the widely disseminated explanation of natural rights in Paine's *Rights of Man*.

Women were not at the top of Spence's agenda. References to women are infrequent in the rest of Spence's writings and it is difficult to know to what extent he is merely inciting and urging male activity by appealing to traditional constructions of masculine physical intervention. When he does, specifically, include women in a political role, there is a sense of its being a rhetorical rather than a practical proposition. Urged on by the recent publication of Paine's *Agrarian Justice* in 1797 ('Mr. Paine will object to such an equal distribution of the rents'), Spence's *The Rights of Infants* ('Written in the Latter End of the year 1796', Spence pre-emptively subtitles) describes the mechanics of the plan for 'parochial property'.[53] Spence grafts a feminist politics onto his usual explanation of his property plan but merely by highlighting the political inactivity of men: 'As I said before, we women (because the men are not to be depended on) will appoint, in every parish, a committee of our own sex, (which we presume our gallant lock-jawed spouses and paramours will at least, for their own interest, not oppose) to receive the rents of the houses and lands already tenanted.'[54] Perhaps what is most important about Spence's discussion of women is his ability to figure their agency at all. Although female equality was a logical aspect of his overall plan, Spence's first thoughts were for how he would get his plan implemented. The means were never in doubt.

Spence put the case for armed insurrection most clearly in his pamphlet *The End of Oppression* which was sold by him in at least two editions in 1795: a year not only of continuing war with France but also of high prices and food shortages and not long after Spence's imprisonment without trial. *The End of Oppression*, like many other of Spence's pamphlets, is written in the form of a dialogue: in this instance between a Young Man and an Old Man. It begins:

> *Young Man*: I hear there is another RIGHTS OF MAN by Spence, that goes farther than Paine's.
> *Old Man*: Yet it goes no farther than it ought.[55]

Before long the Old Man, faced with this sympathetic, eager and intelligent Young Man, says: 'Why, I find you are at least half a Spensonian: you understand something of the nature of enemy'. The 'enemy' are landlords and this is the cue for a reference to Spence's Plan for land reform which he says can be found fully explained in *Pigs' Meat*.[56] This avuncular and good-spirited dialogue takes a sudden change of tack when the Young Man plants Spence's Old Man with a golden opportunity to explain the principles and purpose of revolution.

> *Young Man*: I thank you. I will take the first opportunity of perusing that excellent book. But in the mean time, for the sake of conversation, let us suppose that a whole nation no matter whether America, France, Holland or any other, but as to England, it is entirely out of the question, were fully convinced of the excellence of this system and universally wishing its establishment, I should be glad to know the most easy method of doing so and with *least bloodshed*.[57]

Although the Young Man carefully rules out England from his considerations, the Old Man's reply leaves no doubt about the insurrectionary path Spence is recommending:

> *Old Man*: In a country so prepared, let us suppose a few thousands of hearty determined fellows well armed and appointed with officers, and

33

having a committee of honest, firm, and intelligent men to act as a provisionary government and to direct their actions to the proper object.[58]

This is one of Spence's most fundamental political statements. Without revolution, the plan for the corporate or parochial ownership of land would not be implemented. The vision of 'a few thousands of hearty determined fellows well armed' and organized by a 'committee of honest, firm, and intelligent men' succinctly describes the organization of the Spenceans in the London of the second decade of the nineteenth century. Its essential revolutionary ideology was laid down by Spence in *The End of Oppression* in 1795.

Having stated that this armed committee will seek to set up a provisional government, Spence's pamphlet goes on to explain the land plan once again. Here, shorn of subclauses relating to penalties and the repayments of rents, the Old Man describes the consequences of resistance for the land-owning classes: 'if the aristocracy arose to contend the matter, let the people be firm and desperate, destroying them root and branch and strengthening their hands by the rich confiscations'. Curiously, Spence was not prosecuted for publishing this pamphlet. One reason might be because, elaborately, Spence has the Young Man say that this question does not apply to England. Spence may also have escaped prosecution because he published another pamphlet, the next year, called *Spence's Recantation of the End of Oppression*.

The *Recantation* is an interesting document because of the sophisticated way it plays off representation against meaning. To read the pamphlet po-faced, Spence is 'publicly retracting, denying and recanting, all those doctrines of an offensive nature propagated by me' and which have caused 'uneasiness and alarm to many well-meaning Democrats and Friends of Reform'. He does this in order to 'regain the good-will and applause of my fellow citizens'. The *Recantation* would have made *The End of Oppression* difficult to prosecute but, within his own political culture, the *Recantation* would have firmly defined Spence's position as more radical than the 'Democrats and Friends of Reform'. They may be 'Friends of Reform' but Spence addressed Jacobin 'fellow-citizens'.

Spence turned irony into rhapsody: 'this renunciation' recommends that 'plebians [sic]' live by 'the crumbs that fall, from the tables of the landed interest'. Spence's 'system which I *foolishly* conceived for their happiness' will ensure that 'penniless beggars may yet have a right to buy land!!!' Indeed, 'Up with landed interest! huzza!' says Spence.[59]

THE PANTON STREET DEBATING CLUB, 1795

If the burlesque obsequiousness of the *Recantation* contains both crude and sophisticated commentary on Spencean principles, this is because of the way in which the Treasonable Practices Bills had clamped down on speech and writing. Although very severe food supply problems in the autumn of 1795 were sharp economic determinants, the Government also had to worry about middle- or professional-class political radicalism and its discursive intervention. If Thomas Spence played cat-and-mouse with the authorities in his writings and coinage, the effects of repression and surveillance on speech were just as dramatic. Take, for example, one variety of middle-class discursive intervention: the metropolitan debating club.

In late 1795 the Home Office spy system covered a number of John Thelwall's speeches at Beaufort Buildings and these have passed into the history of 1790s radicalism.[60] This was not the only debating club in London and spies also visited one in Panton Street run by a man called Bull.[61] Thelwall spoke at this club on occasion, announcing 'I am a *Sans Culotte* and stand here the Advocate of those of my fellow Creatures who are Shivering in Nakedness' but he also tempered his more fiery invective by advocating 'Good order' because 'that Sort of Conduct would more Effectively defeat the Enemies of Liberty than any other'.[62] Thelwall's lecture had its statutory spy in the audience and what such reports reveal is the mixed political character of clubs like the one in Panton Street and, more especially, the dramatic silencing which occurred when the 'Convention and Sedition Bills' (as they were referred to at the time) became law on 18 December 1795.

Compared to the rough, scruffy solidarity of post-war Spencean debating clubs, Panton Street in 1795 was usually characterized by a genteel deportment which encouraged a range of opinions and speakers. The metropolitan debating clubs, cheaper than the theatre gallery, were an important forum in which radicals could test the temperature of the times, deliver themselves (like Allen Davenport twenty years later) of long-held thoughts and perhaps even assemble a small following: not for nothing was one of them named the 'School of Eloquence'.[63] Like Wedderburn's Hopkins Street Chapel of 1819, Panton Street had a star speaker at this time: John Gale Jones. Jones was a semi-professional radical speaker living precariously in the shadow of revolutionary activists. In the aftermath of the Cato Street arrests twenty-five years later, the spy and police officer John Stafford quizzed Jones about his knowledge of Arthur Thistlewood. Thistlewood had twice called on Jones in January 1820 'but not liking Thistlewood he was denied to him & did not see him himself'.

Stafford seems to have been satisfied with this answer and he pushed on elsewhere, pursuing a trail of evidence concerning the conspirator William 'Black' Davidson on the information of someone who thought he had made a 'Sale of Gun power to a black Man in Company with [Robert] George in November last'. George had taken a pot-shot at Stafford's spy Banks on 29 December 1819 so Stafford may have relegated Jones to a low priority.[64] Back in November 1795, it was Jones, with John Thelwall, who was the centre of attention.

On the same day that Prime Minister Pitt introduced the Convention Bill to the House of Commons (10 November 1795) 'Jones was frequently interrupted by a well dressed Man, he thanked God he was a friend to King & Constitution – he belonged to no traitorous Society and therefore was not so much in the Secret [*sic*] as that Gentleman (Jones) might be.' This forthright opposition and insinuation did not arouse much interest in the auditors: 'The debate was little attended to: some amused themselves by Chalking upon the Back of a Man, and others by laughing at it.'[65] A week later another 'King & Constitution' loyalist spoke at Panton Street:

> A Young Man in a low tone of Voice said, the Convention Bill was rendered necessary by the Conduct of certain Societies, and the declamatory nonsense of Beaufort Buildings.

Here there was 'some hissing' and the chairman had to call order. The young man went on to say that the Treasonable Practices Acts, like the Suspension of Habeas Corpus the year before, 'was only a temporary relinquishment of a part of our Liberties, for the greater security of the whole' and all the measures were 'well received by the People in general (Much hissing)'.[66] In Bristol the same day, the young Samuel Taylor Coleridge spoke at a politer public meeting of 'respectable tradesmen' until 'authoritatively stopped' by 'the countenance of some person on the Bench'.[67] Panton Street was much more unpredictable.

Although loyalist sympathizers attended Panton Street, there were enough 'Much hissings' to point to a more radical set of speakers and auditors. Like the debating clubs of the post-war era, Panton Street fielded speakers who may have gained a local following. One such Panton Street regular was first described on 25 November as 'A little deformed North Briton (known by the nick name of little David)'.[68] It may be that 'Little David' owed his success to a distinctive appearance and northern accent. Radical debating clubs (and perhaps radical politics in general) may have been socially important in providing the opportunity for people with disabilities to fully realize their own potential: Thomas Preston and Thomas Hazard the post-war Spenceans were both lame while the more famous Samuel Waddington was 4 feet 2 inches tall. Whatever his abilities or disabilities, Panton Street gave him accelerated progress and two weeks later the Home Office was told that 'Little David opened the Debate'.[69] In 1817, Thistlewood's group planned its putative *coup* with Preston's lameness in mind and 'little David' addressed an audience of four hundred at Panton Street. 'Free discussion is the best way to come at truth' claimed Robert Wedderburn, and this play of intervention and opposition, of radicalism and reaction, was what the Two Bills against assembly were designed to repress.[70] Limiting the circulation of ideas in political assemblies and the press was the intended effect of contemporary legislation: the Suppression of Seditious and Treasonable Societies Act (39 Geo. III c. 79), which incorporated some of the earlier 1795 legislation, applied indefinitely after 12 July 1799.

Little David inspired others at Panton Street. 'A Young Man in his Maiden speech' once followed him in such an extreme vein that the Home Office marked the spy's report with a line at the side of the paper to highlight the seditious utterances:

> If the King should sign the Convention and Sedition Bills he would break the Oath he took at his Coronation and be a perjured wretch, that he would no longer be a King, but he would be a Traitor to his Country 'and if he shall dare attempt to trample upon the Liberties of the People', I hope they will trample upon his Head.

The chair intervened, unhelpfully adjudicating that 'however just such expressions might be he could not permit a repetition of them'. It is an indication of the climate of the autumn of 1795 that the chair feared such talk 'would hazard the existence of the institution'. With a plausibility which registered the confident belief in democratic principles, the young man 'insisted that what he had said was perfectly Constitutional'.[71]

The Two Bills were imposed in an atmosphere of increasing tension and the Reevesite bully boys who tormented Thomas Spence two years before also infiltrated Panton Street.[72] There was a rowdy evening on 10 December 1795. The first sign of trouble came when a 'Young Man', who had 'formerly boasted an acquaintance with Mr Reeves', got up to speak. The radical opposition marked its territory when a man, who 'said he was a Member of the L.C.S.', rose to speak. The ability of the Association to eavesdrop and survey radical debates shows the continuing existence of this shadowy and reactionary extra-parliamentary organization. Forewarned (or operating an elaborate bluff), 'The Chairman read a Letter stating that several Persons were to be sent that Evening for the purpose of creating a disturbance'. The bully boy faction sensed a cue: 'A Young Man then rose and said he wished to state a fact' and put 'a plain Question' to Jones, who was sitting opposite and had not yet spoken. He asked him to clarify his suggestion, made by Jones on an earlier evening, that the Whig Club was about to ally itself with the LCS. Such an alliance would have been a political hot potato and the Reevesites must have sensed that Jones had let his oratory get the better of him in notifying an unfounded, if desirable, collusion between a traditional political party and a radical reform group. 'Jones remained silent.' As well he might: he had been thoroughly wrong-footed. Luckily, the home team was fielding an effective opposition: 'Another Young Man rose and said, I never before attempted to speak in publick I hope therefore I shall be excused if I speak improperly.' He then declared himself 'a Member of the L.C.S.'. The rest of the night's events at Panton Street are extremely revealing.

The LCS speaker attempted to deny that the Society was moving towards the centre ground of polite reform. The LCS, he said, 'consists chiefly of Journeymen Mechanics; there are very few members who profess any property among them'. He added that 'I do not think this any disgrace, as Property is no test of Honesty'. What is fascinating about these remarks is that his claim that the LCS continued to represent artisan culture surfaces just at the moment that the Reevesites try to cement the marriage between the old party Whigs and the new Corresponding Society in order to cause maximum embarrassment. The LCS speaker stood on his office: 'From the situation I hold in the C.S. *I know that no deputation* from the Whig Club has been officially received by the C.S.' Astutely turning on his freelance but uninvited advocate, he asked Jones to answer the original Reevesite question which 'I think . . . a very fair and proper one'. Knife-in-the-back time for Jones.

The Panton Street debate fully demonstrates the swift dramas of political speech-making. What was John Gale Jones to do, kebabed by both Reevesites and the LCS? Jones bluffed. He called on the Chair to return the debate to the opening speaker. 'The opener does not intend to reply', countered the Chair. Throwing caution to the winds, he disobligingly invited Jones to speak. By now the room echoed to 'A loud cry of Jones, Jones, Answer, Answer &c'. Jones bluffed again, Since he had been 'so pointedly called upon – he would deliver a few Sentiments lest his Silence should be considered to be a sullen silence, instead of a political one' but Jones seems to have shifted to automatic pilot because 'Instead of answering the Question, he proceeded to defend the principles of Universal Suffrage and Annual Parliaments'. No more bluffs. Next, high drama: 'The same person who interrupted Jones on a former evening' (perhaps the 'well dressed Man' who had 'thanked God he was a friend to King & Constitution' on 10 November) 'with some of his Companions occasioned a Riot'. The bully boys were having their fun with free speech. There was lengthy scuffling and the Reevesite section of the audience were 'turned . . . out by force'. The debate was adjourned, 'which relieved Jones from his embarrassing Situation' noted the spy who, all this time, had been thoughtfully narrating events. One Home Office spy plus several rioting Reevesites versus poor Jones.[73]

For a period of two months beginning in late October, the surveillance of Panton Street was completely effective and the reports of the State's spy were, perhaps quite ignorantly, augmented by Reeves's extra-political Association. Things were to get worse for free debate.

The attack on the King's carriage on 29 October 1795 signalled the opportune beginning of determined Governmental pressure for the Two Bills. Panton Street acted as an immediate forum for the issues and discussed the question 'Can the late outrage on his Majesty be a pretext for the introduction of a Convention Bill?' the same day. However, fear was in the air. 'After half an hours silence, and the Chairman's reading the question five or six times' it looked as if everyone was too scared to speak but that evening democracy was saved by Jones. He entered the room after the first speech and he may have been ignorant of the long silences but, fearlessly, Jones made a committed speech against laws against seditious utterance.[74]

Stretching the last hours of free expression and assembly before the impositions of the Two Bills, Jones delivered a 'Farewell Address' on 18 December at the Assembly Rooms, Brewer Street to an audience of 200 people. 'Yes, I will tell them how this will prevent Sedition,' Jones told them, 'it will make the Man who would have committed an Act which Lawyers might construe into Sedition now think it to be his Interest, as well as his Duty, to resort to Assassination, and to Commit an Act of High Treason.' In a final flourish to 'Loud applause', John Gale Jones tentatively committed treason when he declared that 'should the French invade our Coasts, I would not take up a Musket to oppose them'.[75]

The next day, when the Two Bills were completely effective, there was a perceptible watershed. Panton Street promised a near tautological question for debate: 'Is it not a Duty the House of Commons owes to the People immediately to impeach the Ministers?' No doubt there was satisfaction at the Home Office when the spy reported that 'It was a considerable time before anyone attempted to speak'. 'At length' chairman Bull got up to speak to admonish the room by saying that 'the long silence which had prevailed that Evening convinced him of a Fact which he had long believed to be true: that those who had been the loudest and most violent advocates for reform when there was no danger, would, upon the first appearance of Danger, be the first to shrink from those principles which they had so strenuously recommended for others'. After Bull, there was a cautious speech from his co-manager Adams but then 'another long interval of Silence'. Consciences were obviously pricked because the next speaker, who was a member of the LCS, apologized 'because he didn't think himself qualified, but as nobody else would speak, he would say a few words'. His reasons are interesting: 'it should not be said, that he was a Member of the C.S. and was affraid to speak'. What the speaker went on to say also fits in with the ideology of extreme radicalism: 'He had Children and his daily labour would not support them, as the Children of a working Man ought to be supported. He was born free, and would not be bamboosled out of his Liberty'. Poverty, labour, children and articulacy are the common hallmarks of artisan politics: 'My Children shan't have it to say, My father's Ancestors fought for Liberty & made my father free, but my father was a Coward, that suffered himself to be robbed of his Liberty and has made me a Slave: no, I'll die first, for what's Life good for when one can't support ones family and it makes us think our Children a Burthen instead of a Pleasure'. This speech, in its commitment to succeeding generations, its realization of the historical equation between 'Liberty' and physical force and its belief in the responsibilities and rewards of family life, goes beyond the rhetoric of Jones.[76]

Chairman Bull thought it the 'duty of the other Managers', who included Jones, to speak and 'perform the last requiem to expiring Liberty'. Jones was in the room 'but would not speak'. However, debating clubs had their own dynamics and the audience 'occasioned much Altercation' by bringing a 'vote of Censure upon those Managers who were present and had not spoke'. As Hopkins Street twenty-five years later also shows, the debate is an awkward and exposing forum for those unsure of their political identity. The debate that night, attended by some 150 people, limped to a lame conclusion: 'Bull thanked the Public for their past favours and informed the Company that the Managers intended to apply for a Licence'.[77] Panton Street was a precursor of the more important debates at Hopkins Street Chapel headed by the charismatic Robert Wedderburn. The swift exchanges and sudden reversals of live debate were better handled and more effectively employed by the later Spencean ultra-radicals who approached debating with a committed ideology, a surer knowledge of their sharply defined audience and an effective structural organization which made Hopkins Street a sounding-board for the revolutionary plans gestating in their secret committees.

CHAPTER TWO

Resistance and the Conditions of Discourse in the Early 1800s

THE 1800 LONDON BREAD RIOTS AND WILLIAM BLAKE

When the artist, poet and engraver William Blake and his wife Catherine left Lambeth, where they had been living, in order to move to Felpham in Sussex under the patronage of the veteran writer William Hayley, they were leaving London during the most serious spate of food riots for twenty years.[1] The riots were bread riots and the Blakes were near enough to the breadline for this to be important. The summer of 1800 had been good and hot but the cereal growing season ended with very heavy rain. The harvest failed and by early September 1800 corn prices had shot up throughout England. The factors determining Blake's Sussex experiment were economic and political.

The Sunday before they left (14 September 1800), Catherine Blake wrote to the sculptor John Flaxman's wife, Anna, that everything was ready 'for our setting forth on Tuesday [i.e. 16 September] Morning'. Catherine's letter appended a poetic tribute from William, 'To my dear Friend Mrs Anna Flaxman'. Its last two verses read:

> You stand in the village & look up to heaven
> The precious stones glitter on flights seventy seven
> And My Brother is there & My Friend & Thine
> Descend & Ascend with the Bread & the Wine
>
> The Bread of sweet Thought & the Wine of Delight
> Feeds the Village of Felpham by day & by night
> And at his own door the blessd Hermit does stand
> Dispensing Unceasing to all the whole Land

On the 16th, however, William wrote to Hayley telling him that Catherine had 'Exhausted her strength' and the move would be delayed: 'it will be Thursday [i.e. 18 September] before we can get away from this – City'.[2] What is all this about 'the Bread & the Wine', 'The Bread of sweet Thought & the Wine of Delight'? Why does the 'blessd Hermit' Hayley need to feed the village of Felpham? Why does 'the whole Land' need 'Dispensing Unceasing'?

Events in London in the week of the Blakes' departure for Sussex and the language of the poem to Mrs Flaxman show that William Blake's discourse is filled with that week's ultra-radical rhetoric. On 14 September, the Sunday that Catherine Blake was writing to Anna Flaxman, William C. Coombe, the Lord Mayor of London, began a series of letters carefully informing the Home Office of disorder in the metropolis: 'during last night (between Twelve and Two o'Clock) some violent and inflammatory Papers were stuck up against the Monument tending to excite Commotion and calling upon the Populace to assemble to Morrow at the Corn Market'.[3] The 'inflammatory Paper' announced starkly that 'Bread will-be / Six pence / the / Quartern / If the People will / Assemble at the Corn / Market on Monday'.[4] The handbill successfully gauged the mood of the populace. Every inch the patrician, Coombe appeared in person at the Mark Lane corn market the next day. At first 'no Violence appeared in the Mob' other than 'Hooting and Hissing at some Bakers and I believe in one Instance an Attack upon one Person'. Coombe went away but had to return 'as the Mob continued and some Violence was offered'. Drawing himself, no doubt, to his full height, 'I addressed the Populace admonishing them to disperse or I should discharge my Duty by exercising Force'. 'This Attempt having no Effect I went in the Street and read the Proclaimation of the Riot Act – many went away.' But the Londoners were not to be dispersed so easily: by 6.30 p.m. a 'large Mob had reassembled in Mark Lane committing Violence upon the Houses and shewing a Disposition to Riot'. Coombe finally settled matters for the night by calling out the 'South East District of the Loyal London Volunteers' 'to assist the Civil Power'. This superior force the crowd 'yielded to immediately' and he returned to the Mansion House to write up his account.[5] Coombe's early recourse to the 'South East District of the Loyal London Volunteers' reveals the existence of the local militia men who, when well disciplined, were capable of the excesses epitomized by the Peterloo massacre.

This is the London Blake was leaving. Its pattern of artisan action shows organization, persistence and a refusal to co-operate with the authorities. The next evening, Tuesday 16 September, 'Two or three hundred riotously assembled in Whitechapel High Street and broke the Windows of two Bakers' while another handbill was found on the morning of the 17th at Bankside calling upon 'Starved fellow Creatures' to assemble on Thursday night at 10 p.m. 'with proper weapons in St. Georges fields, where You will meet friends to defend Your Rights Never mind the blood thirsty Soldiers We shall put them to flight . . . The Cause is honourable & ought to be prosecuted as such Rouse to glory Ye slumbering Britons'.[6] The handbill was the adept vehicle of radical agitation. Throughout the metropolis, they found and located their audience. The situation was serious enough for Coombe to distribute his own printed handbill imploring 'well-disposed Inhabitants of this City, upon the Appearance of the Military, to keep themselves away from Windows . . . remain in the Back Room of their Houses'.[7] Sometime 'between Six & Seven in the Morning of Thursday' 18 September, 'on a most glorious day' the Blakes set out due south on their 'journey thro the Petworth road' down to Felpham and avoiding the riots of that day.[8]

Back in the metropolis, the populace continued to organize. Thursday had already been designated by one resistive group for a call to arms at St George's fields while another group called on the people to assemble at St James's on the same day. The language of their handbill reveals great political awareness and quite specific aims. This group aimed 'to Revenge your Wrongs & Be no Longer Slaves or Dupes of a Despotic Tyrannical Government the Reagular Soldiers are your Freands you have only a Few Feather Bed milk sops to oppose you . . . we want Bread & Bread we will have'. Their targets were the 'Bank & St. James & Pitt & his Colleagues', the catch-all enemies of a nation in the midst of an industrial depression.[9] As the Blakes made their way south, the Lord Mayor was writing a running report on the day's events. At 10.30 a.m. 'every thing is perfectly quiet' in the City but radical bill-sticking carried on apace, though now in even more specific language: 'there are arms in the Tower and in the Palace of St. James'. In other words, it was envisaged that the power centres of the state and the metropolis were to be stormed: 'To Arms! To Arms!' 'rouze yourselves from that fatal sleep – awake from that inglorious inactivity', 'Blood must be shed', 'the Aristocrats are your mortal foes – plunge your daggers in their hearts' and 'imitate the example of France'.[10]

The language of Blake's poetry, with its frequent calls to shake off sleep ('I heard the Voice of Albion starting from his sleep' and 'That I may awake Albion from his long & cold repose') seems to be part of the same articulation to 'Rouse to glory Ye slumbering Britons', 'rouze yourselves from that fatal sleep – awake from that inglorious inactivity' that the radical handbills made in calling for insurrection.[11] This much is not surprising. But Blake's poetic language during the riotous days of mid-September 1800 uses the exact language of the insurrectionary handbill transposed up into the register of the effusively grateful artist.

In the immediate political and economic context of the London bread riots, Hayley's ability to feed 'the Village of Felpham by day & by night', 'Dispensing Unceasing to all the whole Land', is a significant immediate economic determinant of Blake's decision to go to Felpham and Hayley's patronage. As soon as he was settled in at Felpham, Blake told Butts that 'Meat is cheaper than in London'.[12] Indeed, the whole of Blake's imagery at the end of *The Four Zoas* is presented using tropes that parallel the contemporary radical agitation. Tharmas says that he and his 'Brethren in their tents' feel 'renewd'[13] while at 'the Golden feast the Eternal Man rejoiced . . . the Vintage is ripe arise / And all they sons O Luvah bear away the families of Earth / I hear the flail of Urizen his barns are full no roo[m] / Remains & in the Vineyards stand the abounding sheaves.'[14] Blake's 'Bread of sweet Thought & . . . Wine of Delight' shares similar tropes to a handbill found on the day of the departure for Felpham: 'Bread or Blood – To your Tents O Israel, O ye Men of England Rouse from your Lethergy – A Land like your own – a Land of Corn and Wine – a Land of Bread and Vineyards, – Arise and form yourselves in own [one?] body – have not Frenchmen shewn you a Pattern to Fight for Liberty'.[15] The language of Blake is the language of the seditious handbill and the articulation of one was the register for the articulation of the other.

If Hayley 'Feeds the Village of Felpham by day & by night' it only shows that the feeding of England was an urgent consideration for the Government in late 1800 as its Home Office department assessed grain stocks in the provinces. Blake's Urthona 'took the Corn out of the Stores of Urizen' and 'ground it in his rumbling Mills Terrible the distress / Of all the Nations of Earth ground in the Mills of Urthona'.[16] Blake defines the condition of England: 'Terrible the distress'. Blake's *The Four Zoas* hints at the radical stance, well articulated in later Spencean circles, that the toil of the agricultural labouring poor was the national repository of wealth entitling them to the shared ownership of the land's natural productivity: 'The poor smite their opressors they awake up to the harvest', 'The Kings & Princes of the Earth cry with a feeble cry / Driven on the unproducing sands & on the hardend rocks'.[17] What is remarkable about the final Night of *The Four Zoas* is that it makes a clear connection between food and revolution. The displacement of 'Kings & Princes' 'on the unproducing sands & . . . hardend rocks' recalls that, in 1800, people of the same social stratum as the benevolent Hayley were calling for quite drastic remedies. Blake's ability to visualize revolutionary overthrow in terms of 'rural work', Urizen beginning 'to sow the seed' with a 'skirt filld with immortal souls' next 'harrowd in while flames heat the black mould & cause / The human harvest to begin', puts together land and revolution in a manner common to Spencean radicalism.[18]

As he journeyed from London on 18 September to political and economic exile on the Sussex coast, Blake left behind a city in sporadic revolt. That night there was a 'riotous' assembly at a baker's shop in Shadwell until the 'Union, Wapping, Limehouse and Ratcliffe Volunteers' came 'forward with the greatest alacrity', Coombe reported, and dispersed the 'numerous' mob.[19] Where committed, the volunteer militia, like the Manchester Yeomanry nineteen years later, could be very effective. Spence's *The Restorer of Society to Its Natural State* had been written as a series of letters which discussed the same problems the rioters were rioting about and to which he gave both analysis and immediate answer. According to Spence, there was only an 'artificial Famine' which he blamed on big farmers combining and hoarding. Spence's answer was 'Farms . . . so small, that the Farmer would hardly be rich enough to hoard much'.[20] His remedy, in his letter of 20 September, was the 'total Destruction of the power of these Samsons' of landed property. 'Simple shaving which leaves the roots of their strength to grow again' would not do, 'No: we must scalp them'.[21] As he glossed in the notes to *The Important Trial*, there was no need to wait: 'Abroad and at Home, in America, France, and in our own Fleets, we have seen enough of public spirit . . . to accomplish Schemes of infinitely greater difficulty . . . the People have only to say "Let the Land be ours," and it will be so.'[22] For expressing such sentiments, Spence was convicted of seditious libel in early 1801.

SPENCE'S SEDITION TRIAL, 1801

At the trial for *The Restorer of Society to its Natural State* on 27 May 1801, Spence conducted his own defence by reading out the entire pamphlet with his own commentary. This was one way round the sedition laws but danger for the defendant lay in the possibility of antagonizing or boring the court. Spence was sentenced to one year's imprisonment plus a fine of twenty pounds. However, reading out a seditious libel in the courtroom had one specific advantage: because the reading out of the pamphlet was a part of the legal defence, it allowed him to publish the entire pamphlet as *The Important Trial of Thomas Spence* quite legally because it constituted the trial proceedings.

Spence's defence shows, once again, the necessity for articulacy. 1801 was the depths of the Napoleonic War and Spence's plan for land reform would have been far-reaching even under the circumstances of peace-time. Spence's *The Restorer of Society to its Natural State* reflected, as it sought to answer, an agricultural system which the year before had suffered spectacularly bad harvests accompanied by food rioting. In these depressing and unoptimistic circumstances, 'wretched [in] appearance', Spence was once again alone in the dock and defending himself.[23] Whatever Spence said, and however he said it, he must have known the likely outcome of the trial.

Spence's defence makes curious reading. The tone is of avuncular irony mixed with idealism. He opened his defence by immediately drawing attention to the politicizing of the trial's context. References to conspiratorial Spencean 'free and easies' had surfaced a few weeks earlier in the Second Report of the House of Lords Committee of Secrecy.[24] Up until the Report's publication, Spence thought he might be 'half inclined to turn a serious Defence into a Burlesque' (which would explain the strand of humour evident in his defence) but now he realized 'I have good grounds to apprehend there is a serious design against my Liberty' and he wondered whether the publication of 'the said Report at such a Time was designed to affect my Trial'.[25] Spence may have had even greater cause for suspicion. The Knightsbridge infidel Spencean George Cullen, who felt honoured to have stood bail for Spence, noted in a British Library copy of *The Important Trial of Thomas Spence* that 'they endevoured to bring on his Trial in his absence for it was absolutely begun Without his knowledge' except that Spence 'went by' at 8 a.m. and realized 'the Trial was ON'. Whether it was a deliberate ploy or a clerical error, Cullen was aware of the gravity of this political trial for himself as well as for Spence, ruefully commenting that if Spence had been judged to have broken his bail, it 'would [then] have ruined Me'.[26] Spence claimed the court had no authority over him:

> Besides Gentlemen, there is another seeming Hardship that I should be tried by Men of Property concerning a Work, the sole object of which is, to now modify Property in such a manner, that many of you Gentlemen

may consider yourselves as highly concerned and interested in the decision. Wherefore I ought to have a jury composed of at least one Half Labourers, who are my equals, and whose cause I have espoused, to defend me against the Prejudices of such Men of Property.[27]

Spence's argument against 'Men of Property' in judge and jury was a complaint echoed by others.

Thomas Bacon, a Derbyshire ideologue and framework knitter transported for his part in the Pentrich rising of 1817, is reported to have complained that the Pentrich men executed after the rising lacked a fair trial:

Old Bacon has been telling the prisoners that they are not tried by their Peers but by men of property. I name this to show you what dreadful principles these men have taught their unfortunate children.

The 'dreadful principles' passed on by Thomas Bacon were about land use and the equal division of property. John Cape, a witness at Bacon's trial, claimed that Bacon had given him a piece of paper 'in which property would be equalized and there would be eight acres of land for each individual'.[28] Although perhaps not specifically Spencean, the appearance of a small-farms ideal and equalization of property objective is analogous to Spence's principles and enough to give a sense of an ideological direction missing from accounts of this event, 'one of the first attempts in history to mount a wholly proletarian insurrection, without middle-class support'.[29]

Hoping, 'as the Proverb says, You will let every Herring hang by his own Neck', Spence good-humouredly distanced himself from his followers and launched into his defence:

I have all my Life thought that the State of Society was capable of much Amendment, and hoped by the Progress of Reason aided by the Art of Printing, that such a State of Justice and Felicity would at Length take place in the Earth as in some Measure to answer the figurative descriptions of the Mileneum, New Jerusalem, or future golden Age.[30]

The rhetoric of millennial prophecy is something of a smokescreen which Spence was adept at manipulating. While Spence's hopes of 'the Progress of Reason aided by the Art of Printing' tells a lot about him, he could speak the language of biblical prophecy like a tap turns on water:

Would it not be better to suppress the Bible than to suffer poor wretched Creatures to delude themselves at the Hazard of Imprisonment, with Hopes of Millenniums and New Jerusalems wherein there is to be no more Sorrow, nor Crying; of a New Heaven or New Earth, wherein dwelleth righteousness that is, Justice. – When Men shall beat their Swords into Plowshares and their Spears into pruning-hooks; when Nation shall not lift up Sword against Nation, neither shall they learn War any more. – When shall sit every Man under his Vine, and under his Fig Tree and none shall make them afraid. When Governors and People shall live in Peace and Amity. When the Wolf shall lie down with the Lamb, and the Leopard shall lie down with the Kid; and the Calf and the young Lion, and the Fatling together, and a little child (in Politics) shall lead them. When the Earth shall yield her Increase and God, even our God shall bless us. Yea, when there shall be showers of Blessings. When the people shall not labour in vain.[31]

The key to this passage of Spence's defence is his phrase 'and a little child (in Politics) shall lead them'. Spence is using religious prophetic discourse to speak to a strict political allegory of agrarian reform. At the beginning of the passage there is an implicit reference to Richard Brothers, one of the 'poor wretched Creatures' who had 'delude[d] themselves at the Hazard of Imprisonment, with Hopes of Millenniums and New Jerusalems'. Brothers's political prophetic announcements had been the cause of his imprisonment in 1795 and the radical memory had not lost the lesson. Speaking at Hopkins Street eighteen years later, Robert Wedderburn feared the authorities were ready to 'emprison him as they did Richard Brothers who had preached for years but when he began to launch out against the Government they had him confined as a madman'.[32] Spence's agrarian allegory is daringly displayed in court under the very nose of the Attorney General, Lord Kenyon: the parochial ownership of land will bring about the time when 'shall sit every Man under his Vine, and under his Fig Tree'. The radical agrarian belief in the superabundance of nature ('When the Earth shall yield her Increase') was to be brought about by the removal of the landowner and the privileging of the producer–labourer ('When the people shall not labour in vain'). No doubt the judge and jury were mystified.

Spence's appropriation of millenarianism is not surprising given the significant date of his pamphlet. It fitted into a pattern of using millennial prophecy with a political intent. The idea of the millennium was used by all radicals as a way of grafting politics onto religion. For the ultras millennial dates could be both summoned and staggered like a kind of a political trigger or date stamp to precipitate revolution or insurrection. In Ireland in 1824 the Pastorini prophecies, first circulated in the 1780s, were widely interpreted amongst the rural poor as denoting the overthrow of Protestantism and, therefore, the date of the removal of the English from their Irish colony.[33] In a wider sense, important anniversaries in the history of recent radical politics could be incorporated into revolutionary plots as manufactured millenniums. In 1817, the annual, frequently riotous and anti-authoritarian, plebeian celebrations commemorating the 5 November Gunpowder Plot to blow up the Houses of Parliament may have combined itself with the entirely secular anniversary of Thomas Hardy's acquittal in 1794 for high treason in the deliberations of Arthur Thistlewood's group who were then contemplating a rising, arranged around 'free and easies' and the firing of two drapers' shops (see below pp. 113ff). The Thistlewood group may well have thought that the combination of their own planning, the popular political mood and the two symbolically significant anniversaries would have been sufficient to activate what was, in effect, a rolling programme of attempts in 1817 to get the revolutionary millennium started. The collusion of the plebeian culture of Gunpower Plot bonfires and effigy burning, which were sometimes aimed at police informers and food price exploitation, may have looked like the sort of trigger Thistlewood required. To try to be doubly sure of the activation of 'the Mob' in the Borough, 'Th^d said all should be busy in the meantime . . . at the free & easy clubs to prepare the populace'.[34] The provisional millennium, the 'free & easy' and carnival rites of misrule were opportune symbols which the ultras hoped to articulate practically.

Spence's sedition trial was a low-key affair attracting no great publicity. Part of its significance lies in this unnewsworthy circumstance. Spence's trial was only another brief interlude in a long series of cuts and thrusts between the Government, judiciary and political pamphleteers. What the trial of the author of *The Restorer of Society to its Natural State* reveals is the ideology and mentality of Spence, whose views became adopted by a wider, more activist group of followers. Spence's quite well documented trial can stand in for the resistive politics of a great many radicals of his kind but even on its own, Spence's sedition trial became significant enough in later years for it to become part of the cultural history of his age. Fifteen years later, the Poet Laureate Robert Southey (whose *Wat Tyler, A Dramatic Poem* was shortly to be exposed to reveal him as a – youthful – closet fellow traveller) paid Spence a perceptive series of unaffected tributes. Although the occasion of the article by Southey in *The Quarterly Review* was a review of Thomas Evans's *Christian Policy the Salvation of Empire* (1816), Southey had by his side a copy of Spence's sedition trial account, *The Important Trial of Thomas Spence*, together with one of Spence's reprintings of his 1775 lecture to the Newcastle Philosophical Society.[35] Comparing Spence to St Francis of Assisi, Southey wrote quite passionately that he was 'poor and despised, but not despicable; for he was sincere, stoical, persevering' and 'single-minded' (though 'self approved').[36] Elsewhere in his review article, Southey took a noticeably sympathetic line on the Spenceans. This is especially significant because, at the time of writing in January or February 1817, the Spenceans were notorious as the instigators of the Spa Fields rising the December before. While he dispatched *Pigs' Meat* as 'a periodical farrago', he was elsewhere equitable in his account of Spence and his followers.[37] Without recourse to irony, Southey wrote that Spencean Philanthropists were 'men who know distinctly what they mean, and tell us honestly what they aim at'.[38] Remarkably, Southey recognized that although Spence at his sedition trial had 'stood alone . . . considered as a lunatic except by a thinking few', he may have been including himself amongst that 'thinking' number when he judged that the Spenceans 'have a distinct and intelligible system'.[39] Considering his establishment status, Southey was surprisingly objective about Spence's land plan: 'Neither is the Agrarian system so foolish, or so devoid of attraction, that it may safely be despised'.[40] It is not that Southey was ignorant of the physical force tactics of the Spenceans ('Let the Ultra-Whigs make the breach, and the Spenceans will level the wall: what the shavers begin the scalpers will finish') and he cannot have been ignorant of the revolutionary implications of the 'Agrarian system' he was treating with such respect.[41] However, it is possible that he may have been reading Evans's *Christian Policy the Salvation of Empire* in ignorance of the author's links with the United Irish and arrest and eleven months' imprisonment under the conditions of the 1798 Suspension of Habeas Corpus: it would have come as a double embarrassment that Thomas Evans and his son were to be arrested and imprisoned under the new Suspension of Habeas Corpus in February 1817, almost as soon as his account in *The Quarterly Review* was published.[42]

If the Evanses' arrest and imprisonment under the Suspension Bill was one sign that Spencean ideals were considered to be dangerous to the State in their circulation and dissemination by the movement's leading ideologues, the wheel had come full circle as far as Spence's 1801 trial for the seditious *The Restorer of Society to its Natural State* was concerned. Southey was prescient enough to realize that Spence's period of imprisonment had done nothing to stop the footing gained by his ideas and his example: 'it appears that for more than twelve years after the termination of his confinement, he was constantly employed in sowing dragon's teeth! The harvest is now beginning to appear.'[43] As for Thomas Evans, when confined without charge or trial in 'Surry gaol', apart from at least one personal letter to his son which was confiscated, the authorities also sent on to the Home

Office Evans's personal 'Inventory Book' of his library. Not surprisingly, carefully listed were both the orthodox English and phonetic editions of *The Important Trial of Thomas Spence*.[44]

COLONEL DESPARD'S TREASON TRIAL AND EXECUTION, 1802–3

At six o'clock on the morning of Monday 21 February 1803 thousands of Londoners packed the narrow thoroughfare outside Horsemonger Lane Gaol. The houses opposite were crowded with spectators. The day before, a scaffold with seven nooses had been erected on a platform adjacent to the prison. On the platform stood about one hundred officials and spectators. At 8.30 a.m. four wheel-less hurdles were dragged by horses out of the prison and bumped the very short distance from Horsemonger Lane Gaol to the foot of the platform. The first hurdle contained Colonel Edward Marcus Despard. Behind him, in pairs, followed six soldiers: Macnamara, Graham, Broughton, Wood, Wratten and Francis. Macnamara read scripture, Graham was silent, Broughton, Wood and Francis smiled as they reached the bottom of the scaffold platform: they all looked round at the scene, in the words of *The Times*'s reporter, 'with much indifference'.[45] It could have been worse. The prisoners were not told the time of their execution until the day before. At the same time, they were told that part of the sentence for High Treason had been remitted. Instead of being taken down from the scaffold while still alive and their bowels taken out and burnt before them, they were now only to be hanged and decapitated after death.

Dispersed amongst the crowd that Monday morning was 'a very strong party' of Bow Street runners who had stayed overnight at a public house opposite the gaol. 'A report prevailing that a riot was to take place', the surrounding streets were firmly stationed with soldiers: two troops of horse soldiers were at the Obelisk; a regiment of cavalry had been brought up from Croydon and put on call at the Elephant and Castle; 'several companies' of infantry were strung out from the King's Bench to Blackman Street. 'Parties of the Life Guards' rode up and down. The authorities had also considered the logistics of communication: in the event of a riot, 'six rockets, of a pound each' were to be fired off to call up the military.

The prisoners were brought up to the scaffold, their hands tied behind their backs and nooses placed round their necks. Colonel Despard then moved to the very edge of the platform and spoke to the crowd. His speech, bare minutes away from death, was remarkable in its sentiments, structure and force: 'His address to the multitude was delivered with uncommon animation. Although pinioned . . . the gestures of his body, almost conveyed to the distant spectators an idea of the sentiments he was expressing.'

Despard's death was a moment of Foucauldian transition: the body of the condemned was to be seen but only indistinctly heard. The articulations of the State's power in dismembering the still-living body were benevolently restrained while the discourses of the trial and execution proliferated in printed trial transcripts and newspaper reports. Despard, according to the Home Office's intelligence, had planned to attack the Tower of London, the Bank of England, the Woolwich arsenal and both Houses of Parliament: all on 23 November 1802. In a glance at the Spencean ideal of small farms, all soldiers were to have been given 'ten Acres of Land with a Proportion of Money to cultivate it with'.[46] In the event, Despard and a number of soldiers and civilians were arrested while they met at the Oakley Arms, Oakley Street, Lambeth on 16 November 1802. The police raid on the Oakley Arms was a rout.

At 9 p.m. on 16 November the Oakley Arms had been visited by a posse of Bow Street runners led by the Bow Street official and spy, John Stafford. He was still infiltrating London ultra-radical organizations nearly twenty years later. They 'ran up one pair of stairs into the club-room as nearly together as possible' and found 'thirty persons in the room altogether'. 'They appeared most of them to be working men; some were soldiers, and in regimentals', said Stafford while another runner reported their appearance as 'some dirty, some clean'.[47] What principally disturbed the authorities was the collusion of disaffection between civilians and military. The Home Office's deeply covert spy on the fringes of the Despard group, 'Notary', had long reported back directly to Richard Ford who co-ordinated the work of the Bow Street magistracy and the Alien Office which was the centre of the secret service. Roger Wells has convincingly argued that a large body of surveillance information, including details of the Despard conspiracy, based at the secretive Alien Office has been officially destroyed.[48] London radicalism survived Despard's débâcle but never forgot his example. In the aftermath of the abortive Bartholomew Fair plotting, Arthur Thistlewood told his followers that 'we must have the mechanics [of Lambeth] and not do as they did in Col. Despard's times. The great men promised 10,000 Spital Fields weavers and the[n] brought only 50. We shall have America in England before long.'[49] Despite the inauspicious beginning to the century, the Oakley Arms became a veteran tavern for revolutionary discussion. Seventeen years later, the Thistlewood group assembled there to continue the discussion of 'Physical Force' begun the day before. Two spies (George Edwards, alias 'W—— r——', and 'B') were at the ready to report all they found.[50]

Behind and beyond official discourses concerning Despard lies the bewildering and shadowy world of spy reports and Despard's revolutionary activities in organizing a committee to co-ordinate two extreme radical and covert organizations, the United Irishmen and the United Britons. Both sides kept themselves highly covert and recent historians of Despard and his context have performed a Herculean labour in piecing together the development of English and Irish revolutionary collaboration.[51]

Despard's appearance on the execution platform that February day in 1803 seems to have been the only time he spoke openly about his politics, aims and beliefs. The mounting of the multiple public execution just outside the perimeter of the prison allowed Despard the opportunity to make one last address to the people. There seem to be two principal extant records of Despard's execution speech: they differ only slightly and must have emanated from at least one eye-witness who was within hearing distance. The report in *The Times* is the fuller:

'Fellow Citizens, I come here, as you see, after having served my country, – faithfully, honourably, and usefully served it, for thirty years and upwards, to suffer death upon a scaffold for a crime of which I protest am not guilty. I solemnly declare that I am no more guilty of it than any of you who may be now hearing me. – But, though his Majesty's Ministers know as well as I do, that I am not guilty, yet they avail themselves of a legal pretext to destroy a man, because he has been a friend to truth, to liberty and to justice'. (Here there was a considerable huzza from part of the populace the nearest to him.) The Colonel proceeded: – 'Because he has been a friend to the poor and the oppressed. But, Citizens, I hope and trust, notwithstanding my fate, and the fate of those who no doubt will soon follow me, that the principles of freedom, of humanity, and of justice, will finally triumph over falsehood, tyranny, and delusion, and every principle inimical to the interests of the human race' (On the delivery of these expressions several shouts were raised by the mob nearest to the platform, and it was found necessary to admonish him of the impropriety of using such inflammatory language.) He concluded in the following manner: – 'I have little more to add, except to wish you all health, happiness, and freedom, which I have endeavoured, as far as was in my power, to procure for you and for mankind in general'.[52]

Despard's last speech discloses the depth, maturity and fortitude of radical articulacy.

Both versions agree that Despard used the Jacobin address of 'Fellow Citizens'; that he spoke of 'having served my country, – faithfully, honourably, and usefully served it, for thirty years and upwards'; that he was prepared 'to suffer death' for 'a crime of which I protest I am not guilty' and that this was done under a 'legal pretext'. The version in *State Trials . . . With an APPENDIX* forecloses the speech where Despard had begun referring to how he was 'a friend' to 'the poor' and to 'liberty'. It is possible that at this point, if *The Times* account is taken as pre-eminent, the 'considerable huzza from part of the populace the nearest to him' prevented the shorthand writer's catching the rest of the speech. However, both versions agree to the general effect that Despard said he had 'little more to add' and that there would be a 'triumph' over 'falsehood, tyranny, and delusion' (or else over 'Tyranny Cruelty, and Oppression').

Despard's last speech is impressive, even taking into account the terminal circumstances of the speaker. It reveals the articulacy of someone used to addressing large groups of people using the discourse of republican politics. The speech is also highly structured so as to gain the greatest rhetorical and persuasive effect. The Jacobinical greeting establishes the political framework; the speech then turns to the speaker's personal circumstances (how he has served his country, how he is innocent, how he was wrongly convicted). From there the speech makes a transition from personal history to the political abstract by way of commenting on how he was always 'a friend' to 'the poor'. The speech concluded with three abstractions: 'Tyranny Cruelty, and Oppression' or else wishing everyone 'health, happiness, and freedom'. The sense of the speech being highly structured is conveyed by Despard's ability to group his main points into sets of three. The simplest group is the three-part structural scheme already mentioned (personal history, friendship with the poor, political abstractions). Within this three-part scheme Despard further subdivided ideas into other groups of three. For example, Despard served his country 'faithfully, honourably, and usefully' and was a friend to 'truth, to liberty and to justice' (or else a 'friend of liberty, suffering humanity, and especially of the poor'). He also prophesied a 'triumph' over 'falsehood, tyranny, and delusion' (or over 'Tyranny Cruelty, and Oppression'). These are the habitual speech-making structures of a person well used to speaking so as to be both persuasive and understood.

In this Foucauldian transitional moment, Despard stands at the centre of a series of textual events. In Despard's last speech, state surveillance reaches its limit. An official at the spectacle of Despard's death stepped forward to 'admonish' Despard on the 'impropriety of using such inflammatory language' but the tradition of public execution as a spectacular event allows him to speak. Despard is seconds away from the seditionless full presence of death. Even in this last speech, the body also spoke: 'Although pinioned . . . the gestures of his body, almost conveyed to the distant spectators an idea of the sentiments he was expressing.' Despard sought to maximize his contact with the crowd by stepping close to the edge of the scaffold platform to speak. If the audible contact between Despard and the crowd was restricted, the crowd seem to have been on his side. In the days before the execution a magistrate warned that people were asking 'When are these poor Men to be murdered?' The authorities had only 'with difficulty procured a person to erect a Scaffold'.[53] Robert Southey was impressed by Despard's execution speech and was fearful that 'The temper of what is called the mob . . . has been manifested at the death of Despard, and there is no reason to suppose that it is not the same in all other great towns as in London'.[54]

The revolutionary discourse of Despard's speech and his rapport with the crowd was the antithesis of the State's spectacular apparatus of execution. Despard's speech may have been highly effective in its proselytizing role: among the spectators was the young Jeremiah Brandreth, executed in the same fashion fourteen years later for his part in the Pentrich rising.[55] The execution is worth pausing over because it was the fate every ultra-radical revolutionary knew might lie ahead:

> Colonel Despard had not one struggle; twice he opened and clenched his hands together convulsively; he stirred no more. Macnamara, Graham, Wood, and Wratten, were motionless after a few struggles. Broughton and Francis struggled violently for some moments after all the rest were without motion. The executioner pulled their legs to put an end to their pain more speedily.
>
> After hanging thirty-seven minutes, the Colonel's body was cut down at half an hour past nine o'clock, and being stripped of his coat and waistcoat, it was laid upon sawdust, with the head reclined upon the block. A Surgeon then in attempting to sever the head from the body by a common dessecting knife, missed the particular joint aimed at, when he kept haggling it, till the executioner was obliged to take the head between his hands, and to twist it several times round, when it with difficulty severed from the body. It was then held up by the executioner, who exclaimed – 'Behold the head of Edward Marcus Despard, *a Traitor!*'[56]

The spectacle of the spectacle was unrelenting. According to *The Times*, the executioner 'took the head by the hair . . . carrying it up to the edge of the parapet on the right hand' before making the announcement of Despard's treachery which was a part of the execution protocol. The State's interdiction on Despard's last speech is directly replaced by the State's visual discourse. The sedition of the subject is replaced by the spectacle of the State. Finally, reported *The Times* at Despard's burial on 2 March, 'An artist, it is said, took a cast of Mr. Despard's face, a few minutes before the lid of the coffin was screwed down'. Right into the middle of the nineteenth century you could go to see Colonel Despard at Madame Tussaud's.

Despard's execution speech is all the more remarkable because of its contrast with his virtual silence at his trial for high treason. Despard's courtroom silence, which mystified Sir Francis Burdett and Horne Tooke on Despard's defence committee, was bravely directed at covering the tracks of fellow activists in the United Irishmen and United Britons while the Government was handicapped by the necessity to keep its spies well hidden.[57] What emerges on reading the trial transcript is the extremely flimsy material evidence the Crown was able to muster subsequent to its tactical decision not to bring forward into open court its deep spy John Moody, alias 'Notary'. Despard had offered no violent act against the Government or its agents. There were no firearms, no bombs, no edged weapons, none of the paraphernalia of the urban revolutionary. The Bow Street runner John Stafford reported that, at the time of the Oakley Arms raid, Colonel Despard was in possession of 'a green silk umbrella with a hooked yellow stick': although the colour was probably well chosen to signify Despard's United Irish background, the court may not have recognized the silent allusion to his nationalist and anti-colonialist ideology.[58]

The only other material objects which could be presented in court were types of text: five printed cards which carried an oath and a constitution. Roger Wells has noted that the same printed oaths had been linked to the United Britons as early as 1801 and that this was known by the Home Office.[59] A new act, with an indefinite period, to forestall 'Administering Unlawful Oaths' (37 Geo. III, c. 123), and carrying a seven-year sentence of transportation on conviction, had been in effect since 19 July 1797.[60] The printed cards were the only legally admissible *material* evidence of conspiracy in the Despard case. Their discursive status and operation is profoundly revealing.

One of the Crown's major witnesses was a person heavily involved in the conspiracy, Thomas Windsor, a private in the 3rd battalion of

Foot Guards. The evidence he gave was crucial because he claimed that John Francis, one of the conspirators eventually executed, had given him a 'printed paper' which contained the oath.[61] Windsor also alleged that Francis had told him that the purpose of the conspiracy was 'To unite ourselves to overthrow the present tyrannical system of government' but it was the existence of the printed oath which was more telling because it was both explicitly illegal and could be produced as evidence.[62] For the oath to be 'administered' did not require it to be repeated aloud: being within sight of it was enough.

In court, Windsor was asked whether he read it out aloud: 'No; secretly to myself, and in a low tone of voice, and he desired me to kiss it . . . for that is the form of the oath.'[63] The Crown's other conspirator–witness, Thomas Blades, also kissed the card and read it silently to himself.[64] The Crown set great store on reports of toasts and verbal oaths. John Pike told of how he visited the Ham and Windmill tavern in Windmill Street and heard the toast 'May the wings of Liberty never lose a feather' given by Despard.[65] Blades also told the court that the conspirators spoke amongst themselves using a secret, and metaphorical, political code. For example, 'the Den of Thieves' was Parliament.[66] It is in the context of symbolic languages that the ultra-radical propensity for wearing military-style uniforms can be understood. Arthur Thistlewood went to some trouble to procure a general's uniform in 1817 but the Despardians also knew the attraction of military nomenclature. According to Windsor, they were organized into metropolitan divisions in the Borough, Mary-le-bone, Spital Field, Blackwall and the City. Each group had ten men headed by an eleventh who took the title of 'Captain'.[67] Blades also told the court that there were 'Colonels' appointed who were to form 'the first regiment of national guards'.[68] The radicals' appointment of 'Colonels' in a 'national' guard illustrates the ways in which revolutionary activism occupied the signifiers of the State's system of nomenclature. This kind of symbolic discursive transaction was of enormous importance to the Crown in seeking to prove its case against Despard and his associates. It is worth repeating that all of this verbal testimony had to carry the burden of the Crown's inability to produce anything more material than the six cards with their printed oaths and Colonel Despard's green silk umbrella, and it is difficult to imagine what other physical evidence they would have had available even if they had decided to allow 'Notary' to testify. Control and surveillance of the origination and circulation of texts was a crucial concern of the Government. Its response to words and ideas it could not control, even though it had found ways to survey them, was to voice its reply by the spectacular apparatus of the process of execution, a ritual dismemberment of the radical body and the threatened opening up of its workings on the holiday Monday of execution and display.

So fascinated was the court by the threatening fragility of the conspiratorial symbolism unfolded before it that a significant trick was missed by the defence. Thomas Windsor testified that he had felt troubled by the company he was keeping and that he was being drawn into an organization he did not fully understand (although he knew enough about ultra-radical political movements to allege that 'united Irishmen' were present at some meetings).[69] Windsor decided to confide in an 'Army Agent' called William Bownas. With hindsight, it seems possible that Bownas sent Windsor back to the Despard group as an *agent provocateur*. In court, Windsor said that 'Mr. Bownas told me to keep an eye upon these people, and to put myself as forward as possible.'[70] Subsequently Bownas was cross-examined by the prosecution: 'Did you give him [Windsor] any directions or advice as to his conduct?' Bownas said: 'I certainly gave him advice as to his conduct, when he maintained that such a meeting as this existed. The advice I gave him was –.' Astonishingly, at this point Despard's defence counsel, a Mr Gurney, sharply interrupted Bownas and said 'We do not want your advice'.[71] Radical defence lawyers of later years, such as the ones at the trials of Watson and Brandreth in 1817, were alert enough to seize on such openings in order to try to expose Government *agents provocateurs* like Oliver-the-Spy and John Castle. Back in 1802, defence lawyers may well have been complicit with the wartime Government.

The network of the informer system, where spies report on what is said or written, and prosecutions for sedition and treason illustrate the workings of the hermeneutics of the State: the strategies with which the State decided on its operations using its interpretation of reported language. The State fancied that it was able fully to recover intention from language. This hermeneutic and its politics are very powerfully visible at the trial of Colonel Despard because Despard's projected *coup* was entirely a construct of language. Other than talk, the only other illegality of which Despard could be accused was that he had held meetings and sworn illegal oaths.

The State's case against Despard hinged strongly on the interpretation of what witnesses alleged had been said by Despard or by his accomplices. With Despard unable or unwilling to provide enough details to mount a satisfactory defence, his counsel argued about the relationship between language and intention. Like the marathon conditions of the Hardy and Horne Tooke trials, the trial of Colonel Despard had begun at 9 a.m. and simply carried on until it was over.

It must have been around midnight that Despard's defence counsel began summing up. Perhaps the defence's most telling argument was to point out, precisely and authoritatively, the problematics of the signifier. Serjeant Best, Despard's defence counsel, quoted Montesquieu on language and intentionality:

> Words do not constitute an overt act – they remain only in idea. They generally, when considered by themselves, have no determinate signification; for this depends upon the tone in which they are uttered. It often happens that in repeating the same words, they have not the same meaning; this meaning depends on their connection with other things; and sometimes more is expressed by silence than by any discourse whatever.[72]

In late-eighteenth-century and early-nineteenth-century England to speak covertly was dangerous because of the informer network, to speak publicly was also dangerous because of the laws of sedition. To speak or write in any oppositional or interventionist manner posed problems of personal safety because of the remorselessness with which the State maintained that it could pluck out of a spoken or written text a politics of intention. The case of Colonel Despard shows that, having fully recovered what Despard had planned from spoken evidence alone, the State was then able to summon up its own terrifying signifying practices of execution in the excessive ritual of the spectacle outside Horsemonger Lane Gaol.

Despard's silence during his trial was worrying to the authorities. The fear of a riot at the execution prompted the interruption of Despard's last speech. Beyond the scaffold, the Home Office feared his example and ideas would have a wider circulation. Behind the scenes, in its most covert moments, the State was regulating the discursivity of its prisoners.

In Horsemonger Lane Gaol after his conviction and sentence, with only the date of the execution waiting to be announced, Colonel Despard was writing. The Home Office wrote an agonized letter of careful deliberation: was Colonel Despard to be allowed the use of pen and ink? On balance, it was thought his writing materials should be confiscated:

> We think that it may be safely assumed that so extensive & Voluminous a correspondence cannot be [?] after his own private Business and therefore there would be no objection unless he should explain satisfactorily the innocence of his Employment to prevent his having the opportunity of writing.

The Home Office feared his writings were 'something that he is preparing for publication', something 'which probably would be most mischeivious & libellous'. Quite legitimately, Despard was using his wife's visits to take his writings out of prison and the Home Office needed to advise on the risks to its reputation of having Mrs Despard searched every time she visited: 'if nothing mischevious was found it would be thought a harsh measure & open to some remark which one would wish to avoid'. On the other hand, if 'the occasion & object for exposing one to it was of importance enough to render it worthwhile', the Home Office was willing to accept the risk.[73] Whatever Despard wrote has never come to light again and there must be a good chance that he was writing to his colleagues in the United Irish or United Britons, perhaps by use of a code.

While the Home Office pursued the ratchet-like logic of weighing up the politics of restricting Despard's writing, it also went about the business of attempting to discover more about the plot since so little had been revealed at the trial. A chief agent on the Government's behalf was the prison chaplain, the Reverend W. Wirkworth. On Saturday 19 February, the weekend prior to the execution, Wirkworth wrote to the Home Office that 'I am fearful, from the general disposition of the prisoners, that they will not discover any thing material'. 'However,' Wirkworth added, 'I shall do my utmost for that purpose.' The prison chaplain was entirely complicit with the Government's attempt to glean all it could about Despard and the Anglo-Irish revolutionary organization he represented. Wirkworth cautioned that 'previous to their knowledge of their fate' (the date of the execution), 'they will not entirely abandon hope, and if they say any thing, it will be a made up tale'. A fictitious story dreamed up while they lived in hope, Wirkworth said, 'would most probably defeat the whole design'.[74] The next day, Sunday 20 February, the keeper of the gaol wrote personally to the Home Office repeating Wirkworth's opinion that 'there appears no probability of any important discoveries'.[75] The prisoners maintained a code of silence to the end.

None of the Despard associates broke ranks and Wirkworth's surveillance of their last hours reveals them as determined and principled men. Wirkworth's strategies were a failure. In an important letter, written only hours after the execution, he reported back his attempts at furthering 'the whole design' of making 'important discoveries'. Wirkworth told the Home Office how he had officiated at the execution but had come up with nothing. It was not through want of trying. Immediately after the trial Wirkworth had introduced himself to Despard in his cell. Despard was more than a match for the unctuous clergyman. When offered the solace of a good book, Doddridge's *Evidences of Christianity*, Despard answered him with grim humour that he 'requested that I should not attempt to put shackles on his mind as his Body (pointing to the Iron on his legs) was under such a fanciful restraint'. More revealing of Despard's opposition to religion is that he told Wirkworth 'that he had as much right to ask me [Wirkworth] to read the Book he had in his hand (a Treatise on Logic) as I had to ask him to read mine'. 'I left the Book on the table but fear he never read it.' Despard's Enlightenment deism or theism fits into the pattern of English ultra-radicalism in its trajectory towards the fervent Hopkins Street anti-clerical revolutionary polemics in the second decade of the century.

The dissemination of radical infidel ideas and writings amongst the London artisan class is one of the most notable features of this period. In the same way that the Revd Wirkworth had grappled with the followers of Despard, eighteen years later the Revd David Ruell, chaplain to the House of Correction and New Prison, Clerkenwell, went to call on the Cato Street conspirators before their execution.

The lengths to which the State was prepared to go in its effort to keep Despard under total surveillance is revealed in Wirkworth's report to the Home Office. It fell to Wirkworth to, 'in the presence of the Keeper', tell Despard 'of his Fate' (Wirkworth's circumlocution for the day of the execution). Despard 'was a little agitated and complained of the shortness of the notice' but gave nothing away. The execution was to be the next day.

Eavesdropping on the condemned men was also carried out and Wirkworth reported on Despard's soliloquies. The conditions of Despard's imprisonment from 1798 to 1801 under the Suspension of Habeas Corpus had made Cold Bath Fields House of Correction notorious as the British Bastille. At Horsemonger Lane Gaol the authorities had taken care to imprison him separately from the other prisoners in a glazed room with a 'large fire constantly kept' even though his supporters were providing the newspapers with the disinformation that Despard and the other prisoners were kept 'chained together in a string'.[76] Despard was allowed frequent visits from his wife but it is not surprising that he felt the extremity of his position. Despard's gaoler told Wirkworth that at night Despard 'walked about the Room apparently in deep distress frequently sighing and in a kind of soliloquy, exclaimed "No–never–No–Not for all the Treasure in the Treasury nor for all the Jewels the King had got" '. It is difficult to resist the temptation to speculate that Despard is caught here referring to his will and commitment to maintain silence about the extent and identity of the *coup* organization. Francis was also overheard to say that he ' "hoped his Children as they was his blood would also have his [own] principles" '. The strength and resilience of ultra-radicalism is nowhere seen more clearly than here.

Revolutionary radicalism had a set of 'principles' which were sufficiently well defined for condemned men to abide by them to the end. Wirkworth persisted in his attempts to discover more information. Having got nowhere, before offering them the sacrament, Wirkworth 'thought it my duty to address them severally on the subject of their Crime'. All the prisoners, 'except Francis' and Despard, 'acknowledged their guilt'. The weight of Wirkworth's devious and scheming administrations must have been oppressive to the prisoners and his office as the political and religious agent of the State continued right to the very end when he reported that Despard 'did not join with his Fellow Sufferers in Prayer, not even in the Lords Prayer, though repeated in his hearing with the Rope about his neck'.[77] The crowd, as *The Times* reported, were more sympathetic: 'The last and most dreadful part of the ceremony was now to be performed. The most awful silence prevailed, and the thousands present all with one accord stood uncovered. At seven minutes to nine o'clock, the signal was given, the platform dropped, and they were all launched into eternity.'[78]

Despard supporters were not to be cowed into silence by the execution. Funerals (even of Queen Caroline) were important opportunities to take advantage of semi-officially sanctioned gatherings to spring a disturbance. The highly covert spy 'Notary' was asked by Sir Richard Ford to send details of anything he heard 'relative to the funerals'. 'I do not apprehend any disturbance, but several persons think something of the kind will be attempted, so that at any rate it will be necessary to be attentive and prepared.'[79] As it happened, the funeral passed off quietly.

It must have been shortly after Despard's burial, or perhaps to coincide with it, that someone published an anonymous, undated and low-key commemorative print of Despard. The picture shows a sculpted bust, in the Classical heroic style, seemingly fitted in a niche and inscribed simply 'E.M. △'. In the British Museum copy the flesh parts have been delicately and accurately coloured. A space beneath the bust, which forms a kind of plinth, has been left for an absent inscription, perhaps revealing the dangerous politics of commemorating one of ultra-radicalism's physical force vanguards.[80] In later years it was the informer George Edwards, the Cato Street spy, who was

Figure 2.1 Anon., portrait bust engraving of Colonel Edward Marcus Despard, *c*. 1803. The copy in the British Museum Department of Prints and Drawings has been carefully coloured, where appropriate, in a flesh shade. D. George BM Catalogue No. 9969. (Courtesy of the British Museum: Department of Prints and Drawings).

commissioned to make 'fiveteen' commemorative plaster portrait busts of Thomas Spence and it seems likely that the Despard print may have been part of a systematic project to honour a dead hero.[81] Another obscure sympathizer also produced an extraordinary broadside poem. C.F. Mortimer's *A Christian Effort To Exalt The Goodness Of The Divine Majesty, Even In A Momento, On Edward Marcus Despard, Esq. And Six Other Citizens, Undoubtedly now with God in Glory, An Heroic Poem: in Six Parts* scatters radical allusions in its path, from notice of the Despardians as Jacobin 'Citizens' through to a reference to John Doyle, the United Irishman, publican and organizer of Spencean post-war 'free and easies'.[82] Mortimer's religious discourse is a co-existent parallel to Despard's infidelity. *A Christian Effort* matches the anonymous print in its heroic undertones and it strains in a broken rhythm:

SEV'N late state prisoners JESUS raise,
What bosom could not wish them happily,
When one spark glows of Christian charity?
Not greater sinners than those gone before,
Methinks, I see, to them, open'd heaven's door.
With FABIUS WASHINGTON rank glorious high,
Hark! sing their SAVIOUR'S love in endless joy,
With Christ betray'd to Calv'ry, in peace rest.
This Paul desir'd, and said, 'Twas for the best.'
Said DESPARD, 'I die bright', (God knows how true)
'My innocence the Ministers well knew;' –
Said all, like JOB, when Sever'd limb from limb,
Thus, DESPARD, said, and FRANCIS, WOOD, and BROUGHTON,
Thus GRAHAM, MACNAMARA, said, and WRATTEN;
Then victims (SEV'N) in hist'ry, not forgotten.[83]

Mortimer's poem is carefully placed: Despardians are 'Not greater sinners than those gone before'. Despard could 'die bright', but the poem opened with a deliberately equivocating advocacy of Despard's treason:

God give all Britons Grace to speak aright!
I say, Take warning by late dreadful Sight!
Not DESPARD sever'd! nor SEV'N, headless! dead!
Had civil, loyal tongue been in each head.
Survivors live in hopes, by faith, not Sight
With Christ, these SEV'N, reign kings majestic bright.
For God in mercy ever doth delight.[84]

Mortimer's repeated emphasis on the 'sever'd' 'SEV'N' emphasizes the injustice done to them because of their failure to 'speak aright' which is a reminder of the flimsiness of the Crown's material evidence and its reliance on verbal testimony.

Mortimer's poem is also manifestly Spencean and it seems to come in an orthodox line from Spence's dissemination of his ideas. Part 5 of *A Christian Effort* is 'A Commentary on Dr. GOLDSMITH'S Deserted Village', a favourite touchstone of Spence's *Pigs' Meat* and token coinage:

Let retail profits of the land disperse
'Mongst SECOND POOR to fill their empty purse
If Emigration, Ministers Sore feel
Four acred farms renew'd, that wound would heal.
This law of Queen Elizabeth restor'd
The CONSTITUTION, then, by all ador'd;
The AUTHOR'S heart with LOYALTY well stor'd.[85]

The dispersal of 'retail' profits is, presumably, a reference to the redistribution of rents envisaged by Spence from his beloved small ('Four acred') farms. Only the Spencean system, Mortimer declares, will gain his loyalty. Mortimer seems to have written other works with Spencean titles (such as *Cottage Farms Renewed By Law*, advertised on the broadside), and his poem forms an important textual bridge between Despardian physical force and Spencean agrarian ideology. The broadside format is particularly important because of the likelihood of its reaching the poorest audience, the very people Spenceanism continued to appeal to.

Despard's example struck an immediate chord of sympathy: not long after the execution John Wilkinson walked into a public house in Leeds and said 'Damn the Jury that found Colonel Despard guilty – I wish they were all in Hell – and Colonel Despard's head cramm'd down the King's throat'. Major Allen and Corporal O'Connor of the Dragoons saw to it that he was brought before the authorities.[86] Despard and Spence provided English and metropolitan ultra-radicalism with two complementary and distinct types of leader: Despard the heroic martyr, Spence the ideological activist.[87]

WILLIAM BLAKE'S INDICTMENT FOR SEDITION, 1803

On Friday 12 August 1803, shortly after the resumption of the war, John Scholfield, a private soldier in the '1st or Royal Dragoons', stepped into William Blake's cottage garden at Felpham. Blake objected to his having come into the garden 'without my knowledge'. 'I desired him as politely as was possible to go out of the Garden, he made me an impertinent answer' 'saying something that I thought insulting.' There was an argument and a struggle during which Blake 'pushed him forwards down the road about fifty yards'.[88] On 15 August Scholfield and another soldier swore a deposition before Justices of the Peace that Blake had uttered seditious words. Blake made his own memorandum of the event ('The Soldier's Comrade swore before the Magistrates . . . that he had heard me utter seditious words . . . that he heard me D——n the K——g') and went around the village collecting witnesses. The legal machinery quickly got into gear.

The practice of prosecuting seditious utterances has its own textual structure of text and counter-text, speech and written discourse. The legal system within which Blake found himself was a textual system, a semiotic of precedent and protocol and a narrative of events and speech acts with their own hermeneutic orthodoxies. Perhaps more sharply than any other event in his life, Blake's trial for sedition must have brought an awareness of how the private individual is, always and already, a public subject.

John Scholfield made detailed allegations when he went up before Justices of the Peace. Blake's seditious utterances (minus legal redundancies) were:

> The English know within themselves that Buonaparte could take possession of England in an hour's time, and then it would be put to every Englishman's choice for to either fight for the French or have his throat cut. I think that I am as strong a man as most, and it shall be throat cut for throat cut, and the strongest man will be the conqueror. You will not fight against the French. Damn the King and Country and all his subjects. I have told this before to greater people than you. Damn the King and his Country; his subjects and all you soldiers are sold for slaves.[89]

A True Bill was found at the Michaelmas Quarter Sessions at Petworth on 4 October 1803 and Blake's trial took place on 11 January 1804. He was found Not Guilty.

Blake's alleged crime was expressly political. He immediately took care to tell his friend and patron Thomas Butts a few days after the incident that 'as to Sedition not one Word relating to the King or Government was spoken by either him or me'.[90] Blake is unique in being the only canonical Romantic-period writer to have been indicted for a political crime.

Blake's crime fell under English common law rather than the new legislation enacted in the 1790s to deal with internal dissent. The Seditious Meetings Act (36 Geo. III c. 8 of 1795) and the Traitorous Correspondence Act (33 Geo. III c. 27 of 1793) were irrelevant. Blake was not prosecuted under the Treasonable Practices Act (36 Geo. III c. 7 of 1795) because, according to Clive Emsley, 'No one was prosecuted under the provisions of the Treasonable Practices Act'.[91] Although some of the wording at the end of Blake's indictment makes reference to his attempt to 'seduce and encourage his Majesty's Subjects to resist and oppose our said Lord and King', Blake seems not to have been in contravention of the 'Seduction from Duty and Allegiance Act (37 Geo. III c. 70 of 1797) which was the Government's response to the Spithead and Nore naval mutinies. This Act remained in force until 1807 and carried the death penalty.[92] Blake's prosecution for seditious utterance was brought under English common law.

What were the chances of Blake's being prosecuted for sedition in August 1803? Blake immediately realized he was in some potential danger. In a letter which ends with greetings from his 'much terrified Wife' Catherine, Blake indicated that he already knew something about the dragoon when he asked for the aid of Butts, who worked as chief clerk in the War Office's Commission of Musters: 'my Accuser is a disgraced Sergeant his name is John Scholfield, perhaps it will be in your power to learn somewhat about the Man I am very ignorant of what I am requesting of you.'[93] According to Clive Emsley's study of sedition in the English provinces, there had been only one case of sedition in the county of Sussex from the beginning of the 1790s through to 1801 while the adjacent county of Kent had eleven cases in the same period.[94]

Emsley also notes that it was the practice of local magistrates to write to the Home Office seeking authority to go ahead with the prosecutions and asking for advice and financial assistance. In this way the magistrates' reports became part of the Government's increasingly efficient intelligence gathering system. No correspondence appears to have taken place concerning Blake's case although the story of Sussex's single action for sedition in the 1790s is told by Emsley because the case of defendant Thomas Lempriere of Lewes in July 1797 resulted in correspondence with the Home Office after he had been bound over to the next Assizes. The Home Office, on the advice of the Crown Law Officers, expressed regret that Lempriere's case had been brought forward and refused to support it. Lempriere was acquitted. It is significant for judging the seriousness of Blake's alleged crime that, Emsley writes, the Home Office tended to be rather hesitant about advising proceeding with prosecutions ('If there was the slightest chance of the man being acquitted the advice was against prosecution'). Approximately one in three of sedition cases came to trial, but 'with the exception of those tried for treason the majority of men brought before the English courts during the 1790s for "political" offences were convicted.'[95] In other words, Blake's sedition case was exceptional for Sussex and it was fairly exceptional in a national context that he should be acquitted once brought to trial.

Sentences varied markedly. Emsley shows that sentences could range from a few shillings with recognizances for future good behaviour to, at the other extreme, a 1798 Hampshire sentence on a Milford carpenter of three years in gaol, with solitary confinement for the first three months, followed by a surety of £500 for five years' good behaviour. The man had recited 'a lengthy seditious doggerel, declaring himself to be a republican ready to fight alongside a French invasion force, and hoping for a revolution in England' – in other words, sentiments not very dissimilar from Blake's long and alleged fulmination.[96]

Blake wrote to Butts that 'I have been before a Bench of Justices at Chichester this morning, but they as the Lawyer who wrote down the Accusation told me in private are compelld by the Military to suffer a prosecution to be enterd into altho they must know & it is manifest that the whole is a Fabricated Perjury'.[97] Decisions to prosecute, however, were less systematic than Blake imagined. Emsley cites the instance of a man in York committed for prosecution on the evidence of four dragoons in April 1803 (only five months before Blake's alleged sedition). The Home Office advised that he should be discharged if he showed remorse before magistrates. On a different occasion in Yorkshire, the Government both recommended prosecution and bore the expense in the case of David Norcliffe at Huddersfield in March 1798 because his seditious words were spoken in front of soldiers. The Home Office said that this made a 'marked difference' to their attitude. He received one year's imprisonment.[98] There can be little doubt that Blake was thought to have committed a fairly serious offence and the authorities thought the balance of probability was against him.

What else was happening around the time of Blake's sedition? The war with France had recommenced in May 1803 and England was alive with rumours of French spies; Blake was thought to be one of them:

> The Soldier said to Mrs. Grinder [wife of the landlord of The Fox inn], that it would be right to have my House searched, as I might have plans of the Country which I intended to send to the Enemy; he called me a Military Painter; I suppose mistaking the Words Miniature Painter, which he might have heard me called.[99]

Neither was Scholfield's suggestion that Blake might have 'plans of the Country . . . to sent to the Enemy' without local parallel. The enemy were, in one sense, already on the Sussex coast: on 23 August 1803 the Chichester authorities had written to the Home Office saying that two persons paralleling Scholfield's description of 'Military Painters' with 'plans of the Country' were found 'taking a drawing near this Town'. More than twenty years before, in company with the painter Thomas Stothard and another artist on a sketching excursion, Blake had been briefly arrested in the Medway on suspicion of surveying for the enemy. Showing just how jumpy the Sussex coast authorities could be in the dangerous summer of 1803, this pair of ruin-bibbers with 'the appearance of Gentlemen' were clapped into Rye Gaol.[100]

If the Picturesque was still being pursued in invasion-scared Sussex, the countrywide documentation on sedition and rebellion coming into the Home Office was disturbingly similar to Blake's case. Four days before Blake's alleged sedition, authorities in Bristol asked for advice on proceeding when a sergeant in the 7th Regiment of Foot had sworn a deposition that he had heard a man say that he 'thought Bonaparte was a fine fellow'.[101] The next day, the authorities in Newcastle upon Tyne sent to the Home Office a copy of their printed handbill warning the populace of 'A SPY' in the vicinity.[102] On the day Blake and Scholfield were wrestling in Felpham, John Nicolson, a London silversmith and jeweller, had sworn that he knew Lewis Wells of Leadenhall Street, an engraver, and that Wells had shown him a drawing of a harp 'which he said was the Drawing for a seal he was Employed to make and he apprehended was for the Rebels in Ireland' (presumably the abortive *coup* of Robert Emmett which followed in the aftermath of Colonel Despard's execution).[103] The next day, the authorities in Tynemouth simply asked whether they would be reimbursed if they prosecuted a man who had offered a toast to Tom Paine's *Rights of Man*.[104] Four weeks before Blake's trial, the Home Office received information about a number of suspects, smugglers and 'furious republicans' in the Flushing area which included '*Blake* with one eye, his right – an Irishman' who 'has been in prison once or twice for talking openly . . . and speaks his mind freely to those who [?] dare not'.[105]

What emerges from the papers on sedition in the Home Office is both the relative confusion and simplicity of the local authorities, allied to a great sense of their earnest attention to detail and nit-picking fastidiousness in displaying their loyalty to the Crown. To get closer to Blake's alleged sedition it is necessary to go more deeply into the motives and political context of informing soldiers and politically aware engravers.

As well as being informed on, engravers were also informers. Blake must have known that at the trial of Horne Tooke for high treason in 1794, William Sharp (a member of the Society for Constitutional Information) had turned King's evidence. William Sharp, as a Swedenborgian, would have been known to Blake because they were occasional associates on engraving commissions during the 1790s.[106] A reading of the trial transcript persuades me that Sharp and Horne Tooke were a double act, with Horne Tooke 'playing off' Sharp as a Crown witness whom he knew would be able to add little to the Crown's case against him. Blake may not have known that, however, even supposing it were the case: to Blake, Sharp must have looked rather similar to an informer.[107]

Blake would have been aware that the LCS in the early 1790s was thoroughly infiltrated by informers and spies. One of these was Frederick Pollydore Nodder, a Tavistock Street engraver and artist who exhibited at the Royal Academy in 1786 and who styled himself the Queen's botanical painter. Little is known about Nodder except that, like Blake, he was capable of producing complete books of engravings drawn, etched and coloured by himself.[108]

Frederick Pollydore Nodder's letters to the Home Office are full of the workings of an informer who spied routinely on the LCS and on the Spence-associated Lambeth Loyal Association (LLA) in order to help the Crown assemble its evidence for the 1794 treason trials. Nodder sent very detailed reports on the LLA: 'Between 9 & 10. o'clock Frankloe [organizer of the LLA] came into the room – he was dressed in a blue Coat & red Coll^r. – buff on white Cloth waistct. & breeches, black Stiff Stock and a military Cock'd Hat with a large Cockade'.[109] Nodder's report shows very clearly how he had been tipped off to report on the significant symbolism of radical clothing but, as a person likely to be familiar and unsuspected amongst London's printing trade, Nodder's job was to find out information such as the names of the LCS's printers. Nodder's information was the Government's principal source for the idea that the LLA trained to arms: 'I think sir that the Person of the Name xxxxxx Cummins a Journayman Printer who I have Named, – (And who I believe printed some of the Cards for the society) This Man I veryly Believe knows almost every Man that belongs to the Armd Meetings.'[110] That Nodder was known to the LCS defendants is certain. His letters reveal his anxiety at having been taken, perhaps at the Privy Council hearings, 'threw the room that the Prisoners was in'. What Nodder most feared was having to appear as a Crown witness: 'But sir as a Man of Honour I rely upon your Word Given, That I am not to be Brought forward on the Trials of those Men – I have Sir suffered much in this Business – For My Loyalty to my King & Country and Likley to suffer More. If I was Brought fowar'd against these Men it would be my Ruin.'[111] However, Nodder's pleas went unheeded: he appeared as a Crown witness at the trial of Hardy, and everyone would have been able to draw their own conclusions. Even before the trial Nodder had received threats against his life and he felt it prudent to carry a pair of pistols whenever he went out.[112]

Activists like Thomas Spence knew the dangers of informers and spies and warned others of their presence. In his pamphlet *A Letter from Ralph Hodge, To His Cousin Thomas Bull* (*c.* 1795) Spence depicted Bull as an informer. When the people rose one night to pull down enclosure fences and commit 'some other outrages' the fictitious Bull 'turned informer and every spirited man in the village was transported'. This is how Bull had gained a Government post as police 'runner', turnkey, 'door-keeper', 'ticket-porter' or even grave digger and he feared a reform of Parliament would remove him from his job.[113] There is a possibility that a safe, and suitable, Government job was eventually found for Frederick Pollydore Nodder. At the trial in 1817 of Dr James Watson for high treason for his part in the Spa Fields rising, someone called 'Nodder' was the custodian of the spy John Castle. Spies, it would appear, look after spies.[114]

Such were the conditions in England in the summer of 1803 that Blake may have had good reason to think that Scholfield was an informer or *agent provocateur*. Blake's suspicions are far from unreasonable. Informers and spies were endemic and this possibility has been discussed by David Erdman.[115] Blake wrote that Scholfield had come into his garden 'with some Intention, or at least with a prejudiced Mind'[116] and in Scholfield's formal deposition about Blake's alleged sedition there is a curious phrase where the legal document states that 'this Informant [i.e. Scholfield] was sent by his Captain on [to?] Esquire Hayley to hear what he had to say and to go and tell them'.[117] The indefinite pronoun 'he' is crucial: is the 'he' Blake? This would make sense of Blake's suspicion that Scholfield had 'a prejudiced Mind' and had been sent to spy or inform on him, sent by the army Captain to report back to them. Whatever Blake thought, engravers were known to be active both as informers and as radicals.

The context of engraver–spies or engraver–Crown witnesses, like Frederick Pollydore Nodder and William Sharp in the famous treason trials of 1794, may not have seemed so very distant to Blake ten years later. The chair of the magistrates at Blake's hearing in October 1803 as well as the trial in January 1804 was Charles Lennox, 3rd Duke of Richmond. At the trial of Hardy and of Horne Tooke, the Duke of Richmond's plans for parliamentary reform published in his *Letter to Colonel Sharman*, 1783 (and frequently reprinted, in Spence's *Pigs' Meat*, for example) had been consistently claimed to justify and support the legitimacy and precedence of the aims and ambitions of the LCS and Society for Constitutional Information. That the LCS members were only implementing the reform plan of the Duke of Richmond became a cornerstone of the defence. The LCS tactic was a piece of highly successful political appropriation and the Duke of Richmond was summoned to appear as a witness for the defence at the trial of Horne Tooke. The Duke's biographer, Alison Olson, writes that 'Richmond was held indirectly responsible for the government's defeat in prosecuting for treason the leaders of radical reform societies.'[118]

The irony may have been a grim one for William Blake as he stood in the dock. According to a note of Blake's patron, William Hayley, 'the old Duke of Richmond was bitterly prejudiced against Blake; & had made some unwarrantable observations in the course of the trial, that might have excited prejudice in the Jury'.[119] Although the trial ended in Blake being acquitted, the literary texts Blake has left behind betray some evidence of the extent to which it continued to have an enormous effect on him psychologically.[120] Blake may also have felt very strongly that the trial jeopardized his livelihood and career. In the claustrophobic atmosphere of Sussex, Blake found that the bench of magistrates contained two potential patrons. Listed as appearing on the bench at both the Michaelmas Quarter Sessions and at his trial was William Stephen Poyntz to whom William Hayley, on 28 June 1803, had recommended Blake as an engraver for 'Mrs Poyntz's *Prize Bull*'. This would have been humble enough work but the Quarter Sessions bench also contained the more notable George O'Brien, Earl of Egremont, who was later to become a minor buyer and patron of Blake as well as the more substantial patron of W.M. Turner. The accused artist in the dock can have had nothing with which to be able to predict the effect of the trial on his subsequent patronage.[121]

The uncertainty of the attitude of future employers, as well as the possible exposure and incrimination of an individual's political outlook, were possible future punitive consequences of indictment. Guilty or acquitted, the political accused had an insecure future to face from both employers and friends. Over the long period of time, perhaps from 1804 to 1820, that Blake was working on his illuminated poem *Jerusalem: The Emanation of the Giant Albion*, he felt sufficiently bitter to burn with acid into his engraved text the names of at least three of the magistrates who sat in judgement at his trial. Justices John Quantock, William Brereton and John Peachey appear in hostile contexts in several parts of Blake's poem, often placed in close association with Scholfield and Cock, the dragoons who made the allegations.[122] If the Duke of Richmond was an unknown quantity, a patrician whose career had been ignominiously curtailed by the reformist movement, Blake seems to have been more keen to pillory these lesser notables of the magistracy, perhaps a reminder that these local dignitaries could, if they wished, do Blake much damage by further insinuation and obstruction after his trial and acquittal. 'Scofield, Kox' are predictable subjects for Blake to have wished to give immortal notoriety to in *Jerusalem* but it is also possible that Blake may have experienced some sense of discomfort, and even alienation, at having these two soldiers so firmly remind him that, whatever radical causes he had espoused in his poems of the 1790s such as *The*

French Revolution (1791) or *America: A Prophecy* (1793), Blake was now explicitly detached from his artisan roots and living under the patronage of a person perceived by the soldiers as belonging to the minor gentry. The ability of Scholfield and Cox to initiate, forward and prosecute their accusation is testimony to the growing political confidence and aggression of their social class.

CHAPTER THREE

'A Free and Easy Society to Overthrow the Government': Post-War Spenceans

TWO SPENCEAN ACTIVISTS: THOMAS PRESTON AND ALLEN DAVENPORT

Sedition was the dominant law of discourse in late-eighteenth- and early-nineteenth-century England: it suppressed writing and it suppressed speech. Some of this suppression was exerted by the spectacular and celebrated Two Bills of 1795 but the workings of English common law, ably assisted by the loyal predisposition to turn informer, exerted just as much effect. Artisan radicals developed their own strategies for circumventing the regulation of discourse, registering their political autonomy through the autonomy of speech. Speech was more immediate than writing, less prone to indictment unless there was the testimony of witnesses who could be proven to have been physically present at the time of the seditious utterance. Speech was also more suited to the outlawed strategies of the physical force ideology popular amongst some radicals. Thomas Spence's assertiveness in front of a succession of magistrates shows how robust speech could be. In *The Important Trial* he told the bench that:

> My Father used to make my Brothers and me read the Bible to him while working at his Business and at the End of every Chapter encouraged us to give our opinions on what we had just read. By these Means I acquired an early habit of reflecting on every Occurrence which past before me as well as on what I read.[1]

It is this articulacy that Spence sought to develop in his 'Pronouncing' books.

Spence stated in at his trial that:

> When I began to Study I found every Thing erected on certain unalterable Principles. I found every Art and Science a perfect Whole. Nothing was in Anarchy but Language and Politics: But both of these I reduced to order: The one by a New Alphabet, and the other by a New Constitution.

But as well as being a reading aid, Spence's elaborate phonetic alphabet is ideally suited to being an aid to speaking.[2] As long as written words are recognized and their meaning understood, there is not much point in knowing how they are pronounced unless the reader is going to speak. Radical discourse was the raid of the articulate. This is why Spence devoted so much effort to developing his strange phonetic alphabet. *Dh´e imp´ortant Triál ŏv Tóm´is Sp´ens For a Pól´it´ikal Pámfl´et ´entitld 'Dhĕ Rĕstorr ŏv Sosiĕte tw ĭts nătĕural Stat'*, with its full recollection of how Spence had himself conducted his own defence, is an obviously important radical document to publish in phonetic form. *Dh´e imp´ortant Triál* would enable the inarticulate. Thomas Evans, the Spencean activist, had listed in his 'Inventory Book', confiscated during his imprisonment under the 1817 Suspension of Habeas Corpus, not only a set in orthodox and phonetic writing of Spence's *Important Trial* but also a copy of William Enfield's popular *The Speaker: or, Miscellaneous Pieces, Selected . . . with a View to Facilitate the Improvement of Youth in Reading and Speaking* which, in some of its many editions, had plates engraved by Blake.[3]

This assault of articulate speech was something Spence continued with steady conviction. Every time Spence sold a pamphlet in the 1790s at the 'Hive of Liberty', Little Turnstile, the radical publisher William Hone noted that he 'recommended others with strong expressions of hate' and 'prophecies of what would happen to the whole race of "Land-Lords" ' while the exterior of the shop was 'decorated with Lines in prose and verse' carrying similar messages.[4] Two people who became dedicated and active Spenceans were Thomas Preston and Allen Davenport. Both were shoemakers, both were involved in post-war ultra-radicalism: Preston as a leading organizer and ideologue heavily associated with Thistlewood and Watson Snr; Davenport as a poet, speaker and polemicist at Hopkins Street and in the ultra-radical press. Both have left autobiographical writings which can be collated with information from other sources. Significantly, both men seem to have first encountered Spence's ideas in the years after 1800, a time when information about him, and radical activity as whole, is particularly sparse.[5]

Just as Spence had his bookstall 'decorated with Lines in prose and verse', quite independently Thomas Preston was also interested in fascinating passers-by with compact messages and enigmatic pictures. Long before he met Spence, the shoemaker Thomas Preston, in the late 1790s or early 1800s, nailed up a political picture with accompanying mottoes outside his shoemaking shop in Walworth:

> Here it was I had a picture (which I have now by me) painted expressly for me as my sign, which I, with all due formality, nailed to the wall on the outside of my house. It attracted considerable attention, and drew some customers to the shop. The subject was somewhat *ominous*, as the chief character in the picture had a halter round his neck. Among the many, the worthy magistrates of Surry deigned to pay me a visit on the occasion, and seemed very desirous to have the key, the better to decypher the subject. I told them they could contemplate as long as it might prove convenient to them, but that the mottos were sufficiently expressive, and that I had no key – They conn'd over the mottos, which were as follows, '*A warning to the Oppressor, and a lesson to the Oppressed;*' and at the bottom, '*The King and Constitution Pure. – Burdett the Pilot!*'[6]

The local notoriety of Preston's relatively obscure political statement is a typical aspect of contemporary casual surveillance, despite his imagery being firmly within the traditions of political print caricatures. This type of low-level intimidation could easily be administered by the authorities on those suspected of even silent disloyalty. Preston learned to couch such explanations as he chose to give in ambivalent language:

> Some would peep in on me, saying, *my good man, whereof do you place the rope around that gentleman's neck? – 'For the same reason,'* quoth I, '*that they really do so at a place of execution. – to deter men from acting wrongfully.'* This usually silenced the enquirer.

Preston became a great convivial organizer and propagandist, one whose conversations were routinely reported by spies and informers in the post-war years. Preston's arrival at Spenceanism is worth tracing.[7]

Despite a lameness caused by a childhood accident, Preston 'acquired a strong inclination for travelling' and he went to Manchester, Liverpool, Nottingham, Birmingham, Warrington, Dublin, Cork and St Kitts in the Caribbean. He stayed long enough in 'Ireland, the essence of fertility' to become the 'advocate' of a Cork shoemaker union and there can be little doubt of his close association and sympathies with the Irish anti-colonialist United movements.

When he set up in London he was a frequent visitor to its literary societies and to the Polemic Society debating club in particular.[8] For Preston, Spence's simple ideology contained both a theory of revolution and a theory of conspiracy. Preston claimed that the land issue was well understood by those in power but that they 'regulate matters' so that 'the poor man wants food *even in the midst of plenty*'. The land, 'the natural source of vivification is frequently mismanaged and abused' and 'the "people's stores" ' denied to the producers.[9]

Preston's involvement in Spencean ideology led him to be indicted for high treason after the Spa Fields riots of December 1816. When the case against James Watson Snr collapsed with the exposure of the spy John Castle, Preston's case was not pursued but his *Life and Opinions* is a defiant discussion of his background and beliefs written on the roller-coaster of his contemporary notoriety. He included accounts of his arrest at his house (in the unfortunately suspicious 'Gunpowder Alley') and midnight visits and interrogations by the Lord Mayor. Preston's own account of these interviews in his *Life* is fairly modest compared with the actual records filed to the Home Office which reveal a principled and steadfast character. He told the Lord Mayor:

> There is nothing in my view can save the country than the great landholders and fundholders giving up something – I have seen such distress about Spitalfields that I have prayed to God to swallow us up I have seen a fine young woman who has not lain in bed for 9 months, I have ruined myself I have not a pound I have kept forty men at work but I never could see a fellow creature in distress without relieving them.[10]

Preston's sensitivity about homeless young women may have been sharpened by his own family of daughters. His generosity to those in distress (actual as well as philosophical philanthropy), is independently supported by an informer who reported on Preston at the Red Hart in Shoe Lane in 1816:

> He usually asked, in the Tap-room he visited, if there were any Men out of Work; if there were, he immediately sent for Bread, Cheese & Beer, saying, 'It is the Duty of every one not to see any one in distress, but to divide all equally'.[11]

At his examination, Preston daringly referred to the disaffection of the armed forces: 'I am convinced the Troops are not [as] satisfied at the present time as they are imagined to be'.[12] This is another reminder of a long and wishful belief of Spenceans.

Preston straddles all sides of radical activity. His boast of having 'kept forty men at work' is testimony to his relative success as a businessman (in the Thomas Hardy tradition) but he is also glimpsed carrying out the humdrum work of circulating Spencean ideas. He does not seem to have written any Spencean tracts himself but, at the Red Hart in 1816, Preston was reportedly selling a pamphlet by Thomas Evans 'entitled "Spence's Plan" ' and employing three men to distribute handbills. Like Spence, Preston accompanied sales of pamphlets with verbal observations about 'the present calamities'.[13] His career, in many ways, is paralleled by that of another Spencean shoemaker, Allen Davenport.

Davenport, like Preston, seems to have had considerable skills as a speaker but Davenport was also aspirant in literature. Gaunt and high-cheekboned in appearance, perhaps from the prolonged periods of subsistence-level existence which he details in his autobiography, Davenport 'was never in any school, for the purpose of instruction, in all my life' but as a child his 'greatest ambition was to acquire the art of reading and writing'. Fallen to 'catching a letter at a time as I best could' from other children fortunate enough to have been to dame school, he bought printed songsheets and 'proceeded to match all the words in my printed songs, with those I had previously stored in my mind, and by remembering the words thus learnt, by comparing notes, I knew them again whenever they met my eye.' Davenport's arduous acquisition of literacy may have been typical of his exceptionally deprived class. In the 'small and obscure village' of Ewen on the Wiltshire–Gloucestershire border, Davenport's labouring father ('allowed to be the best scholar in the village') seems to have had no leisure time to devote to the education of his ten children.[14] By comparison, Davenport's contemporary, the field labourer poet John Clare in the village of Helpstone, Northamptonshire, was much more advantaged in educational opportunities. It took initiative, independence, labour and careful planning to learn to read and write. The result, in adulthood, was that Davenport 'could not shake off' the 'ruling passion' of poetry.[15]

Two friends taught Davenport how to make a pair of shoes and 'From that moment I called myself a shoe-maker, and have followed that trade ever since'.[16] Davenport's semi-skilled status enabled him to work 'at a starvation price' for a similarly struggling Cirencester shoemaker in 1800:

Irons were not used then in the country; we set the stitch with the thumb nail; and in that style, I soon made a pretty good shoe, and should have got on tolerably well, had it not been for the extravagant price of provisions, which lasted nearly two years, during which time, the people in the villages of that district were literally starving.[17]

Davenport's occupation of the lowest rung of the shoemaking trade coincided with the food price increases which provoked riots in London, even as William Blake escaped to Sussex.

Davenport's status as an unindentured, periodically itinerant shoemaker, 'very diffident of my ability in regard to my trade', made him circumspect about his prospects for making a livelihood, but on reaching London in 1804 he walked smartly into a shoemaking shop in the Edgware Road (to 'occasion, as we call it') and was taken on despite his 'country style of work'. When Davenport's first London master got into debt and died in prison, he found employment with another Edgware Road shoemaker. It was at this second London shoemaking shop that, in 1805, he became acquainted with Spence's ideas.

What is fascinating about Davenport's recollection of his first acquaintanceship with Spencean ideas is that it came during the course of a new literary friendship:

> One of this master's apprentices, a young man, on reading some of my verses, became quite enamoured with poetry, and evinced considerable genius, and tact in some of his poetical productions; and we became a sort of kindred spirits; but he died at the age of twenty four years.

Davenport and the apprentice clubbed together to buy 'Cooke's edition of the British Poets' at sixpence per number. This appears to have been Davenport's first experience of English canonical poetry. Cooke's poets, but Pope's especially, 'were complete dampers, and went very near to extinguish every spark of my poetic genius. I felt ashamed of my own, as I now thought, wretched doggerel.'[18] The unknown door-to-door bookseller of Cooke's poets, plying the Edgware Road, also brought about a considerable political event in Davenport's life.

One day 'the man that brought our numbers, brought also a book, which he said ought to be in the hands of every Englishman in the country' 'and lo! behold! what should this wonderful book be, but the *Spencean System*?'[19] T.J. Evans recalled that Spence eked out a living as 'a numbers carrier' in Oxford Street in the years just before his death in 1814 and it is conceivable that Davenport's first knowledge of 'the *Spencean System*' came directly from Spence's peripatetic book-selling activities.[20] By his own account, the effect on Davenport was electric: 'I read the book, and immediately became an out and out Spencean'. He underwent a political transformation: 'I had been a sort of Whig Reformer before; but I now saw clearly, that all Whig, Tory, or even Radical Reformers, were as rush-lights to the meridian sun, in comparison with that proposed by the clear headed, and honest hearted Thomas Spence.' Davenport may even have been a Spence bore: 'I preached the doctrine to my shop-mates, and to every body else, wherever, and whenever I could find an opportunity.' No doubt he was cordially tolerated in the workplace, but 'all the reformers that I met with' 'generally laughed at me, and called me a visionary.'[21]

Davenport's testimony forms one of the most complete records of how an artisan entered and acquired his contemporary symbolic culture of literacy, literary aspiration and ultra-radical politics. The *Life* contains other remarkable evidence of the literature and politics of the obscure tavern world of London radical culture. He published poetry, essays ('it was gently hinted that pieces in prose would be preferred') and letters in the 'very fiery political publication' *Sherwin's Political Register*.[22] Daveport was politically highly active, claiming to have attended 'all the great political meetings in Spa-fields, in Smithfield, and wherever and whenever any such meetings took place'. This dates his active political involvement as far back as 1816 but he was to take an even greater part as the decade wore on.[23]

'During the perilous years of 1818 and 1819, I strained every nerve, and called every faculty into action to inspire the people with the spirit of Reform', Davenport recalled. Spence's land plan formed the basis of his political ideology but Davenport was also responding to contemporary political hegemony when he sought 'to expose the deceit, the treachery, and the base doings of the higher powers, with Lords, and Commons, under the suspension of *habeas corpus*'.[24] One of his vehicles was 'a sort of dramatic poem' called *The Kings, or Legitimacy Unmasked*.

The Kings, or Legitimacy Unmasked, A Satirical Poem was printed on the Oxford Street printing press of the Spencean activist Samuel Waddington in 1819. A copy was bought by a spy directly from Robert Wedderburn and sent to the Home Office. According to the *Life*, it was printed at the author's expense and 'written in great haste'. Waddington was probably too volatile a character to make a good proof-reader and Davenport complained that 'instead of the errors of the author being corrected, in passing through the press, they were doubled by typographical errors and blunders.'[25] It may seem a small point to today's reader but Davenport was sensitive about the issue of language and literacy. Language was a political issue, so when the *Courier*'s editor Daniel Stewart employed terms like 'the rabble' and the 'ignorant mob', Davenport took exception.

As far as he was concerned, insistence on grammatical correctness was a device to disable and ignore the complaints of the 'labouring classes':

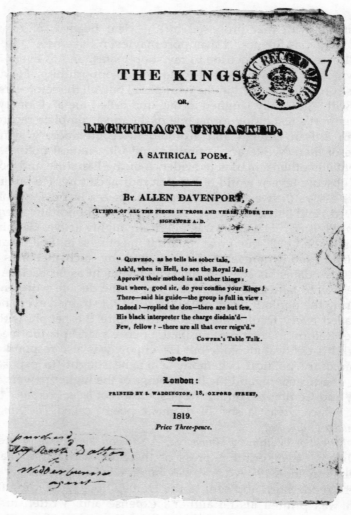

Figure 3.1 Title page of Allen Davenport's *The Kings, Or, Legitimacy Unmasked, A Satirical Poem*, London, 1819. HO 42/ 202. 7. (Courtesy of the Public Record Office)

If we attempt to express our sentiments in writing, they tell us that we, the labouring classes, not having a competent knowledge of grammar, must of course write nonsense, and therefore for one trifling error, or a mere mistake, tell the writer that he has a very bad meaning, or that he has no meaning at all. Oh! the grammatical fools! Was it with points in grammar that the famous battle of Naseby was decided, which wrested the liberties and property of England from the grasp of a lawless tyrant;

or that of Waterloo which has enslaved Europe? Certainly not, – it was
with the points of swords and bayonets, that both the good and the
mischief were peformed.[26]

Davenport had learned his linguistic fluency in the rough-and-tumble
of Thomas Evans's post-war Archer Street debating club. Sticklers for
grammar and spelling were employing a device to ignore political
aspirants and also ignoring the production economics of writing. His
writings had typographical errors because he was 'too poor to employ
a grammatical reader, to correct his manuscripts, and of too little
importance to command the press to attend to his own corrections'.
Ultra-radicals like him did not figure very highly in the hierarchy of
conventional publishing and the condition of the ultra-radical press
itself was probably too rough-and-ready for pedantic accuracy.[27]

Nevertheless, Davenport was proud of the poem's 'bold and
democratic style'.[28] Written in the form of a dialogue, *The Kings* is one
of Davenport's more successful writings. Easy, fairly memorable
couplets vividly illustrate his politics: 'Ancient kings as I've already
shewn, / Robb'd foreign states, the modern rob their own' and 'The
people have it in their pow'r I own, / Either to set up kings, or put
them down'. Politically, the poem is representative of the broad
ground of radicalism: a history of kings and kingship ends with the
exemplary republic of 'Columbia', or America, which 'owns no
pension'd knaves, or titled fools; / Her laws accord with nature's
glorious plan, / By which her sons enjoy the rights of man'.

Davenport was highly sympathetic to Napoleon. When he dis-
cusses him in *The Kings* Davenport carefully puts republican ideology
before considerations of national politics. Davenport is sympathetic
to Napoleon in exile but within a strictly republican ethic: 'Had he
[Napoleon] remained, as he at first began, / The foe of princes, but
the friend of man; – / Ah! had he nobly spurn'd the guilty
crown, / No human force could e'er have put him down!'. Davenport's interlocutor tries to catch him out: 'He is your favourite then,
the thing is plain, / You wish to see him reassume his reign.' The
reply is precise and succinct: 'You much mistake, I wish for no such
thing, / Let him be free, but let him not be king.'[29] Davenport's view
of Napoleon was that of a strict republican: Napoleon had been the
first man to threaten all of the European monarchies.

As far as Davenport was concerned the battle of Waterloo was the
victory of oppression. 'The plains of Waterloo became alike the grave
of heroism, and of the liberties of Europe', Davenport wrote in
Sherwin's Political Register, which was one of the most radical journals
of its day, having been earlier called *The Republican* before fears

engendered by the 1817 Suspension of Habeas Corpus brought about the change of name.[30] Davenport's contributions to *Sherwin's* put him in the midst of an ultra-radical press of bewildering vigour and ephemerality, including journals such as Robert Wedderburn's *The Axe Laid to the Root, Or, a Fatal Blow to the Oppressors* (1817), *The White Hat* (1819), Richard Carlile's *Republican* (1819–29), James Watson Snr's *Shamrock, Thistle and Rose* (1819) as well as the semi-permanence of *Cobbett's Weekly Political Register*, which went through a phase of being edited by Cobbett from the political safety of the USA.[31]

Napoleon, expressly in his republican context, was Davenport's hero because he headed a military force dedicated to crushing the monarchies of Europe. Davenport's *The Kings* steered a circumspect course around the figure of Napoleon but his poem 'The Musiad', printed in his collection *The Muses Wreath* in 1827, called for Napoleon to be celebrated as the central subject of epic poetry ('Napoleon! can no muse be found to sing / A matchless hero . . . / Whose deeds make *Iliads* seem realities').[32] Davenport never wrote his Napoleonic epic but in *Sherwin's* he visualized a hero dramatically flawed by monarchic tendencies:

> [Napoleon] held up tottering royalty for a season, by accepting of a crown himself . . . and was the chief cause of his final overthrow; for had he remained the citizen soldier, and retained the same principles that he professed when he was placed in the consular chair, there would not at this moment have remained one single crowned head in Europe![33]

Davenport's idea of Napoleon as a powerful republican model only makes sense if one appreciates Davenport's willingness to embrace physical force revolutionary politics.

Sherwin's Political Register became an important and sympathetic vehicle for Allen Davenport's writings. W.T. Sherwin had originally called his radical journal *The Republican* but in 1817, in the shadow of the Suspension of Habeas Corpus from February of that year and its sweep of radical arrests and departure of William Cobbett for the USA, he felt it prudent to offer a less provocative title.[34] After publishing one of his poems, *Sherwin's* 'gently hinted' that it would prefer 'pieces in prose' and Davenport 'took the hint, and [I] tried my hand in that department'. The result was 'eminently successful' and sometimes, he claimed proudly, 'I occupied half the space of the Register' and the 'signature of "A.D." became very popular': he had become 'a public writer'.[35] What is fascinating about his pieces for *Sherwin's Political Register* is that they are so obviously indebted to the confidence and fluency of the platform at the Archer Street debating club. *Sherwin's* allowed Davenport to develop his ideas in a swift and uncomplicated style, a simple language, devoid of subclauses and shot with the occasional metaphor:

> From time to time there has always been some king bee spring up, a Pitt, a Grey, a Burdett, or God knows who, 'all honourable men,' no doubt, and where they buzzed the People swarmed, and whenever they made a stand, the People both generously and firmly stood with them, till the leaders at length becoming inflated with popularity and intoxicated with their own success in gulling the People, their hearts became vain; they fancied themselves too great or too good to be the leaders of a crowd, and thought that their splendid abilities would correspond much better with the splendour of a Court. One of these worthies easily got what he wanted, – a good place; another sunk into a lord, and third seems to be 'like a young girl struggling between pleasure and reputation'. Thus have the People, from time to time been deserted by their leaders . . .[36]

This is from Davenport's first piece for *Sherwin's* and it shows a characteristic wariness of popular radical leaders like Burdett. The political autonomy of Davenport's artisan class is an important ultra-radical feature.

For Davenport, the difference between the pages of *Sherwin's Political Register* and the platform of Archer Street (or, later, Hopkins Street) was the difference between allusion and direct reference. What should be the fate of the 'accursed borough-mongering system', asked Davenport in *Sherwin's*? 'Let the shades of Cashman, Brandreth, Ludlam and Turner, answer the question!', he replied to himself, referring to the 1817 executions following Pentrich and Spa Fields. This was the trouble with writing to an unknown audience. Language was a species of haunting and this is probably why Davenport was steadily drawn towards the debating club forum. Print summoned up political ghosts but it lacked the immediacy, the connected presence, of speech: 'why then should we hesitate', declared Davenport under his Ferguson alias at Hopkins Street, 'I am ready now'.[37]

Davenport is an important figure in the history of the development of Spencean ultra-radicalism because his career can be followed from its earliest beginnings – from the moment of his reception of the Spencean ideology right through his involvement with Spenceanism's evolution into the National Union of the Working Classes, and the Co-operative and Chartist movements.[38] Davenport's serious literary aspirations also make him a significant figure typifying the movement away from physical force and towards respectable political commentary. To some extent, Davenport's eagerness to be fully incorporated into the growing myths of Romanticism in the mid-1820s shows how fully he had relinquished some of the earlier violence of his revolutionary views. In his collection of poetry *The Muses Wreath*, the materialist philosophy of d'Holbach, which had been mediated into ultra-radical circles by the publication of most of P.B. Shelley's *Queen Mab* in the 1815 *Theological Inquirer*, was vying for its place with new Romantic tropes like 'The Eolean Harp' which Davenport made relevant to infidel materialism simply by skipping Romanticism's dominating requirement to make everything metaphysical: Davenport's understanding of the organic had more to do with natural growth than with a reified concept of 'Nature'.[39] By the time of writing his autobiography in the mid-1840s, Davenport could confidently pinpoint an enigmatic artisan parallel for John Keats in a recollection of a shoemaker workmate who 'became quite enamoured with poetry, and evinced considerable genius' but who 'died at the age of twenty four years'.[40] Home Office surveillance was also so extensive that it is possible to corroborate much of Davenport's later *Life* and to see that his political commitment and active involvement in Hopkins Street debates of 1819, which were shadowed by revolutionary organization behind the scenes, was not compromised by his love of literature. With Allen Davenport, by courtesy of the Home Office, it is possible to see ultra-radical speech and writing functioning together. In the end Davenport, who had been operating under an unsuccessful alias, seems to have thought the Thistlewood group too violent or ill-led and he disappears from the scene towards the end of October 1819. At about the same time as he made his last recorded appearance at Wedderburn's chapel, Davenport seems to have stopped publication in the radical press. The *Theological Comet* had to ask 'What is become of A.D.?' before printing his 'Saint Ethelstone's Day', a bitter poem on the Peterloo Massacre with its 'Yeomanry Butchers' who 'hack'd off the breasts of women, and then, / . . . cut off the ears and the noses of men'.[41]

Davenport published in the ultra-radical press knowing that other booksellers thought his *The Kings* 'too strong': 'whenever it was exposed, it was suppressed by the new police.'[42] The fear of seditious prosecution continued to be a material regulation on the dissemination of discourse in the second decade of the nineteenth century, but Davenport's *The Kings* found another route into his radical culture. Although suppressed, Davenport's poem 'became a little popular among the radicals, some of whom got it by heart, and recited, or rather acted it in small assemblies, with some applause.'[43] What

Davenport is talking about is the 'Harmony' sessions which concluded Spencean 'free and easy' clubs. The tranposition of Davenport's suppressed written text into the orality of the 'free and easies' sheds yet another light on the culture of ultra-radical London.

'FREE AND EASIES'

At Colonel Despard's trial in 1803, the guardsman Robert Tomlinson gave evidence that he had attended a conspiratorial meeting at the Ham and Windmill tavern in Windmill Street which had been attended by about forty other soldiers: 'They were drinking, and a man asked me "If I would be sworn in;" I asked what that was; he said, "A free and easy society." '[44] 'Free and easies' were the preferred mode of ultra-radical discussion in the period following. This is how insurrectionary radicalism survived: as a culture whose discourses were oral rather than written, employing speech and song rather than writing. Unlike Spence's coins or pamphlets, speech and carnival have left few authored records.

Not all 'free and easies' were Spencean, but this was the format Spence and his followers developed to discuss and promote revolutionary politics. The best work on these has been done by Iain McCalman in his article 'Ultra-radicalism and Convivial Debating-clubs in London, 1795–1838'.[45] 'Free and easies' were informal political meetings and entertainments which took place in public houses in working-class areas of London. They grew out of the political and *ir*religious debating clubs of the 1790s. The Government took these clubs extremely seriously and in the years following the Spa Fields riots up to the Cato Street conspiracy, it would have been difficult to attend a 'free and easy' without at least one Home Office spy being present.

What was wrong with writing? Writing could be seized and conclusively identified; the new repressive laws and the old common laws of treason and sedition could be used against those who wrote. Even speech was dangerous enough: virtually all of the evidence against Colonel Despard came from reports on speech, things alleged to have been said. Robert Tomlinson's testimony at Despard's trial shows just how close the culture of 'free and easies' was to the revolutionary ideology. Asked to clarify what it was he had been asked to join, Tomlinson said it was 'A free and easy society to overthrow the Government, and have our nation the same as France.'[46] What is important about Tomlinson's statement is not its truth to the event but its performativity. 'Free and easies' were associated with the 'overthrow of Government': the court understood as much and Tomlinson was not further examined on the meaning of his words. For Despard, it was enough to hang him.

What was it like to attend a 'free and easy'? Perhaps the best reactionary account of their 1790s phase, the pre-Spencean era, is given in William Hamilton Reid's *The Rise and Dissolution of the Infidel Societies in this Metropolis* of 1800. Reid's colourful eye-witness account is especially fascinating in view of his turncoat background. In 1793 he was in the LCS; in 1798 he was arrested at the same time as Thomas Evans and Thomas Spence, but by 1800 he had written a book which is an exposé of radical debating culture.[47] Reid's account is principally directed at religious infidelity but he writes of the convivial atmosphere which he had experienced at first hand:

> Next to songs, in which the clergy were a standing subject of abuse; in conjunction with pipes and tobacco, the tables of the club-rooms were frequently strewed with penny, two-penny and three-penny publications, as it were so many swivels against established opinions; while to enable the members to furnish themselves with the heavy artillery of Voltaire, Godwin, &c. reading clubs were formed.[48]

Reid's new reactionism led him to warn that 'these clubs were only frequented by low and obscure characters'.[49] According to Reid, 'the whole system of domestic economy seems reversed, by the introduction of deistical notions' in the infidel debating societies: women no longer dressed up or attended church on Sundays because their husbands were become rationalists and allowed their children to run wild in the fields.[50]

This subverting of social hierarchies was something Reid found especially worrying. 'It should be observed, that as apprentices were admitted into these assemblies; and, according to the modern notions of equality, eligible to the chair, so sudden a transition, from domestic inferiority to professional importance, often turned a weak head . . .'[51] The danger of spreading disaffection to the lowest sections of society via these convivial debating clubs was a fear frequently voiced by Reid, who must have written his slim volume in the latter half of 1800 because he notes that the high price of provisions meant that 'the herding principles has been checked' and the labouring class can no longer associate in the taverns of London.[52] Reid's comments are revealing of London life before and after the food shortages. 'The passengers, who, in the piping times of peace, were frequently obstructed, can now pass, unmolested by ballad singers, and drunken squabbles in the streets' and this 'has prevented many of them from being introduced to the the Infidel or Political Societies at the public houses.'[53] This tavern-based political activity denounced by Reid was to become much more raucous in the next two decades.

Accounts of tavern polemics are fragmentary but can be gauged by using Spencean publications and spy reports in conjunction. Around 1811 Thomas Evans published his *A Humorous Catalogue of SPENCE'S SONGS*, Parts I, II and III.[54] The pamphlet would have been inexpensive in any case, but publication in three parts ensured that even the poorest of the tavern song-fanciers could take home some of it. In 1817 a Home Office spy dispatched one back to headquarters where it can be seen as a rough-bound pamphlet, its cover iconoclastically recycled from the title page of a book on English law.[55] Evans's 'Address To All Mankind' contained a kind of ideological manifesto of the Spencean 'free and easy':

> If but two or three meet together in so good a cause, a blessing will attend them. Even under the modern Tyrannies of China, France, Turkey, &c. what could hinder small Companies from meeting, in a free and easy convivial Manner, and singing their Rights and instructing each other in Songs? Can Tyrants hinder People from singing at their Work, or in their Families? If not despair no longer but begin immediately, too much time has already been lost. Sing and meet and meet and sing, and your Chains will drop off like burnt Thread.[56]

The prose here has some of the obstructive quietism exhibited by Spence when he remonstrated with the runners who bundled him into their carriage in 1792. This is 'so good a cause' that 'a blessing will attend' all who meet 'in a free and easy convivial Manner'. The place of songs in the Spencean 'free and easy' is interesting.

Evans's 'Address' seems to make it clear that 'small Companies' gathering 'in a free and easy convivial Manner' could evade political repression. Nobody could clamp down on singing in the workplace, yet this was exactly where activists like Davenport were discussing Spencean principles with the unconverted. A populace who 'sing their rights' and instruct each other in song eluded surveillance in their chorus of numbers. Though there were spies in the tavern, they could sing Spencean songs 'in their Families'. The music of the 'free and easy' is the music of carnival, harlequin with an apocalyptic dagger: 'Sing and meet and meet and sing, and your Chains will drop off like burnt Thread'. Evans's prose here is measured and symmetrical, ending with a comparatively rare example of a vivid and wholly memorable Spencean metaphor.

What were the songs like? They tend to come across as a didactic carousal of Tommy Spence and his plan grafted over well-known tunes in the same way that Spence's slogans were stamped over common coins. The songs proclaimed Spence's cheap publications to the 'Swine': *Pigs' Meat* for the swinish frequenters 'At the Sign of the Fleece' in Little Windmill Street where 'Spence treats all the Swine with a Book; / But not for vile pelf / 'Tis all wrote by himself / To instruct you by Hook or by Crook'. There was no necessity to learn the words, just listen and then join in at the universal 'Tol de rol' refrain, possibly led by Thomas Preston or Thomas Porter. The Home Office's copy of *A Humorous Catalogue of SPENCE'S SONGS* is accompanied by a slip of paper with the spy's hastily scribbled notes: 'Porter —— will be in Old Street, St. Luke's singing, supposed, Thursday'. Porter's plans conveyed, the spy added a brief physical description which fixes the fact that Porter must have gone to the tavern in his stone-mason's work clothes, the spy thinking the colour denotative of politics: '– Ab$^{t.}$ 5f. 5I – with a white apron on. – dark short hair – sings loud'.[57] Evans's song 'THE INEFFICACY OF THE FRENCH REVOLUTION', grafted over the tune 'Malbrouk', seems to threaten that the Spencean-next-time would be different. Napoleon lacked an ideology but the Spenceans do not:

> The Gallic Revolution,
> Pretended Restitution,
> But where's their Distribution
> On the Agrarian Plan?
>
> They wanted Tommy Spence,
> To teach them Common Sense,
> And then their Hills and Dales, Sir,
> Their Rivers Plains and Fields, Sir,
> Had not been bought at Sales, Sir,
> They're just where they began.

Evans's song visualizes a redistribution of land under an 'Agrarian Plan' while 'Spence' conveniently rhymes with 'sense'. Disillusionment with Napoleonic France is obvious, the English alternative being Spence's plan.

Official surveillance became much more systematic in the aftermath of the Spa Fields rising which was attended by an entwining of politics and violence. The report of the spy Williamson, alias 'C', on a late September 1817 visit to the Waterman's Arms, Castle Street, Bethnal Green, gives one of the fullest eye-witness accounts of the procedures, protocol and culture of a 'free and easy'. The detail of this record also gives some idea of the extent of Government surveillance at that time. 'C' is 'Examin^t.' and his report is taken up about two-thirds of the way through:

> It wanted about 10 minutes to 7 when they got there – they went first into the Tap Room then up stairs – The room upstairs is two Rooms made into one, it is a cosy room. They waited in the tap Room till the Company became very numerous, then they went up – Before they went up stairs one of the Sailors was dispatched after Preston to know why he did not come – After they got up stairs Porter came in and took the Chair – This had been settled at Preston's the day before that he should take the Chair – Then Porter called Silence and gave the first Song – It was a song against the Prince Regent, about the fat Pig in Hyde Park, and the King gone to St. Paul's – then others sang a great many Songs all against Government and after each Man had done singing he gave a toast – Examin^t. remembers two of the toasts – One was given by Porter and was this 'May the Skin of the tyrants be burnt into Parchment and the Rights of Man written on it' – The other toast was 'Here's wishing the old Dog may be hung, the old Bitch drowned, and the Young Whelps smothered' – Examin^t. does not know the name of the Man who gave that – The toasts were received with great acclamation – During the txxx the Landlord (Byer) sent up to say there were two Officers in the place and they must not be singing such kind of things – This was told Massey and Porter and they gave it [?] round to the [?] next – some of the Company went away when they heard of the Officers – Then some one sang a merry making Song – Preston came in before the Song began he took his seat alongside the Chairman He made an apology for Thistlewood and Watson being absent, he said they were on other particular business of as much consequence as there was there, and he hoped the Company would excuse them – Before the Company separated Preston made a speech 'That he hoped they would have the hearts of Englishmen, not to be Slaves any longer, but turn out & fight and xxx those d——d infernal Villains' – the Company gave thre Cheers with their hats off when he had done – The Room was very full
> _58

This report is a rich field for study. The organizers arrive first and wait in the 'tap' until the top 'cosy' is packed with about 140 people, some of whom are sailors. They pay on entry. The 'free and easy' is chaired, Porter previously having been delegated to carry out this function. Porter calls for silence and delivers the first song and then others join in singing 'a great many Songs' all of them 'against Government'. Each singer finishes his song with a toast, received 'with great acclamation'. The landlord is identified by name in order that the authorities could consider revoking his licence. On this night the landlord is complicit enough with the political gathering to be prepared to warn of the arrival of police officers but cautious enough to ask them to pipe down. Some of the gathering are intimidated at the mere mention of the presence of police and they drift away. Political singing is tactically exchanged for a 'merry making Song'. Preston enters the room and has to apologize for the absence of Thistlewood and Watson who would have been star-turns for the evening. Afterwards, the sailor who organized future tavern venues refused to circulate word of the next meeting unless Thistlewood and Watson were 'promised'. After merry singing, Preston commands sufficient quiet to make a 'long Speech about Government' and sufficient respect to have the speech raucously concluded by 'three Cheers' with hats off.[59] Whether or not Preston knew of the presence of the police officers, he proceeds with a physical force speech, appropriating the national identity of 'Englishmen' to get them to 'turn out & fight' 'those d——d infernal villains' of rulers. Earlier toasts had called for the smothering and drowning of royalty and its offspring while Porter's toast, ' "May the Skin of the tyrants be burnt into Parchment and the Rights of Man written on it" ', reminds us that natural 'Rights' need to be written where it counts, where everything is written, on the body. The evening concluded with the nucleus of organizers having a separate 'Gin' (*sans* tonic?) to discuss the next meeting.

Some of these ultra-radical songs were learned by heart. A Home Office trawl for information about the coloured man William Davidson (in prison in 1820 and soon to be executed for his part in Cato Street) reported him singing 'Songs . . . of a Political kind', according to the information of one R.I. Chaff, musician. Some personal belongings of Chaff's brother had been left with Davidson while he went off 'in the employ of a Person who travels about the County with wild Beasts'. Clearly, the circus was proximate with the conspirator. Chaff, on rummaging through his brother's things, came across a marbled exercise book entered up in something which looks like Davidson's handwriting and containing a list of the names and addresses of the Cabinet: in other words, a Cato Street 'hit' list. Chaff was sufficiently friendly with Davidson to have once been invited 'to an Entertainment given by Davison [*sic*]' where 'There was singing & Dancing & the Songs were of a Political kind, & reflecting in very bad Language upon the Ministry, & also alluding to the Regent'. Chaff swore that 'Davison sung himself a particularly bad Song, when he appeared to sing Extempore & not to read from any Paper'.[60] Davidson's memorizing of political songs tallies with Allen Davenport's claim that *The Kings* was 'got . . . by heart' by radicals.[61] It is likely that, for a time, Davidson and Davenport would have mixed in the same Hopkins Street circles.

By the end of 1816, the Mulberry Tree in Moorfields had become the regular Thursday venue 'for the avowed purpose of debating on the Spencean Philanthropy'. Details gathered by the Home Office revealed seven London sections which blanketed the week with political gatherings, usually on the 'free and easy' model. Some were Spencean, others were more loosely defined as being 'for the Purpose of hearing Cobbets Register read'.[62] While the Spenceans may have been taking the same organization to different venues round the week, it is quite probable that auditors and participants passed between the different debates on offer. It was thought that there were political meetings and readings in 'one twentieth part of the Public Houses in London' and many more were centres 'for the Purposes of receiving signatures for a Reform'. The Home Office was able to draw up its own description of both kinds of activity:

> The meetings . . . Generally Commence ab^t 8 oclock – Sunday is the General evening for reading Cobbett, – frequently after which the Examiner & Independant Whig are read & other Political tracts Calculated xxxx the heart and inflame the unthinking – the mode is this – the Chairman Calls on a reader from those appropriated to that part who Generally takes his place at a Desk – there is not much Argument on these evenings – but in proportion as the Company is select – the reader shapes his comments – on the other Evenings there is Generally some abstract Political Question debated – but it is remarkable that the speakers soon forsake the bearings of the original Question and deviate into such a path as gives scope for the most violent invectives against Ministers Parliament and every part of the Government – . . . there Appears nearly throughout the whole Class of the regular attendants of these meetings dispositions to become disciples of the wildest wickedst Theories that every [sic] destroy'd the Social Happiness of Civil Society – these meetings are always attended by Pamphleteers (vendors of them) who bring for sale the most seditious cheap tracts that are in print the number of which attend these meetings are from 60 to 100 at the Mulberry Tree there has been nearly 150.[63]

All the fears of the authorities can be seen in this report. The reading aloud of *The Independent Whig* and Cobbett's *Political Register* ensured that the intentions of the restrictive stamp duties were partially alleviated and illiteracy bypassed. Newspapers read aloud in the pubs of Clerkenwell and the Borough would 'inflame the unthinking' into becoming 'disciples of the wildest wickedst Theories'. It may have been in this sort of context that Allen Davenport's *The Kings* was performed. Notably, it seems to have been the practice for readers to enlarge and 'shape' 'comments' on what was being read and the fact that 'there is not much Argument on these evenings' implies that audiences were attentive. The presence of 'Pamphleteers' selling 'the most seditious cheap tracts . . . in print' provided a significant support for all of these activities. On other nights, the debates ranged widely. Scrutiny by the authorities of pre-published topics and questions for debate (stuck up on handbills or carried in the press) would yield no reliable information on the likely degree of contentiousness because radical debates could adapt themselves to the audience or to the speakers. 'Abstract Political Questions' formed a notional starting point but soon the debates 'forsake the bearings of the original Question and deviate into such a path as gives scope for the most violent invectives' against authority.[64]

The regularity of the provision of 'free and easies' ensured that the Spencean philosophy and all aspects of topical radical politics could be discussed in an atmosphere of solidarity and conviviality. Sometimes the spies were alarmist, as when one visited the ' "Polemics" ' club at the pro-Spencean Mulberry Tree and found them 'disseminating the Poison of their Principles to sap the foundation of Society'. Not only that but they discussed the Pentrich trials 'with an Accuracy that showed they had studied the Law'.[65] The spy may have been exaggerating his fears, but the Spenceans were sufficiently active over a sufficient number of years to suppose that the 'disseminating' of 'Principles' had some measure of effectiveness. The relationship between Spence's pronouncing books and the 'free and easy' is now an easy one to see because articulacy and intervention were both enabled and encouraged by the informal atmosphere of these tavern clubs. Well-known local speakers were listened to with respect but it was the leading ideologues such as Thomas Evans and Robert Wedderburn who encouraged and set up the Archer Street and Hopkins Street debating clubs to provide specific forums for the audience's articulation and intervention. There is enough evidence from the whole series of insurrections planned around the time of Bartholomew Fair 1817 to believe that the Spenceans thought there was a vivid connection between the 'free and easy' and the popular uprising. The principal event which led them to believe that this formula would be crowned with success was the uprising at Spa Fields in December 1816.

CHAPTER FOUR

Articulacy and Action

THE SPA FIELDS RISING, 1816

It is about 1 p.m. on the afternoon of Monday 2 December 1816. The place is the open ground of Spa Fields, London.[1] By 11.30 a.m. that morning a crowd of some 2000 people had assembled near the Merlin's Cave public house and 'a still greater concourse' of people are 'dispersed in various parts of the fields' in the direction of Cold Bath Fields prison. The famous demagogue Henry 'Orator' Hunt is expected but is now overdue. At 12.30 a.m. some 'Shabby looking Men' draw a waggon onto the grounds, halting it across a path running over Spa Fields.[2] Thinking 'Orator' Hunt had arrived, 'a large proportion of the Populace . . . came running in all directions' towards it. The men carry two 'Tri Coloured' flags and a banner which is a canvas frame ('like a picture frame') on a pole.[3] They stick them up on the waggon. On the banner there is an inscription: 'The Brave soldiers are our Brothers, treat them kindly'. One of the flags, it will emerge in court later, also carries an inscription – you need to look carefully because the cold wind is causing the flag to flap about, making it difficult to read: 'NATURE TO FEED THE HUNGRY'.[4] As you approach, you can see a number of men standing on the waggon. Thinking that one of them is 'Orator' Hunt, a considerable crowd has gathered. Unknown to anyone there, Hunt was still continuing 'a long speech' elsewhere on the fields.[5] The leader of the shabbily dressed men is the surgeon–apothecary 'Dr.' James Watson Snr. He is accompanied by his son, James Watson Jnr, Thomas Preston and Arthur Thistlewood and the United Irish emissary William Putnam McCabe, direct from Paris.[6] The men are members of the small organizing group who arranged and publicized the meeting. Hand-bills have been posted up well in advance. With the 'Orator' absent, 'The Gentlemen in the Waggon . . . seemed to have a plan of their own independent of their former leader.'

The Watsons and their political comrades have laid out their scarce money to hire the waggon on which they stand. They have made meticulous preparations to have suitable flags. The crowd is big. The conditions are right. The opportunity is not to be missed. Someone must speak. 'Mr. Watson Sn' prepared to address his auditors by waving his hand and giving other indications of intention . . . Comparative silence being at length obtained Mr Watson spoke as follows.' Watson Snr's speech is highly accomplished; the audience is sympathetic. Watson speaks for them and to them and they cry out their responses throughout.

About ten yards from the waggon, and clearly visible to the crowd, stands Vincent George Dowling, pencil at the ready. He is acting on behalf of the Home Office and will take down the speeches in shorthand. He will also note the responses of the crowd but these will be slightly doctored for the purposes of the trial. He will also tell the court at James Watson Snr's trial for high treason that 'While the two speeches were going on, they [the crowd] were extremely quiet, and were all attentive to the speeches; occasionally there were shouts, and these shouts did always end immediately.'[7] In court he says, at first, that he was there on behalf of *The Observer*. Pressed further, he will acknowledge that he files his copy directly to Mr Beckett, Under-Secretary of State at the Home Department, the man who had advised on P.B. Shelley's surveillance a few years earlier.[8] The crowd do not interfere with Dowling. Somewhere close to the waggon, but incognito, are two Bow Street runners, Despard veteran John Stafford and John Limbrick: they will testify directly at Watson's trial.[9]

James Watson Snr first made a statement of organization and intention: 'Fellow Countrymen we are Convened here this day in consequence of the resolution passed at the last Meeting to hear the Answer to the petition which we agreed should be presented to the Prince Regent'; and solidarity: 'those who were present when we last assembled together because they will best know how to appreciate the manner in which their prayers have been received (Cheers).' Then, a question which stirs the audience, fixes the current situation and makes the first implication that power is in the hands of those present:

> Mr. Hunt it will be recollected was the person deputed to present our Petition to the Prince Regent but what answer did he receive? none

Figure 4.1 'The Cart', from *The Dorchester Guide; Or, a House that Jack Built*, London, [Dec.], 1819. D. George BM Catalogue No. 13324. (Courtesy of the British Museum: Department of Prints and Drawings)

Whatever hopes we might entertain that our voices would be heard have all proved groundless – we are left to the full enjoyment of our miseries, without one ray of consolation (Groans and Cries of Shame).

Warming to the theme, more questions follow. Watson takes care to give the crowd its opportunity to respond: 'Is this the treatment which Englishmen have a right to expect? (Cries of No!) Ought we not to give vent to our feelings (Yes) Why did we call upon the Prince Regent to affect us redress?' Then there are answers, closely followed by more questions: 'because four Millions are overwhelmed with distress – while half a Million only are living in a state of splendid Luxury I ask is such a number as this to dictate to all England? (No!).'[10]

This repeated the claims of a handbill so firmly stuck to a wall that a passing agent of the Home Office had to write it out by hand. The three men, and others like them, employed to distribute handbills by Thomas Preston at the Red Hart in Shoe Lane that month had obviously done their work conscientiously.[11] The new language of class developed towards the end of the eighteenth century enabled adjectives to be stuck onto nouns: there was no longer just a 'lower' class but a class which 'laboured' and a class which did not.[12]

Fully involved with this responsive audience, Watson momentarily misjudges and puts a foot wrong:

> It is not only in this Country that we suffer In the sister Country, Ireland, our brethren are still more oppressed (murmurs of disapprobation from some of the Crowd as if they did not wish to Combine the Cause of Ireland with their own) There the Climax of misery is brought to a close – Thus it is impossible to carry oppression further!

This was the language of the handbill, the Irish dimension which was the true background of London physical force ultra-radicalism. An Irish-led insurrection, French backed, was the revolutionary blueprint going way back to Despard's time and beyond but it was still a locally unpopular cause. As it happened, the Home Office will sharpen its case for Watson's rabble-rousing by doctoring out this minor disagreement with the crowd when the speeches are read out at Watson's trial.[13] Watson retrieves the situation, he steers the issues back to action, back to the concept of a nation but one which has his own appropriation of 'Englishmen', in this time and this place:

> Are we then to go on from time to time – from month to month – from year to year crying to the Father of his People, as he is called for redress (cries of no – no – no!) Then if anything is to be done the present is the time in which it should be done! (Cheers Huzzas!) Can the minds and hearts of Englishmen remain inactive in such a State of things? (no, no!).

The next move is significant: discussion *and* writing have failed: 'How then are we to be restored to our rights – not by talking not by long speeches not by petition, for our Petitions are not heard (bravo!

Cheers).' The new language of 'rights', multiplied by Tom Paine, has been fully assimilated.

Crucially, Watson now began to suggest that authority has shifted from Parliament to those present in Spa Fields that afternoon:

> In this state of things we are assembled together to take into consideration the case of the dying Multitude the Calamatous state of the Nation It remains with ourselves to consider how we shall relieve ourselves in these Calamatous times (bravo!).

'It remains with ourselves to consider how we shall relieve ourselves' but with what authority and ideology? The ideology is Spencean:

> We have been truly told that Trade and Commerce are at an end but we still have the Earth – which Nature designed for the support of mankind The Earth is capable of affording us all the means of allaying our wants and of averting starvation – But how is this to be accomplished?

This is the essence of Spencean ideology and Watson gives it as a distillation and refraction into its simplest components. 'Nature designed' something: what 'Nature designed' has been taken away. The word 'Nature' is fixed, appropriated as a material. 'Nature' gives food. Just as it says on the banner, 'NATURE' will 'FEED THE HUNGRY.' The banner flaps in the breeze.

This is an ideology shorn of the name of its originator, although some will have heard Spence's name bandied about the local 'free and easies' or hawked about by vendors of pamphlets or even by the house-to-house booksellers who 'recommended' Spence's pamphlets while they sold Pope's poetry in part-works. One month after the rising, in mid-January 1817, a spy went to the Spencean haunt at the Cock in Grafton Street to hear Robert Wedderburn and fifty others debate the question 'Woud the Practical Establishment of Spences Plan be an effectual remedy for the present distresses' at which Thomas Preston 'told us that the landholder was a Monster that must be hunted down.'[14] At Watson Snr's subsequent trial for high treason a piece of inadmissible evidence will be a paper which reads 'Query. Have all men a right to an equal participation in land – A. Yes, as all men require the productions of the earth and water to exist, it is clear, nature intended those elements equally for all mankind'.[15] Put like this, the truth of Spenceanism was self-evident: 'But how is this to be accomplished?' Watson asked the crowd:

> I will tell you I have said the Bonds of Society have been neglected what then is our situation? They have (His Majesty's Ministers) placed us in a

state of Misery – they have neglected the Cries of the hungry and the starving people (Shouts and cries of 'they have' 'they have') There is not a day in which we pass the street that we do not see our miserable Countrymen starving to death Of this his Majestys Ministers ought not to be ignorant, if they are, but they are not. They know that the People are starving in every part of the Kingdom but they will not admit of any measures for their relieve (groans).

Those in power have broken their promise, spurned our rights: its effects are visible on the streets of London. The ignorance of ministers and Regent is not accidental, says Watson, it is wilful: 'Do they hear our Cries? (no, no).' The speech is reaching its climax. The 'language of Men', that Romantic myth, has not been heard. Watson's speech sweeps to its conclusion:

Have they not been supplicated respectfully and in the language of Men in the language of forbearance and patient suffering to afford us relieve (yes, yes!) Have they listened to us? (no, no!) must we not then act for ourselves (yes, yes!) Ever since the Norman Conquest Kings have deluded you and have in many instance converted you to their own wicked purposes (Cheers) This must not last any longer (Shouts and Cries of No, no!).

At this point, 'the Orator then stood down and made way for . . . Mr. Watson Jun.' James Watson Jnr came even nearer to the pulse of the crowd.

Watson Jnr picked up a vital thread from his father: the Prince Regent provided the continuity.

This Man calls himself the father of his people (cries of 'damn him!' 'down with him!') Is not the duty of Father to protect his Children? (Yes!) ought he when in the hour of distress they appeal to his Justice and assail him with their Complaints to spurn them and treat them with scorn? (no!) Ought he to trample on their rights and privileges as Englishmen? (no!) Ought he to spend in idle extravagance and luxury the money which as been wrung out your pockets? (no! no!) Are we to submit patiently to such treatment (no!) Will Englishmen any longer suffer themselves to be trod upon like the Poor African slaves are in the West Indies? (no, no, we must have relief!).

As the Bow Street runner (and spy) John Stafford testified in court, Watson Junior's speech 'seemed to consist principally of interrogatories'.[16] The crowd's responses became more articulate, swinging, in tune with the orator, between groans and huzzas amidst the crushing, unifying levelling of laughter:

But how are you to be relieved? It is true that since we last met, from the Resolutions which we then passed and the firmness with which we acted, that Meetings have been called and subscriptions entered into to give us ox-cheek Soup and Old bones Broth (laughter and cries of shame!) on these occasions some come forward with their two hundreds who ought to have come forward with one or two hundred thousand Can you believe then that these People meant sincerely to obey the wishes of the Multitudes? (No! No!) Do you not believe that they would still come forward and rob you of all you possess? (yes, yes!) and then give you a Penny to pay the Turnpike? (laughter) The Prince Regent in his great generosity has given you £6000 out of funds which did not touch his own pocket – yes and then too when he possesses plenty and spends a Million a year taken from your Pockets in Wasteful profusion (Groans) A Friend of mine here had been designated by the Treasury Journals as a second Watt Tyler – no bad title – for be it recollected that Watt Tyler rose for the purpose of putting down an oppressive Tax and would have succeeded had he not been basely murdered by William Walworth then Lord Walworth then Lord Mayor of London but if he was surrounded by thousands of his fellow Country as I now am no Lord Mayor that ever existed would have stopped his Career (Huzzas) It seems to be the determined Resolution of Ministers to carry every thing their own way – or as they state – our Sovereign Lord the King intends to carry every thing with firmness – In that they mean to carry the business in defiance of the voices of the people (groans) Now I will ask, if they will not give us what we want shall we not take it (yes! yes!) Are you willing to take it? (yes, yes! from all quarters) Will you go and take it? (Yes, yes) If I jump among you will you follow me? (cries of yes and loud acclamations).[17]

'At that instant,' wrote the spy, 'the Orator seized the largest of the tri coloured Flags and heading the Mob marched off towards Clarkenwell amidst loud shouts.' According to the runner, John Stafford, a small part of the mob ran ahead of the flags.[18] As they ran past, Stafford seized the motto-less, tricolour flag and tried to break it but, amazingly, he claimed 'it was the stem of a young tree . . . too strong for me' and he managed to grab only a green strip of cloth to produce in court.[19] His runner colleague, John Limbrick, attempted to pull down the other flag and the situation turned briefly ugly ('Cut him – cut his bloody head') before Stafford came to the rescue.[20] The crowd was armed with 'guns, pistols, cutlasses, dirks of various description, and also a small brass carronade . . . on wheels, drawn by men,' according to *The Observer*'s man while, at Watson's trial, there was talk of pikes concealed in privies.[21] In the mayhem, 'some were discharging their pieces in the air, not to do mischief' and someone overcharged a pistol heavily enough for it to explode and blow their finger off.[22] James Watson Snr, John Hooper, Arthur Thistlewood and Thomas Preston were all subsequently arrested and charged with high treason. James Watson Jnr escaped and eventually got a passage to America.[23]

Everything about this Spa Fields meeting suggests that it was an uprising rather than a riot: 'the commencement of an insurrection, as I should describe it', the experienced chief Bow Street clerk John Stafford told the court.[24] The Spa Fields uprising had been prepared and made possible by radical articulacy, the culture of the 'free and easy' coupled to the twin Spencean ideologies of land incorporation and physical force. Watson Jnr's speech jettisons the false largesse of the rich with their pennies for the vagrant sent off down the turnpike to the next parish, and it closes on the authority of history. Wat Tyler's revolt is Watson's precedent (this explains why Southey's *Wat Tyler, A Dramatic Poem* was published the next year). The historical counter-culture of England has been well inculcated in a thousand Spencean debates.

The importance of Spa Fields is that it can be identified as a moment when a linguistic event turned into a revolutionary event. It happened because language is always transgressive. Revolutions are where language transgresses into another order of discourse, the discourse of action. The physical results of Spa Fields were, at best, inconclusive. E.P. Thompson justly notes that all it amounted to was that the area of the Minories, to the north of the Tower, were haphazardly held for several hours. However, there can be no doubt that the discursive properties of the Spa Fields, laden with the Spencean ideology, survived intact. Three weeks after the rising, the spy George Ruthven called on Thomas Evans 'to buy one of the Books in Evans's Window – entitled "Christian Policy" [*Christian Policy the Salvation of Empire*, 1816, one of Evans's own pro-Spencean pamphlets] and asked "Did not you think it an imprudent thing to begin the Riot so early in the Day"?' Evans disagreed and told Ruthven that he thought the crowd should have headed immediately for the Minories where Evans thought there was a 'large quantity' of arms and where the soldiers would have admitted them into the Tower. Whatever Evans's views about the inconclusiveness of the rising, he was in no doubt about the strength of the Spenceans: 'He expressed a perfect Confidence that the Spencean System would sooner or later prevail', he told Ruthven. Two months later, in the Nag's Head, Carnaby Market, Thomas Evans made sure symbolic rituals of collective affirmation took place when he 'stated &c that the Land was the Peoples right &c. asked every Individual present if they agreed, and each answered Yes upon their Honour . . .' There were fifty people present that night and all of them, 'Mr. Clarke' reported, pledged themselves to Spencean land redistribution.[25]

The Spa Fields 'riot' had been carefully planned to be an uprising. In late October 1816 a number of people had found handwritten bills 'put under their Doors in the course of last Night' reading:

> Britons to Arms!
> The whole *country* waits the Signal from *London* to fly to *Arms! Hasten* break open all *Guns* & Sword shops! or other likely places to find Arms! – Run all Constables thro who touch a man of us! – No rise of *Bread!* – No Regent! No *Castlereagh!* Off with their *Heads! –* No Place-men *Tythes,* or *Enclosures! –* down with them all – Stand true or we are *Slaves* for Ever! – NB printed Bills with farther particulars will be sent out in due time. 500 written ones are now up in different parts of the Town.[26]

The breaking open of gunshops was faithfully followed on the night of Spa Fields and the denunciation of *'Enclosures!'* betrays typically Spencean preoccupations. The laborious production of handwritten bills coupled with the odd assurance that 'printed Bills' will soon be produced indicates a little local difficulty caused by the propensity for Londoners to turn informer.

Thomas Storer, a printer, had been approached by the two Watsons (in late October or early November 1816) to print handbills. Storer thought the handbills too inflammatory and tipped off 'Mr Beckett the Under Secretary of State' at the Home Office. Storer is a run-of-the-mill sort of informer by the standards of the times but Beckett of the Home Office was a significant person: he was the one who directly received Dowling's transcript of the Spa Fields speeches. Storer's information provides a fascinating context for the Watsons' preparations.

The physical force philosophy of the uprising was also manifested behind the scenes. When Storer refused to print the bills, the Watsons dropped in on him. Storer sought to give his information as if verbatim. Watson had said: 'I suppose you are afraid of having your house about your ears, and by your refusing me the Bills and disappointing me is enough to bring it upon you.' This scarcely veiled threat was backed with apocalyptic imagery: 'there is a Revolution in the Country which cannot exist a week longer unless something is done, and when it takes place it will be like the rolling of the sea and overwhelming all before it . . .'[27] The prophetic idiom is consistent with other examples of Spencean discourse. That the Watsons' ideas were Spencean is corroborated by another handbill Storer claims Watson Snr gave him. This stated that 'the Royal Family were to be placed as Pensioners and the Land to be divided, and things completely changed'. The Watsons backed the theory of their physical force philosophy with weapons as well as threats.

By late evening on the night of Spa Fields the failure of the rising was evident. James Watson Snr seems to have realized his exposed position and by 11 p.m. he was trudging northwards out of London on foot in company with two men. Charles Miell of the Bow Street 'horse-patrole' had been tipped off about Watson's route and knew that he was expected to be armed. He and other officers galloped in pursuit. The results were both dangerous and hilarious:

> I rode up to the prisoner at the Bar [Watson] which was the first man, and I said 'Gentlemen, I beg your pardon, but where are you travelling to', the prisoner at the bar replied, 'to Northampton' I told him it was a late hour of the night to be travelling so near London.[28]

The next thing that happened was that Watson took 'a bundle up from under his right-arm' and passed it up to Miell who was mounted on his horse:

> Instead of my taking hold of the bundle, I passed my left-hand into the breast of his coat, and I catched hold of the butt-end of a pistol; I drew the pistol from the prisoner, and told him that if he offered to move, I would blow his brains out.

Miell's colleagues sounded rattles to call for help, whereupon 'the other two persons who were with the prisoner, drew a pistol a-piece from their [greatcoat] pocket'. Both men aimed their pistols at Miell, one of them pulled the trigger. There was a flash in the pan – the gun failed to fire and Miell lived to tell the tale in court to a solicitous Solicitor General.[29] Watson Snr was arrested there and then but his son, James Watson Jnr, eventually escaped to the USA assisted by Watson's friends. Rumours abounded that he had scarred his face with caustic but, according to the examination of Robert Moggridge – a fellow radical and friend of the family – 'Watson was not disguised, he had a mark or mole on the right Cheek and a dropping of the left Eye lid, he told me he had applied Caustic to the Mole, but it did not appear to have produced any effect.'[30] Different versions of this rumour seem to have persisted at least into the autumn. One spy gave a particularly ruthless account of how he had been in conversation with Arthur Thistlewood and Thomas Preston at the Salmon and Ball in Bethnal Green Road when they had seen a sailor in the tavern who looked like 'Young Watson'. Thistlewood and Preston 'proposed to burn a Scar in his face with caustic', dress him up like Watson Jnr, hand him over and collect the reward 'to put the Government to the Expence'. Nothing came of it.[31]

Perhaps put on by Mr Beckett of the Home Office, Thomas Storer had dogged the movements of the Watsons and their friends right into the tavern world of London's radical culture. John Dyall, engine-weaver and founder chairman of the Spa Fields meeting organization, was found by Storer in the Carlisle public house, Shoreditch.[32] Dyall 'appeared about half Drunk and was reciting a passage from Shakespeare's Tempest ending with "like the baseless fabric of a Vision leaving not a Wrack behind"'. Storer provides little context or comment for this quotation but Shakespeare seems to be appropriated to signify the coming insurrection rather than the stately harmonies of the Bard's last plays.

Fraternity between soldiery and citizenry was at the forefront of their concerns:

> Dr Watson declared that for three Months past he had been sounding the inclination of the Army and he found they would not interfere with the Mob unless they were insulted for they had all Families and relatives in the same distress as ourselves.

They would get the people to 'Cheer' the soldiers and get them to 'act with them', Storer reported.[33] According to the spy John Castle, the Watsons planned to send in a parade of young women dressed in white carrying small flags and cockades 'in order to take off the attention of soldiers, so that they should not ride over us, and to give us time to address them'. The symbolic use of white fits in with radical preferences of the time. So too, unfortunately, does the symbolic use of women dragooned to face the bayonets in the fashion of male ultra-radical opportunism of the time.[34] Even if Dr Watson eventually got it wrong about the army, the possibility of such a collusion would not have seemed an unusual suggestion to his auditors. 'They could fight as well in a black Coat, as in a blue or a red', Watson told them, 'and there was plenty who knew the use of Arms as well as them', that is, citizens were as well armed as soldiers. Watson's language was appropriately within the apocalyptic register of revolutionary situations ('It was time for something to be done', 'there was a kind of dark cloud hung over them').[35] If Spencean ideas were pledged in public, private conversations were also faithfully reported to the Home Office:

> Last night I was in Company with Preston alone but cannot get correct information of the Proceedings to be acted on Friday next – It is my

Opinion from what I collect from his Utterance the Bank is to be attacked by the People in a Body led on by him his End he says is to do away with Land Owners and Fund holders and produce a New Order of Things – I wish to know how you mean to Act as I am positive I can assist in a Measure . . . .[36]

Whatever Storer thought was going to happen on Friday 29 November never happened, but the existence of a *coup* plan some days before the meeting proves that the riot had a planned spontaneity and Preston's reference to the seizure of the Bank of England harks back to the insurrectionary objectives of Colonel Despard in 1802 and may have been a satisfactory result of Cobbett's ceaseless attacks on paper currency and fundholders. Although capturing the Bank would have been of great symbolic appeal, it is a useful reminder that Spencean ideas had always been based upon economics as well as natural rights.

Storer's offer to assist the Home Office was probably not taken up. The Government had its own spy and *agent provocateur* in place: John Castle. Castle's evidence runs to over 150 pages in the printed transcript of Watson's trial.[37] The defence successfully managed to prove Castle's murky background which included an obscure episode in Abergavenny when Castle was a soldier and had been involved in an attempt to free a French prisoner of war alleged to be an eminent artillery officer in Bonaparte's army.[38] Castle's testimony was brilliantly contradicted by 'Orator' Hunt whose testimony at Watson's trial was crucial. Hunt retained the aura of respectability that the obscure apothecary lacked and he was regarded as a notable, if notorious, politician whose credentials were still intact after Spa Fields because he did not get there until after the mob headed off for the gunshops of Clerkenwell. However, he had spent some time with the Watsons and Castle before the riot at the Merlin's Cave tavern on the edge of the fields.

Hunt swore that at Merlin's Cave everybody drank the King's health except for Castle who had offered a toast beginning 'May the last of Kings be strangled' until interrupted by Hunt's outraged protests. Echoing the Spa Fields flag, Castle was also alleged to have said that 'the Soldiers are our friends' to which the rest of the company remained indifferent. Indeed, Hunt recollected that James Watson Snr had remonstrated with Castle about the violence of his language. To cap it all, Hunt calmly announced that the 'NATURE TO FEED THE HUNGRY' banner belonged to John Castle. Hunt stitched Castle up – good and proper.[39]

Reading Watson's trial transcript, it is not just Hunt's testimony or the reduction of Castle's credibility by defence counsel Topping which is remarkable but also the part played in it by the steady persistence and strategic information-sowing of ultra-radical witnesses. The Crown set about its case of arguing that Spa Fields was not a riot but an insurrection. To do this they concentrated not only on the alleged treachery of the two Watsons' speeches but also their production of handbills. The handbills would be used to clinch the argument about the premeditation and organization of the plot.

One of the first witnesses to be brought forward was Arthur Seale of Tottenham Court Road who was one of the most active and prolific of the radical printers associated with Spence and the later Spenceans.[40] Seale was at the cutting edge of the case against Watson. If it could be proven, consecutively, that Watson had ordered the handbills to be printed, that Watson knew what was on the handbills, that the crowd had assembled because of Watson's bills, that it was his speech which spurred the crowd to insurrection and that, finally, all of this was part of a deliberate plot and plan, Watson would be guilty.

Seale was asked to swear that Watson had heard the handbill read out prior to its being printed (this was the only way to prove that Watson was conscious of its contents and that the handbill's text belonged to Watson):

Q: Will you take upon yourself to swear that he heard it?
Seale: I have already sworn, and I cannot go any further.
Q: What have you sworn?
Seale: That he was present when the manuscript was given to me.
Q: Was it read over so that you can take upon yourself to swear that he heard its contents?
Seale: It is impossible to swear that a man heard, for a man may turn a deaf ear to what is read.
Q: Will you swear that he heard it?
Seale: I cannot understand the meaning of the word swear further.[41]

Seale is under quite a bit of pressure here. He cannot know what the outcome of this line of questioning will be but he sticks closely to the proposition that language addressed does not mean language arrived. Seale's is a brilliant piece of deconstruction of the word 'swear': that which the court wants confirmed as a promissory note of the spoken handbill text fully arrived at the receiver, Watson. Remarkably, Seale's interlocutor is the defence counsel, Copley, who seems to have been very confident or else very daring in pursuing this line of questioning. To make a convincing connection between

Seale, Watson and the handbill would be very damaging and it is difficult to see where Copley's line of questioning was intended to lead given that his ostensible purpose was Watson's defence.

Arthur Seale had been the printer of many of Spence's pamphlets, including *The Important Trial of Thomas Spence* (1803), so he would have learned lawyer-handling at the master's feet.[42] Seale was persistent in his extempore caution about the effective communication of language:

> Q: Upon the oath you have taken, do you believe Mr. Watson heard it?
> Seale: The only thing I could do would be to read it as I read it then, and then their Lordships and the Jury may judge whether he must not have heard it.
> Q: Will you listen to the question? Do you believe that Mr. Watson heard it?
> Seale: It is impossible to swear that another heard it.
> Q: The question is not that, and you must understand the question.[43]

At this point, Lord Ellenborough interrupted to try to clarify the question:

> Lord Ellenborough: The question now put to you is not of the description which might be objectionable; but the question is, whether you swear that you believe he heard it.
> Seale: Certainly.[44]

How intimidated was Seale? He was being pressed to answer a question which, in all probability, had been put to him in the hope that it might seem innocuous. Lord Ellenborough's intervention put a full stop to a definitive answer to the question of the communicative process of language. Instead, Seale was merely being asked to give advice about his 'belief' about what took place. Nevertheless, Ellenborough was a hated figure: in June 1817 a spy claimed that he was on a list of prominent people on the Spenceans' assassination list and that the publisher William Hone 'had been heard to say "it was a Pity no bold fellow could be found to murder Lord Ellenborough" '.[45]

Mounting a more clearly relevant defence of Watson, Copley insisted that the original manuscript of Watson's handbill be produced in court. Who had brought the original manuscript to Seale's printing shop? The answer was like a time-bomb lobbed into the courtroom:

> Mr. Topping (for the Crown): Who made the application to you to print these bills?

Seale: A Mr. Castle.

Mr. Topping: Was any paper brought by him?

Mr. Wetherell (defence): We do not know who this Mr. Castle is at present.

Mr. Topping: It is a fact –

Mr. Wetherell: But he is not connected at present.

Lord Ellenborough: He must be either a person connected with the purpose or not; now whether he is or is not it is a mere simple bringing of the bill: he is at present a mere human being, by whom this act was done.[46]

The importance of Seale's naming Castle was that, once he had been established as the bringer of the handbills, all the subsequent revelations about his dubious past as a soldier and his bigamy needed to be referred back to this point: Castle had been involved from the start and that was what Seale's very early testimony established beyond doubt. Topping probably did not know about Castle's manipulation as a Government spy and possible *agent provocateur*. Wetherell's caution about introducing Castle's name probably stems from his wish not to introduce an unknown quantity, but there may well have been some degree of moral posturing going on in the background, beyond the courtroom.

The separation of the judiciary from the police and from the Home Office may have been intact in the early nineteenth century but the gulf between them could be easily breached. Sir Richard Ford, although perfectly capable of planting moles, giving spies instructions and paying them for their service, had crises of conscience when their covert dealings were bearing fruit. Before Despard's trial back in 1803, Ford had written to the spy 'Notary' telling him:

I do not wish to be made acquainted with any thing that passes in your Committee that may tend to the prejudice of the State P—— on their approaching Trial, I do not think that would be fair – but whatever falsehood, or perjuries are in contemplation, there can be no impropriety in being informed of . . . I will never permit myself to go beyond the boundary of Honour and Candour.[47]

This is Sir Richard Ford putting his hands over his eyes and peeping between his fingers. Perhaps it is even more reckless than that because, in the case of such covert information, the master is at the mercy of the minion when it comes to the supply of news: Ford's 'Honour and Candour' are a slender guarantor against his own perjury.

During Watson's trial John Castle was officially under arrest (in the custody of 'Nodder') and charged with high treason. Did Seale have a suspicion of Castle's duplicity and, if so, was he deliberately originating the handbill with him? Such a cross-incrimination, a mirroring of Castle's own treachery to Seale's political friends, is not as far-fetched as it sounds because feints and hoaxes were Spencean counter-strategies developed to meet the surveillance of the authorities. The dragooning of young maidens dressed in white to talk to soldiers would be one example of planned hoaxing, but such tactics were a persistent feature of ultra-radicalism.

On 7 February 1817, two full months after the Spa Fields rising, John Stafford reported that Preston was already planning the symbolic trappings of the next insurrection: 'Preston told me to night that he had a suit making the Coat to be Green – Waistcoat Red – Pantaloons white with Hessin Boots and tri coloured cockades'. In a variation on the colour codes of the dragooned women of Spa Fields, next time Preston envisaged '2 or 3 hundred young women . . . got with Green Gowns Red Handkerchiefs, White caps and Cockades'. As before, their purpose was 'to go first and meet the soldiers' in order to provide a feint and to gain fraternal co-operation with the soldiers: Preston had also thoughtfully 'asked' his two daughters to go. It is a measure of the significance placed on uniforms that Stafford reported that 'I expect to be measured for cloathes tomorrow'.[48] Such clothing was easy to run up from those amongst them who earned their living at tailoring but Stafford's remark remains a poignant one about the extent to which he had thoroughly infiltrated himself.

After the fiasco of the later Bartholomew Fair *coup* plot of September 1817, intended to be virtually an anniversary event of the 1816 rising, the Spenceans contemplated hoaxing the Home Office and police. Arthur Thistlewood, then vying with Watson for leadership of the Spenceans, dreamed up a complex hoax:

> Thistlewood said that a few Men with the Populace would do every thing – when he was at Paris 50 Greeks puzzled the whole German Army – He said the Beggar's Opera would be performed tomorrow, and he would get a Paragraph into Bells Paper stating that Thistlewood & Preston would be there – this would bring a Number of his Friends together – and he would write a Hoax to Lord Sidmouth, and Sir N Conant who would order the Police Officers to the theatre and the Scheme at Paddington would not be interrupted.[49]

The 'Scheme at Paddington' was yet another *coup* contemplated in the aftermath of the damp squib which was the Bartholomew Fair plot. Had it been pulled off, it would have been an elaborate piece of theatre to send police to the theatre. They would have got there to find that the beggars were performing elsewhere.

Seale's trailing of Castle's scent at the beginning of Watson's trial would not be without precedent as far as innovative ultra-radical use of the courtroom is concerned. The Duke of Richmond had been called by the defence at Thomas Hardy's 1794 treason trial to discuss a pro-reform pamphlet he had written in the 1780s. Despard went a dangerous step further in seeking to embarrass Sir Evan Nepean by calling him as a character witness. In the 1790s Nepean had been one of two permanent Under-Secretaries at the Home Office and, in this capacity, had helped preside over and administer an enormous expansion in its intelligence gathering activities.[50] Nepean told the court he had known Despard since 1784 but he had only the politest of deferences and ignorances to relate.[51]

Seale's creative incrimination is a good clue to the persistence and determination of the ultra-radicals. The trial proceedings and preparations were suffered to be no impediment to the roller-coaster of Spencean opportunism: as soon as Watson, Hooper, Preston and Thistlewood were acquitted in June 1817 they began plotting again.

THE REVOLUTIONARY PLANNING FOR BARTHOLOMEW FAIR, 1817

The reports of the spy 'B', John Shegog, for 30 June 1817, barely weeks after the acquittal of Watson Snr, Hooper, Preston and Thistlewood, are double entered at the Home Office in separate files and with slightly different wording.[52] One of the principal differences between late 1816 and mid-1817 is that, after the débâcle of the Spa Fields trials, Government surveillance was increased:

> The leaders of sedition are very active and consider the present moment as favourable to the revival of Spencean Principles –

> As there is great activity and boldness among the Leaders of Sedition and Treason (whatever may be said to the contrary) I beg leave to inform you of their proceedings – They consider the time favorable for reviving the Spencean principles.[53]

Clearly, the Spenceans were losing no time before organizing again.

Acquittal celebratory dinners had been *de rigueur* in London radical circles since the LCS treason trials of 1794. The dinner, at first planned for the Spencean venue of the Cock in Grafton Street, to celebrate the radicals' escape was to be combined with the July anniversary celebrations of Spence's birth and intended to 'propagate his principles'. John Shegog the spy was able to preen and tell the

Home Office that 'I have been invited to it.'[54] One of the event's organizers was the Castle-trailer and Spencean printer, Arthur Seale.[55]

Both versions of Shegog's reports on the subject of Spencean conversations are important because they reveal not only that the Spenceans were undaunted by relatively close calls in the courtroom but also that they were narrowing their contemplation of physical force:

> Some of the blood thirsty and Deistical party are brooding over and consulting how to Murder and Commit assassination on the Privy Council and this is deemed by them the most advisable mode [of] proceeding at present
>
> . . . they entertain their Plan of Assassination, and Lords Castlereagh, Liverpool, Sidmouth, and Ellenborough, have been marked as Objects of their pursuit – Lord Castlereagh has been watched, in the hope of catching him returning alone from the House at night – and it has been said the present Session shall not terminate without some one being assassinated –[56]

June 1817 marks the beginning of a long-term plan to assassinate the Cabinet which finally ended in Cato Street in 1820. As such, it may be said that the events of February 1820 began in June 1817, and Shegog's reference to how the Spenceans 'entertain their Plan of Assassination' may imply that political murders were contemplated even before that date.

This shift towards fiercer physical force was noted again by Shegog in early July. The acquittal dinner was 'put off on account of Hooper's Illness'.[57] Hooper was one of the Spa Fields trial defendants and his illness seems to have become progressive because he died six months later during which time a deliberate attempt was made to recruit Hooper's wife into counter-espionage with the help of a Bow Street runner called Westcoat who knew Mrs Hooper from 'when she was formerly on the Town'. Mrs Hooper said that Thistlewood and his friends 'had behaved so ill to her husband she would do any thing to expose them' and she connected their doings with the enigmatically named '"Tumble down Dick"' from the Borough 'who is very mischievous'.[58] 'Some of the most desperate' continued to meet 'frequently' at Hooper's house. An intention to 'encourage the Principles of the Luddites, rather than those of the Spenceans: – as the Spencean Principles are not considered sufficiently violent to answer their purposes' was expressed by Thistlewood, Hooper and 'many others' and it is probable that a coterie around Thistlewood was marking its territory as distinct from the fairly peaceable two

Evanses. As if to throw spies off the 'free and easy' alehouse circuit, the Thistlewood group also began to 'meet in Coffee Houses in preference to Public Houses'. This change of venue was short-lived but they continued to 'read seditious, and inflammatory Publications'.[59]

The double entries for Shegog's reports in the Home Office files give further colour to the condensed version given above. The alternative entry of Shegog's report, for the same day, seems to be of his own drafting. Shegog had attended the 'Public Meeting' (rather than celebratory dinner) at the Belvidere tavern, Pentonville, and found 'there were many of the Spencean and other seditious characters assembled (in an irregular manner) in some of the Publick Houses in the neighbourhood'. This dispersal of political activists around 'some of the Publick Houses' with no central assembly is interesting. Their mood was far from timid and defeated, however, and once again Shegog reported that they were 'in hopes some enthusiastic characters may be worked upon to commit Assassination'. In an observation which reveals that the radical culture of the 'free and easy' persisted, Shegog noted that 'many' of them were 'disappointed and vexed because there was no Speechifying &c. &c.'. The disposition towards greater physical force, which was also a shift away from Spencean principles as developed by Thomas Evans, is a more clearly ideological shift in Shegog's own draft: 'they intend inculcating the Principles of the Luddites instead of the Spenceans, as some of the most vindictive of them say the Philanthropy and Benevolence of Spencean Principles will never effect any Change and that Ludditism is best calculated for the times'. In effect, this group seems to have been turning away from the model of polite revolution advocated by Thomas Evans and they were now considered by Shegog to be 'impatient and anxious to commit Acts of desperation and depradation [sic]'.[60]

Hooper being 'at present unwell', the acquittal dinner seems not to have taken place.[61] But there was another insurrection on the agenda: the Spenceans planned to use the carnival-like period of London's Bartholomew Fair as a device to cover or precipitate an insurrection. As it turned out, the Spenceans knew that the authorities were on to them and it was eventually called off but its planning was extensive. The importance of the abortive Bartholomew Fair plotting is that the narrative of its planning can be gauged by a lengthy dossier of spy reports. In short, the minutiae of ultra-radical planning and its Government surveillance can be studied.

The spies involved in the Bartholomew Fair surveillance were 'B', John Shegog, and 'C', John Williamson, a trimming-weaver.[62] Shegog (or Shego or Shegoe) of Lambeth Walk was a well-placed spy who was intimate with the culture he reported on although, when the subject was religious infidelity, he exaggerated the suspected dangers. His religious sensitivity probably emanates from his vocation as a Whitechapel preacher but he was also 'employed in the Tower at the Ordnance'.[63] Both the plotting and the spying can be followed on a day-to-day basis and the opening report gives an idea of the scale on which it was planned. The financial and communication centres of London and the nation were top priorities:

> A numerous Mob are to assemble, and to have a Supper during Bartholomew Fair, in Smithfield. They are to go to the Artillery Ground on Saturday night to get the Field Pieces, and also to Gray's Inn Lane, and are afterwards to go to the Bank, and blow open the Gates, and destroy the Books – another Party are to attack the Post Offices – C. has seen two Pikes – The Tickets to the Supper are to be distributed tonight – The Men engaged in it are mostly weavers – they want to get about fifty Men who understand the Use of Great Guns –[64]

It is clear from the conspiratorial planning of these years that all the participants assumed they could expect and command a large following. They were to meet 'at Bunhill Row, opposite the Gates of the Artillery Ground, precisely at 9 o'clock – their object is to break open the Armoury and to take the small Arms, and Field Pieces, and then to distribute these to others'. If they did not succeed in taking the arms 'they are to attack the Bank' assisted by 'two Men, who have worked at the Bank, [and who] have offered to conduct them over it'. Attitudes to spy infiltration were half-hearted. Tickets, and no doubt hints of the plot, were to be circulated to known sympathizers but when 'C began addressing Thistlewood calling him by name, "Mr. Thistlewood" . . . he was called to order with "No Names"'. The group were jittery but committed and some of the fine detail of planning had already been worked out. 'Pikes, and Iron work' were to be 'finished today – they are to be distributed in Bunhill row' near to where they were presently meeting. As a decoy, the weapons were to be brought by a man 'who knows nothing of the Business' but who was to set out at 2 p.m. accompanied by 'a Person who will . . . detain him on the Road, drinking &c' so that he would not arrive until evening. Meanwhile, 'Coaches, carts, &c.' were to be hijacked 'for the purpose of blockading the Street, and the houses are to be taken possession of in order that they may annoy the Troops from the Tops of them'.[65]

As well as giving the organizational details of the plot, Williamson's report for this night is also fascinating because he was able to report on the group's changes of mood. Plans 'were rather checked by a Man, who came in, and informed them that the Lord Mayor had been making Enquiries in Spital fields'.[66] Nevertheless, every man was individually given a 'Turn to speak' and there may have been nearly twenty people in the 'Private Room' of the King's Head by this time. James Watson Snr seems to have been going through a period of being cold-shouldered. His name did not appear in Shegog's list of those present when the more violent 'Principles of the Luddites' were discussed in July. Indeed, it could be that the July acquittal dinner, although suggested to 'commemorate' 'Watson &c;', may have been from the start imagined as an event to allow Thistlewood a chance to steal Watson's timid thunder.[67]

Whatever the truth about Watson Snr, it was Thistlewood that the Home Office tailed. It is the routine nature of the following report which makes it remarkable, its matter-of-factness:

> Thistlewood went from Home about 7 oClock and talked to a young Man in the Shop, returned home – went out again with a Man, a Woman, and a little boy, went towards Temple Bar, round the New Church, up Newcastle Street, and home. – afterwards the Woman looked for some time out of the Window, as if to see whether they were watched – At nine oC Thistlewood went over Waterloo Bridge, stopped to look at the Dragoons who were passing, then went to Oakley Street, and soon returned with a tall Man from thence, and went again to Preston's – They went into a Room behind Preston's Shop, and put out the Candle – after some time Thistlewood came away alone – & went home.[68]

Thistlewood's stroll was actually to reconnoitre the readiness of the soldiery who might oppose them as well as carrying on with the business of calling on political colleagues (which included a visit to someone in Oakley Street, Lambeth, the setting of Despard's arrest fifteen years earlier). It is obvious from the details of the report (the lookout, the snuffed candle) that Thistlewood and his friends expected to be under surveillance but the closeness of the report is also highly revealing of the social and domestic conditions of ultra-radical political activism. Whether used as a decoy for his own movements or not, Thistlewood was able to enlist a family group. The appearance of a woman in the report is rare: to see that she plays an active part (checking 'to see whether they were watched') is even rarer. The blind side of male-dominated ultra-radicalism is the support given by women beyond and within the domestic sphere.

Two days later, the revolution was called off: 'The Intention of the Disaffected to have risen on the last day of Bartholomew Fair, has been postponed' on account of 'the precautionary Measures which were adopted by the Government'.[69] Of course, there is no disguising the fact that risings cannot be 'postponed' when there is a popular weight of numbers combined with a reasonably effective application of force. The lack of popular support may also be indicated by a scatter of letters written at the time. 'An Englishman and True Friend' wrote to the authorities to say that ''Tis for the sake of preventing Bloodshed I make this known to you . . .', explaining that a group had plotted 'to Engage the Populace in a Riot at Bartholomew Fair While they a[nd] a Band of them of 50 in Number Whent to a place Where is Majesty's Ministers Where With a full intent to Masaircre the Whole . . .'[70] The interesting thing about this report is the apparent circulation within the local culture of the assassination policy that the Thistlewood group discussed the previous June. There can be no doubt word had circulated the Smithfield area about a rising. A local inhabitant warned a distant relative (who related the matter to the Home Office) that 'a Dredfull Sloter will Take place to morrow Night at Smithfield' and he intended to 'keep my Children at home – for many would fall to morrow'.[71] If the rising was abortive, in the same way that the Spencean group had propagandized the intended rising, their discursive activity went into reverse gear to deal with the fiasco of deferral.

The first reflex of the leaders was histrionics ('Preston was so vexed at the Disappointment that he declared if he had had a Pistol by him he thought he should have blown out his Brains') followed by some level of personal recrimination plus the tactic of claiming that the rising was 'a Hoax on the Government'. This reaction was reported first hand by the informer 'A', James Hanley, a Spitalfields weaver, who 'met Preston last night in Holles Street' the day after the calling off of the Bartholomew Fair rising. Preston blamed Thistlewood for putting off the insurrection because he was 'intimidated at a few soldiers' and Watson Snr was said to be 'rather lukewarm and fearful of being hanged'. On the other hand, 'Preston spoke throughout of himself as the principal' and boasted that 'for his own part he had not known what Fear was'. Preston's remarks are colourfully vainglorious (presumptive leadership, total absence of fear, the strenuous need for a pistol) but beyond hyperbole it is possible to distinguish a balanced account from Hanley's report. The thoughtful pause, reported on 6 September, as Thistlewood watched the Dragoons pass by Waterloo Bridge, correlates with Hanley's account that Preston was 'not a little chagrined, on looking into the Artillery Ground, to find the Soldiers under Arms, and the City Police on the alert'. The Bartholomew Fair insurrection was planned and rumbled on a large scale.[72]

Hanley's report is fascinating in showing how the local cultural system of politicking dealt with an embarrassing fiasco. Preston seems to have perceived himself as playing to two levels of audience: the local and the national.

Preston's initial inquiry on meeting Hanley was to ask 'if he had heard of it, thro' the Papers'. This would obviously have allowed Preston the opportunity of confirming the exploit as a hoax. Preston's plan was 'to encourage the Idea that the whole was a Hoax' and he had 'directed Individuals to give Currency to such a Report'. '"I would wish it to be represented as such to every body"', he said but he also added, weakly, that 'if the Military had not turned out in such force it would have been something more than a Hoax; we would have upset them, if they had not unfortunately scented us'. Preston seems to have attempted to pass the 'hoax' theory onto Hanley and he was obviously caught in a credibility crisis concerning the lack of popular support for their plans (he admitted during the conversation that 'they had only received £8 towards defraying the Expenses of the late Trials').[73] He may have quickly given up hope of fooling Hanley, whose confidence and bearing were based on personal knowledge supplemented by information from the Home Office (although he may have been unaware that the 'Spenceans' Shegog and Williamson were spies: Ford had kept 'Notary' ignorant of the identities of his other 'good freinds' [sic]).[74] Preston revealed that the original plan had been 'to have made a sudden Attack upon the Bank by the Mob from Smithfield' supported by 'two hundred Pikes, and Pikemen ready' and with 'Colours'. Smithfield was the site of Bartholomew Fair but rather than this being a confidently carnival insurrection, 'The Showmen, and every body they met were to have been compelled to join them'. They were also to have proceeded to free the two Evanses, 'early on Saturday night', from their imprisonment under the Suspension of Habeas Corpus. According to the tenor of his conversation with Hanley, there was to have been no stopping Preston except that, on finding lots of soldiers and police about, he had gone to the Broad Arrow tavern in Grub Street and 'met one of his Daughters, who implored him not to begin on account of the Soldiers'. Perhaps this tender scene, redolent of sensibility, actually happened but it provides a neat excuse as to why Preston proceeded no further himself.[75]

Preston's negotiation of Hanley is intriguing. It runs the whole gamut from guarded secrecy to open bravado and is a complex piece of dissimulation and self-fashioning within his radical culture. However, this is not to dismiss Preston as an eccentric megalomaniac.

His response to the fiasco of the non-uprising at Bartholomew Fair was to pitch in with more 'free and easies': 'Preston suggested the Establishment of twenty good Free and Easy Clubs, at twenty different Parts of the Town, on Saturday Night, and to sally forth on a Signal at the same moment, each with a determined Leader at its head'. By Preston's optimistic and generous calculation, 'this would distract the Government, and if they could stand an hour or two, they would succeed, as the soldiers would certainly join them.' Gauging the extent of support from the soldiery is difficult because the spy reports filter out most of the character of Preston's words while the intricacies of this specific culture make other things obscure. For example, in the report on Preston, one can detect the ironic tones of Hanley who, at this point, knew the rising had been scared off, partly as a result of his own espionage.[76]

If the Bartholomew Fair rising was only a discursive event, the Spenceans grouped around Thistlewood and Preston continued their revolutionary discussions. Just over a week later it was said that 'Thistleton [*sic*] is cool and designing and bent upon mischief'. This report of Shegog's seems to correlate with the atmosphere of persistent determination which had run right from the time of Spa Fields, but amid signs of waning popular support. On the one hand 'Thistleton is endeavouring to enlist some desperate enterprizes' but, on the other, 'Thistleton' was having to go on a political crawl, acting 'in the manner of Despard in going from house to house in search for associates of his own sentiments'.[77] Two weeks later, the bloody example of Despard's solitary *coup* leadership was on Thistlewood's mind: 'Oh said Thistlewood we must have the mechanics and not do as they did in Col. Despard's times'.[78] Significantly, the Spencean plot for political assassination, which first surfaced in June, persisted and Shegog stated that 'I believe his intention is to attack the privy Council in some way.'[79] Far from advocating a departure into vindictive terrorism, Preston and Thistlewood were still maintaining their ideological discussions. Two days later they 'determined to have nothing to do with the old Patriots, or lukewarm and undecided Characters; but to select a body of determined Men, who would fight, and conquer, or die'. Alongside this tactical decision to spurn some of their traditional compatriots ('Dr Watson's name was struck out of their list'), the Spencean ideology persisted as they affirmed yet another post-revolutionary prospectus: 'Monopoly is to be declared at an end, the land is said to belong to the People, and that every one has an equal right to it.'[80] Four days later, Preston once again 'suggested a free and easy club as the best means for accomplishing their Object'.[81]

Tactics and ideology ran hand in hand in late September. Somewhere around this time, Thistlewood was giving attention to his symbolic non-verbal communication when it was reported that 'Thistlewood is to have a Generals Uniform completed by Thursday and Cockades are to be worn'. The importance of Thistlewood's uniform is not Ruritanian grandiloquence but political eloquence conveyed by non-verbal means.[82]

On the first Thursday of October 1817, the Spenceans called a meeting which has every appearance of being a war council rather than an extraordinary general meeting. From inside the Spencean organization Shegog wrote a quick letter warning that 'all arrangements are postponed till the meeting to night' although they 'all are very busy in getting Arms and Ammunition & Cutlasses–'.[83] The meeting was held at the Duke's Arms, Upper Marsh, Lambeth. Two spies were dispatched to report. John Shegog noted that 'There were about 40 or 50 of the Chief leaders present, Some from Bethnalgreen, Spittalfields, Bermondsey, the Borough and Lambeth, Men of the worst description, ready for any desperate enterprize'. Although they had been deeply infiltrated, Shegog reported that they were 'very cautious and circumspect (at present) in communicating any thing to strangers or committing any thing to paper or having any plans drawn out lest that sh[d] be discovered . . .'[84] The other spy was Joseph Champion who took the code-name 'J' and told of how the meeting included a letter read out to the company and sent by the veteran Despard associate Charles Pendrill who was now exiled to the USA in company with James Watson Jnr. 'The letter contained opprobious Language against Government', reported Champion, '& described the distresses of the people who he said were walking about the streets starving without shoes or stockings.' Thomas Preston was excited enough to declare that 'if 25 thousand men would join him he would give Liberty to the World'.[85]

Thistlewood was less histrionic and more pragmatic. In particular, he called on the fraternity of their collective discursive culture when 'He wished the Company would express their sentiments – altho' speaking little signified –'. The revolutionary trajectory which attenuates discourse from writing into speech before shifting discursivity into action is noticeable. For Thistlewood, speech did not much signify but he based his comments on recent radical history: 'The brave Parker at the Mutiny at the Nore failed because nothing was acted upon. The business was to act with decision.' Richard Parker had been the leader of the Nore naval mutinies in 1797 and had been hanged with thirty-six others. The proximity of Irish activism at the Nore mutinies and the United Irish background of the Despard conspiracy in which Pendrill had been prominent, all makes it possible that Thistlewood's reference to Parker's role at the Nore was prompted by the letter from Pendrill. Champion noted that 'There appeared to be a considerable portion of Irishmen among them.'[86] Thistlewood's sense of the political redundancy of speech-making, their distance from higher-ranking political leaders and their preparedness for autonomous action is exemplified in his assertion that 'M[r] Hunt at Spa Fields advised the people to be orderly & peaceable; He said I do not like this Course, he asked every man to come with a Pike on his shoulder.'[87] Even though Champion's is a highly selective account, it is possible to see in his report the vestiges of Thistlewood's use of a considerable degree of argument based on a specifically ultra-radical version of history. The heroism of 'brave Parker', the lost opportunity of the Nore mutinies, the false counsel of Hunt at the Spa Fields rising, collects together radical history spanning twenty years, one which must have been highly meaningful for the '40 or 50' 'Chief leaders' of extreme, physical force, London radicalism in the Duke's Arms, Lambeth.

Joseph Champion's report is a distorting lens on what happened that night but there can be little doubt of the degree of would-be sophistication Thistlewood and Preston were attempting to give to their actions: nor of the Government's steps to keep them under surveillance. It seems to be the case that both ultra-radical leaders had wished to keep their movements a secret and that the Duke's Arms meeting was one of special importance. Earlier that day Thistlewood and Preston tried to establish a hoax, a piece of disinformation. What happened was that the two leaders concocted a written note stating that 'Mess[rs] Thistlewood and Preston will leave town . . . for Derby . . . to tender what Assistance they can to their Unfortunate friends that are to be tried . . . on a Charge of high Treason'. The event they were referring to was the trials subsequent to the Pentrich rising in Derbyshire. Unknown to Thistlewood and Preston, two things happened. The well-placed spy John Shegog immediately reported that they had another, separate, hoax to support the Derbyshire redherring. 'Thistleton', Shegog said, 'sh[d] insert a paragraph in the Paper on Saturday, "that Preston & he were gone to Derby" ' in order that 'they would not be suspected'. Amazingly, it seems that the authorities also had a 'boy employed' to watch Preston's house. As Preston left home that day, 'a paper dropped from his Coat Pocket in the Street, which the boy picked up & brought to Sir. N[athan] C[onant]' at the Home Office. Shegog was in a position to be able to put both pieces of information together and discount their attempts at sowing disinformation.[88]

As the month wore on, Thistlewood and Preston continued their meetings. On 11 October Preston declared that there was ' "No thing so bad as delay – Despard lost his Life by delay & so did Ld Edw Fitzgerald" '.[89] Lord Edward Fitzgerald was the rebel Irish leader who had been captured and who thwarted the English by dying from his wounds during the risings of 1798. Both Despard and Fitzgerald may have been personally known to those in Preston's ultra-radical circle who had their roots in United Irish activities in London by 1797.[90] Despard continued to provide an historical touchstone for Preston and Thistlewood. Preston cited Despard's 'delay' on 11 October and two days later Thistlewood warned 'let us not be taken and Die for doing nothing like Despard'.[91]

One week later Williamson reported a more detailed stage of the physical force planning which included the seizure of four field guns from local barracks which were to be taken to the St Giles's end of Oxford Street to 'prevent the advance of the Troops should they attempt to Sally upon them – the Streets were also to be blockaded with brewers Drays for the purpose of checking the advance of Cavalry'. Preston's role was to be restricted 'because of his lameness but he was to have a free and easy Club at St. Giles where he was to be in readiness with his Men to join the Party as they approached and that he was to give out that the troops had joined them.' Williamson's report shows how closely the culture of the 'free and easy Club' was knitted to the role of revolution and it must have been hoped that the carnivalesque politicking at the 'free and easy' would disguise Preston's ruse that the troops had come over to the revolutionary side. There was also continuing uncertainty about the sympathies of the soldiery:

> It was proposed that the Soldiers at the Barracks should be made to go along with them, and do their duty at the Guns, except elevating them – if they refused to do so they were to be killed – but if they agreed to do it, Thistlewood said he would promise them a free discharge & good Pension and 20£ in their Pockets.[92]

The planning was now reaching a stage where, as at Bartholomew Fair, the subtleties of deploying women in the vanguard of the rising came under discussion. Shegog, who talked with Thistlewood on the morning of Monday 27 October, reported that Thistlewood had:

> told his wife that she and Preston's 4 daughters should be in the Mob & if any thing occurred that was alarming they should have a bottle of inflammable Matter & by knocking off the Cork it would burn like a Torch & give Alarm.[93]

As always, it is difficult to estimate the true role of ultra-radical women but they could hardly be expected to have gone into the flanks of the thickest urban revolutionary combat, Molotov cocktails at the ready, without a large degree of personal political commitment. It is possible that women relatives became more involved the closer things seemed to be moving towards the rising: three days later Shegog commented that 'Mrs Thistlewood grows now to be violent especially against the Regent'.[94]

Planning for a rising continued into the winter and it is difficult not to see the Cato Street conspiracy, an ill-timed surge of dwindling radical enthusiasm, foreshadowed in the various attempts at having Castlereagh 'watched, in the hope of catching him returning alone from the House at night'.[95] On 30 October 1817 'Thistlewood harped again on the Cabinet dinner and said the R[egen]^t was gone a shooting' and 'he wished some good fellow w^d lay it in him then.' In figuring out the next date for a rising, he was probably picking up on the assistance of the popular plebeian culture of Guy Fawkes disturbances when Shegog reported that 'Th^d s^d the 5 November would be a good day to act, & he was determined against delay'.[96]

To put it starkly, nothing came of any of this but the discursive system of the artisan symbolic culture continued unabated. In very early January 1818, Hooper, one of the Spa Fields defendants, died after some six months' illness and the Spenceans set-to once again in an attempt to foment a rising out of the funeral. The political use of radical funerals went back to Despard's burial and Spence's quieter death was also attended by graveside political oration. The pall-bearers were to include Watson Snr, Thistlewood and Preston and they called for two hundred and fifty 'large placards' to be 'stuck up in different parts of town to give notice of the burial' as well as a newspaper notice. Preston was to make a speech 'after the Burial' and, according to Williamson's report at the Cheshire Cheese, they already had 'Cartridges made for the great Guns, sixes, nines, and fours' and had the insurrectionary 'Intention of taking the Field pieces from the Artillery Ground as they return from the Funeral'. The funeral was to be carefully timed so that the 'funeral Procession' would 'start at ½ p. 1. oC so as to reach Stepney about ¼ p. 4. o'C–'. This was all done 'in the hope that it will be dark before the Funeral is over' in order to cover the disturbance on what would have been one of the longest winter nights.[97] As it happened, Williamson attended the funeral and reported that, true to Spencean hopes, 'there was a great Crowd' but that the authorities, obviously alerted by Williamson, were already in place and the Bow Street runners were seen in Newgate Street and near the Mansion House while a 'large body' of officers was stationed in the churchyard where Hooper was to be buried.[98] Mrs Hooper would not have been pleased.

Meanwhile, unknown to any of them, something fatal was beginning to happen to Thistlewood and to the Spencean underground in London. On 27 January 1818, barely three weeks after Hooper's funeral, 'A General Officer', who remained covert and unidentified, wrote to the Home Office to say that 'there is in this place a man, who I found in Distress, and have employed and supported to a certain degree, and who came to me yesterday to say that he has been for some time acquainted with, and employed occasionally by Messrs. Watson, Preston and C° [and] also by Evans'. This was to prove an espionage bombshell because the person 'found in Distress' and who took the code name 'W——r——' was the bust-modeller and Cato Street buster, George Edwards.

Edwards, on being sounded by this intermediary, expressed an immediate anxiety 'not to expose himself to the Revenge of those concerned in these Transactions' but, the officer added, 'he is otherwise willing to disclose all he knows.' Edwards obviously knew what they already knew: 'They [the Spenceans] are meeting in Numbers at secret meetings . . . they carry Arms habitually . . . they have spies everywhere, and are aware of the means, and Men employed to detect their Plans'.[99] But there was more. Edwards, already encoded under the byline of 'W——r——', wrote a semi-formal letter a few days later which stated that he had known Spence personally: 'I was originally acquainted with Thomas Spence, and thro' him, became acquainted with the Evans's, Thistlewood, Preston, the Watsons, and an other . . . I attended the Spencean Meetings occasionally, though I disapproved of their Principles, till about two years ago'.[100] Edwards was an important find to the Home Office because he could report from the centre of the ultra-radical group. At this stage in the internal secret service's development, the authorities were particularly dependent on well-placed sources because their national espionage organization was quite limited and they would have been capable of only a modest amount of cross-referencing and provincial surveillance. 'W——r——', keenly, seems to have deposited a second report that day, one vivid enough for it to be easily understood why the Government found Edwards such a useful and well-positioned intelligence gatherer:

> In answer to an Observation that Thistlewood went about armed with Pistols, old Evans replied he should not wonder if Thistlewood knocked some of the, <People of Rank>, off the Hook; – Evans remarked to Watson that 'Lord S.[idmouth] had said in the House of

Lords that Conspiracies were still on foot' – Watson said with a smile 'There is something, however they got hold of it.' – Watson said they must have some more Hoaxes before, they came to the Real Attempt – He talked of contrivances for throwing detonating Balls and Combustibles into Carriages which would deter persons from taking public Offices . . . Watson is ready to forward a Plot, but not to engage in personal Danger – That was the point of difference between the E[vanse]s & others on the Spa Fields riot.[101]

Edwards's account is an interesting one and rare in purportedly capturing an emotional reaction when Watson smiles at Evans's remark about Sidmouth. A lot can be gleaned from this report, both about its consistency with other spy reports and about the culture Edwards was observing. It could be that Edwards is reporting on Thistlewood's weaponry because they had already received a report from Mrs Hooper about Thistlewood's habitually being armed with a knife, and the elder Evans's remark about Thistlewood knocking 'People of Rank . . . off the Hook' fits in with the assassination plans Shegog had been reporting since the previous June. On this basis, the plan to use grenades and incendiaries against people in public office is only an extension of the tracking and tailing that had gone on before, although now its political effects are envisaged as being more widespread and much more akin to present-day political 'terrorism'. Watson's enigmatic smile seems to be one of satisfaction that the Government continues to take them seriously and it opens up once again the problem of how far the Spencean revolutionaries were operating as the licensed 'low' discourse of the 'high' dominant hegemony. Transgressively, Watson's smile, like Edwards's necessary surveillance, disrupts the possibility of licence following rules. Ideologically, the agency of Thistlewood is restored because his difference is marked out against the timidity of once-tried Watson Snr, and the more discernible, more open, distancing of the Evanses from the core physical force group. Importantly, Edwards's report is a reminder that, as a culture, the Evanses, Watson Snr, and Thistlewood still functioned at the level of immediate discursive exchange.

If Watson Snr's smile is problematically elusive, Edwards's report that 'Watson said they must have some more Hoaxes before, they came to the Real Attempt' fits in with the crop of reports from around the time of Bartholomew Fair that the Thistlewood group strongly supported the use of hoaxes. There would always be a near-impassable gulf between 'more Hoaxes' and 'the Real Attempt', but it would be injudicious to dismiss Watson's scheming as simply a licensed response to Governmental authority. The Government's surveillance machine makes it possible to scrutinize Watson's motives from above and below. As a licensed transgressive, Watson's taunting little pamphlet *More Plots, More Treason, More Green Bags: A Letter to Viscount Sidmouth* (1818) stood upon its ability to safely ridicule authority within a discourse which places it firmly within the genre of satire and lampoon rather than of seditious utterance. In *More Plots*, Watson inflates the Government's surveillance and his radicalism so as to provide it with safely conspicuous visibility:

> Should your friends the SPIES and INFORMERS fail in describing in glowing colours my disaffection, my plots, my plans, my views and intentions . . . I shall be willing, upon receiving a free pardon for all my heinous offences, to give you every information in my power.[102]

If Watson's *More Plots* placarded itself as a word to his friends as much as a warning to his enemies, the textual envelope of a private letter is a good deal less open to view, except that the Government was also adept at the interception of mail.

In July 1818 the Home Office intercepted and filed a copy of a letter from Watson Snr to Thistlewood. It is a suspiciously rare opportunity to cite the private writing of men who, as a practical political principle, infrequently committed their thoughts to written record:

> The people themselves I mean the poor industrious fellows have looked too much up to wealthy men for relief, fatal error, they will never be relieved but by their own exertions and they will not enjoy the fruits of those exertions if they give up the reins into other hands – The Wigs prick up their ears and no doubt expect to come into power, when they will probably give us a Reform in there way a mere Sop to the whole but the people know them and their own wants, and I hope will not now be deceived by any artful manoeuvres of any of the exclusive priviledged gentry – the people have been in leading strings too long and I think are determined to participate in or to rule the necessary change which is coming.
>
> The Mammonites have swayed us too long – we must have no property mongering Jugglers, they have always entailed misery on the most industrious and useful people in every nation. I scarcely ever knew a man of property sound to the core – I have mostly found them proud and intolerant towards all whom they considered below them. Surely such a perversion of reason will in some age have an end.[103]

It is probable that this is a hoax letter similar to the one found by the boy detailed to watch Preston's house. Watson's letter comes across as safely generalized and unspecific as far as his plans are concerned and so very much a casting about of political observations that one wonders why he needed to reapprise Thistlewood of such mild views ending with the woolly and earnest 'Surely such a perversion of reason will in some age have an end.' Nevertheless, Watson's view that he 'scarcely ever knew a man of property sound to the core' and his wish to have 'no property mongering Jugglers' is a useful paraphrase of Spencean attitudes. In particular, Watson's pervasive distrust of 'wealthy men', 'the exclusive priviledged gentry' and opportunistic 'Wigs' denotes the strengthening independence of artisan radicalism, newly prepared to 'be relieved' 'by their own exertions'. These were the attitudes that were to be vehemently expressed at the Hopkins Street debating club the next year and it was a piece of strategic disingenuity for Watson to allow his letter to trail the hope that 'Governments would if wise encourage clubs' because 'while men talk – Ministers have nothing to fear'. The double-sided nature of Hopkins Street was an endeavour to make sure that Government had everything to fear from talk.

On the same day that 'W——r——' filed his first report, he also added another snippet of information which would have alerted the attention of the authorities: 'Wedderburn is publishing a Pamphlet called the Axe laid to the Root, but it has not much sale –'.[104] Wedderburn's journal *The Axe Laid to the Root, Or, a Fatal Blow to Oppressors, Being an Address to the Planters and Negroes of the Island of Jamaica*, printed by Spencean veteran Arthur Seale, was an extraordinary (if short-lived) publication. *The Axe* developed the recantational ironies of some of Spence's tracts of the 1790s, carrying letters which pretended to alert Jamaican plantation owners to the dangers of the spread of London radicalism ('the free Mulattoes are reading Cobbett's Register') and the invincible Spencean doctrine.[105] However, the forum in which Robert Wedderburn most vociferously developed his anti-colonialist and revolutionary polemic was in a ruined loft in Soho's Hopkins Street.

CHAPTER FIVE

Some Ultra-Radicals

ROBERT WEDDERBURN, MAN OF COLOUR

The coloured Spencean orator Robert Wedderburn had already been under surveillance for about a year. Iain McCalman has ably discussed, introduced, and assessed Wedderburn's impact on the London ultra-radical scene: his oratory, his ideas, his charisma, his burlesque and carnival inversions. A spy report in January 1817 gives another illustration of how the two Evanses were beginning to be eased out of their increasingly moderate political stance by Wedderburn's vigour:

> Attended at the Nags Head, upwards of 60 Persons present, Question: Is the American Government to be applauded or Condemned for the means they have taken to civilize the Indians by giving them a Portion of Land. Both the Evans's were present but only the Junr. one spoke. A Mr. Wedderburn made the most Blasphemous, Inflammatory, Incoherent harangue I ever heard. He said we might call him an Infidel 'true he once professed Christianity but now he was an Infidel, Ignorance was better than knowledge, Barbarism better than Christianity, even the founder of Christianity had declared that he came to set Father against Son and Son against Father &c. He sincerely hoped, if there was a God he would prevent Christianity from getting among the Indians give us Nature and we don't want to know God, we can worship the Sun'.[1]

In this post-Spa Fields speech, Wedderburn is articulating orthodox Spencean ideology as it applied to land ownership. America was the democratic utopia, but the Spenceans feared the practice of property ownership would be transferred, unadapted, from Old World to New

Figure 5.1 'A Peep into the City of London Tavern. By An Irish Amateur'. G. Cruikshank sculp. J.L.R. del. D. George BM Catalogue No. 12891. (Courtesy of the British Museum: Department of Prints and Drawings)

World. Wedderburn's Nag's Head speech reveals the persistence of ideas publicized by Spence back in the 1790s. In 1796 Spence had struck his own token die 'IF RENTS I ONCE CONSENT TO PAY / MY LIBERTY IS PAST AWAY /' picturing a feathered North American Indian. Wedderburn's views must have been expressed with Spence's ideas in mind.[2]

The orthodoxy of post-war Spenceans was also revealed two days later when a spy 'Attended at the Cock in Grafton Street', with 'upwards of 50 Persons present', to debate the question 'Woud the Practical Establishment of Spences Plan be an effectual remedy for the present distresses'. This question furthered the agrarianist statements made by James Watson Snr in his speech at Spa Fields which were vividly restated at the Cock by 'Mr. Preston [who] was among the Speakers and told us that the landholder was a Monster that must be hunted down'. The evening was stolen, however, by the performance of Robert Wedderburn, whose speech-patterns come across, even when mediated by the spy, as a series of short jabs of redundant questions and assertive statements:

> Mr. Wedderburn open'd the Debate in his usual inflammatory stile, and gave an additional proof of his infidelity by declaring that we were all born in the same way and must all perish alike, we were but Animals, we might talk of the immortality of a Principle within us, but what was it, he never saw it, never felt it, nor did he believe a word of it.[3]

Rough diamond Wedderburn's oratorical rise in the post-war period is the obverse of figures like John Gale Jones in the 1790s. Wedderburn was deeply aligned to the revolutionary political ideology of the Spenceans whereas John Gale Jones was more clearly (to be anachronistic) a centre-left reformer. Hopkins Street was more boisterous and unpredictable than Panton Street. Wedderburn's Hopkins Street Chapel was a device conjured up by a mature phase of wholly artisan London ultra-radicalism. Its official dissenting licence, granted in April 1819 and brilliantly detailed by Iain McCalman, was a licensing of blasphemous and seditious utterance.[4]

Wedderburn was occupying a discursive site pioneered by Thomas Evans. It was Evans's Archer Street Chapel which was the prototype for Wedderburn's, and Evans and Wedderburn had taken out a joint licence there in early 1818.[5] An irate pedestrian, complaining to the Home Office in March 1819, gives some idea of the set-up:

> Passing yesterday through Archer Street I saw some people going (or I thought) into a Religious meeting, curiosity caused me to go in to hear what doctrine was preached there, upon my entrance I was astonished to find that it was a Political Lecture room where a man of the name of Evans was delivering a Lecture from the Bible, Paines Rights of Man & Age of reason from each of these Books he selects passages and lectures

upon them apparently for the purpose of bringing the Government & Clergy into contempt (the enclosed Songs will clearly prove it).[6]

The songs were printed by Wedderburn (a prosecution-evasion ploy for Wedderburn who was semi-literate?) but such theological sampling aided the Government in its attempts to keep Wedderburn and his friends under continued surveillance. At any rate, Wedderburn seems to have learned the skills of audience-handling at Thomas Evans's Archer Street Chapel because the police spy John Stafford reported that 'a quarrel arose between Wedderburn and a Young Man they called each other Fool &c &c and Wedderburn declared he would never attend again if the Young Man was, suffered to come into the room'.[7] When nearly a year had elapsed and Wedderburn had split from the moderating Evans, Hopkins Street was more carefully elaborated around its host and was, to some, awesomely street-credible.

The Reverend Chetwode Eustace was another outraged passer-by and his information gives a good picture of Hopkins Street and how it alarmed sensitive conservatives:

Yesterday Evening I proceeded to Hopkins St. Chapel to hear the question discussed whether it was right for the People of England to assassinate their Rulers, for this my Lord I conceived to be the real purport of the question tho' proposed in other terms – I had some difficulty to discover the place for it is apparently a ruinous loft to which you ascend by a step-ladder – the assemblage was perfectly suitable to the Place for both Orators and Audience were with few exceptions persons of the very lowest description. The Doctrines were certainly of the most dreadful nature and two persons particularly distinguished themselves by expressions which appeared to me most violently seditious and treasonable – One of these men (who appeared to be the principal in this Concern) is a Mulatto & announced himself as the Descendant of an African Slave – After noticing the [?] persecutions of the Slaves in some of the West India Islands he said they fought in some instances for twenty years for 'Liberty' – and he then appealed to Britons who boasted such superior feeling & principle whether they were ready to fight now but for a short time for their Liberties &c. He stated his name to be Wedderburn and said he was author of a production entitled 'The Axe laid to the Root' or some such name – but two other persons I think went even a greater length – Indeed some of their expressions appeared to have shock'd even the worst of their hearers – The question was adjourned to tomorrow evening as Wedderburn said he had been with about two Hundred persons to whom he gave a promise that the subject should be resumed – but he might have said this merely as an inducement to those present to attend on the succeeding evening – Your Lordship will perceive that these persons are of the most contemptible description – however, I fear they are too successful in their efforts to conscript the lower orders – From what I have observed of their fellows I would most humbly recommend that some proper persons may be sent to watch their proceedings and that prompt measures may be adopted for making examples of Wedderburn & such desperate characters who so fearfully violate the laws and avow their object to be nothing short of the Assassination of their Rulers & the overthrow of the Government.

PS Should it be your Lordships wish at any time to see me you will be pleased to have a note directed to the care of Mr. Stockdale Pall Mall.[8]

This letter says it all, right down to the unctuous offer to be of further assistance in providing information (an offer which seems subsequently to have been taken up).

Chetwode Eustace must have been quite a determined man to penetrate the 'ruinous loft' via the Soho 'step-ladder' and his letter might be taken as an emblematic manifestation of bourgeois anxiety about a vivid and articulate underworld secretly penetrated and eavesdropped. 'The assemblage', Eustace pointed out with delicate symmetry, 'was perfectly suitable for the Place' and the speeches an autonomous meta-discourse in which the 'right' of the 'People' to 'assassinate their Rulers' is discussed, 'tho' proposed in other terms'. What may have shocked Eustace more than anything else was his eavesdropping on an entire cultural history, a radical alterity in which the transgressive 'Mulatto' 'announced himself as the Descendant of an African Slave', one now risen to contemplate 'the overthrow of the Government' proselytized by the seditiously named pamphlet, ' "The Axe laid to the Root" or some such name'. For Eustace, ' "Liberty" ' is a dangerous commodity already successfully wrested from 'some' of the Caribbean islands by 'twenty years' long struggle. Wedderburn, though 'desperate', is 'too successful' in conscripting 'the lower orders' and, throughout, Eustace's account accentuates Wedderburn's transgressive qualities as someone who will 'violate the laws' and whose 'expressions appeared to have shock'd even the worst . . . hearers'.

Chetwode Eustace was right: Wedderburn's perspective was deeply anti-colonial. Wedderburn in a 'ruinous loft' in Soho at the centre of the English empire articulated a perspective different from that of native English dissent. On the evening of 10 November 1819, Wedderburn was accompanied by the verifying presence of 'two west Indian Blacks' to discuss the question 'which is the greater crime, for the wesleyan Missionaries to preach up passive obedience to the poor Black slaves in the West Indies, or, to Extort from them at the rate of

£18,000 per annum, under pretence of Supporting the gospel'. Like many Hopkins Street debates, the politically correct answer is enshrined in the rubric of the question, but:

> as soon as the Question was Given out Wedderburn came forward and addressed himself to the chairman and the two west Indian Blacks which where [sic] invited for last night by Wedderburn and that they might Expose the villiany of our church and state by sending out these vipers of Church Missionaries to Suck the Blood of the poor innocent Blacks in the West Indies and to make them believe that the great God was with them but instead of God, it was the devil and the Missionaries that was sent from London by the Secretary of State for the Home Department and for no other Motives than to Extort Money for by the great Wesleyan pretending to preach the Gospel to poor devils and passive obedience to the planters there marsters, and these villains as he Terms them are not abit Better than a Thief that robs for xxxxx bread he xxxx to them, he moreover contends and will he says swear to the present day that in consequence of these Government Missionaries or rather Church robbers that if these poor black devils as he terms them if they have not Got any money to give these Government Missionaries they are tied up and flogd and most unmercifully indeed.[9]

For Wedderburn, religion was imperialism, a transcendentalist metaphysic 'to make them believe that the great God was with them' and, moreover, from the anti-colonialist perspective, a metaphysic allied to an economic ruse 'by the Secretary of State for the Home Department . . . for no other Motives than to Extort Money'. Wedderburn is quite specific in believing that Wesleyan Methodist dissent was a double colonizing of the racially undifferentiated subject: it is a religion which preached 'the Gospel to poor devils and passive obedience to the planters there marsters'.

It was a tempestous evening:

> There was present last night two or three fresh persons I had not seen there before one particularly annoyd the great Mr. Wedderburn and his two blacks by opposing him in the first Question first set on foot by Mr. Wedderburn whose very language almost shook [the] room by his Exclaiming against the Church, clergy and there Missionaries. Send abroad – it all meant money and that there aim was nothing else the Question did not come to a close agreement as the time not allowing of it it broke up a little before 11 oclock and adjourned.[10]

Like Panton Street at its height, the forum of Hopkins Street Chapel was one which was open to interruption: Wedderburn dished it out but he also had to take it, his only defence being his 'very language' which 'almost shook [the] room'.

Wedderburn and the Hopkins Street Chapel clearly rattled every-one in the vicinity. Wedderburn took care to publicize his debates with irritating effect. One 'W. Porden' (possibly William, the non–freeholding architect of the same name and an ineligible jury-packer for Watson's high treason trial) wrote a letter to the Home Office, on the same day as the above debate, complaining of 'a Bill pasted against a boarded Inclosure' in Rathbone Place at the Soho end of Oxford Street, 'Two similar Bills . . . pasted against an Empty House' nearby and 'many more in different parts of Oxford Street.' Porden knew enough about Hopkins Street to name it 'the Temple of Sedition' and to correctly describe Wedderburn as the 'offspring of an African Slave' who would open the next debate on 'Can it be murder to kill a Tyrant', or, 'Has a slave an inherent right to slay his Master who refuses him his *Liberty*'.[11]

If Wedderburn had by this time lost just a little of the foreground-ing of Spencean ideology, in its place came the upsurge of an artisan discourse which articulated the contemporary culture of Hopkins Street. One October night in 1819 might be taken as an indicative example of what happened at Hopkins Street. The report was endorsed with a note that 'The aforegoing is true in substance and is sometimes verbatim what passed at the meeting' and was signed by William Plush and another man called Lea. Plush was a local parish constable and he seems to have been given the long-term task of attending Hopkins Street to report on Wedderburn. In this capacity, he gave evidence at Wedderburn's trial for blasphemy in early 1820. Lea may have been a civilian informer who had come forward to witness the proceedings and the speeches formally, as a part of an overall attempt in late 1819 to indict Wedderburn for blasphemy. The surveillance of Hopkins Street appears to have been a straightforward task but one which required some delicacy of espionage. Lea seems first to have stayed near to a lower door to the chapel (which was in the loft) where he was 'engaged in observing the conduct of Wedderburn' as he admitted the audience. Significantly, many of them must have been to Hopkins Street Chapel before because 'the greater part of the persons who attended the meeting paid nothing but produced a card with a Seal on it'; this gave free admittance for a month while casual visitors were charged sixpence. Wedderburn seems not to have started the debate himself but stayed at the door admitting auditors and debaters for about an hour.[12]

It could be that this was simply a tactic to corral passers-by but, as most of the auditors had been there before anyway, it is more likely that Wedderburn was carrying out some kind of vetting role to avoid surveillance. Meanwhile, 'The Chair was taken about a quarter before

9. oclock p.m. by a mere Boy apparently about 18 yrs of age (a white man)'. The shudder of horror at 'a mere Boy' acting as the chair repeats a similar anxiety concerning such a sudden 'transition, from domestic inferiority to professional importance' (which 'often turned a weak head') expressed in William Hamilton Reid's survey of London debating club culture twenty years before. The youth's colour was noted not as a routine matter but rather as one specific to the circumstances of Wedderburn's presence. Stationed at the door, Lea 'distinctly heard all that passed and could discover that Wedderburn was the next Speaker having heard him speak before at the Door to the persons who out of curiosity had assembled'. Presumably Plush had previously described Wedderburn's colour to Lea, but on this evening (as on some other evenings) there was at least one other black person in the audience, a 'Young black man' who spoke in the debate after Wedderburn. It is just possible that this coloured man is William Davidson, a Cato Street conspirator who was an effective orator and a relatively recent addition to the Spencean group centred on Wedderburn, Thistlewood and Watson.[13]

The debate was on the question 'ought the public Society to reject all persons of property and their Leaders and Choose from among themselves the men of ability to manage the business of Reform'. The first, unidentified, speaker ('a white man'):

> confined himself to invective against property but more particularly against the national schools, which he said were instituted not to promote learning but rather to subvert it – they were he maintains nothing more or less than a Government Instrument instituted for cramming down the Throats of the xxxxx Branches of the lower Classes of Society the Ridiculous and fulsome Doctrine of Church and King – To see your Children marched to the Teachers House to hear the same nonsense preached up to them by the Gentlemen of the Black Gown of Fear God & Honor the King[.] His Majestys ministers had seen with Alarm that the people of England were becoming more and more enlightened, that the Dissenters were becoming more numerous while their favourite State Religion was sinking into nothing.[14]

The 'invective against property' was true to the Spencean background of Hopkins Street as well as to the question for debate but it soon seems to have branched off into wider considerations. This speaker not only identifies the collusion of 'Church and Kings' in organized education but he also perceives education as a 'Government Instrument' to save the 'sinking' 'State Religion' from increasing numbers of 'enlightened' 'Dissenters'. The caution over the political role of the national schools differentiates early-nineteenth-century ultra-radicalism from its Victorian variety. What is at issue is the loss of artisan control over family life: 'To see your Children marched to the Teachers House' and there to hear priests ('the Gentlemen of the Black Gown') further cram the state religion down the throats of the young. The auto-didacticism of Allen Davenport and his kind was one thing, but to embrace uncritically state-fostered education was another: the 'Gentlemen of the Black Gown' referred to by this Hopkins Street debater in 1819 voices the same caution over 'Government Instrument instituted' education as is found in William Blake's *Songs Of Experience* ('The School Boy') and the 'Priests in black gowns' of 'The GARDEN of LOVE' in the early 1790s.

The second speaker that night, another unidentified white man, thought that the support of men of property would assist the radical cause. Wedderburn had by this time gone 'up the Steps or Ladder into the Room where the meeting was held' in order to catch the end of the second speech and, unwittingly, left the door unattended 'which Lea took advantage of and remained and distinctly heard all that passed'. What Lea heard was one of Wedderburn's better reported speeches, one full of his own personal and cultural history and the ultra-radical politics of Carnaby Market:

The 3ʳᵈ Speaker who is a stout man of colour (Wedderburn) commenced by stating that he was sorry he felt obliged to differ in some trifling degree with the last Speaker, he had recommended hypocrisy to be used for the purposes of obtaining Money from the great ones, it was very well he was willing to allow because Money was a useful Article, but what was the sum that the great Mʳ Coke of Norfolk had given to the Sufferers of Manchester why £50 while he was receiving $200:000 per Annum. – this was a Specimen of what the great ones would do, part of this Sum he himself was paying in Taxes. He could not sit down to the most humble meal, but what three fourths of what he Swallowed was taxed, and for what did he pay those taxes, why to pay the Interest of the national Debt. He appreciated the Idea of the last Speaker, if they were under the necessity of having a man of property – of having some one in the back Ground, and if he decieved You Blow his Brains out – But the people of England are now becoming more enlightened they talk of Military Training, let them call it what they will, Old as I am I mean to learn my Exercises. – Some Years back I was on board of a man of war there I learnt to prime and load and Fire the great Gun I served on board a privateer, My station was in the Top there I learnt to handle Small Arms, but this is not enough every fool knows how to fire a Gun, we must know how to form the Solid Squares from that to extend our Line But not as the Duke of York did at Holland weaken our Centre and let the enemy rush through and oblige us to run away but like the Irish at Vinegar Hill advance in a Body as they did

– they seized by so doing the great Guns of their Enemy We in like manner must advance and seize our Rights. We must learn to use the gun the Dagger, the Cutlass and the Pistols – We shall then be able to defy all the Yeomanry of England – But if we chose a Man among us as a Leader and he takes a Bribe, or if we ever suspect him of being about to take one Chop of his Head, Any man can chop a Stick and a head is as easy chopped off as a Stick – But the Prince Regent is alarmed Lord Castlereagh is alarmed & well he may be when his head is in Danger and per*haps he thinks rightly too.*
[MARGINAL NOTE: This was said with peculiar Emphasis –] but the prince is a fool with his Wonderful Letters of thanks to the Yeomanry of Manchester – but if we learn our Exercise Let Lord Castlereagh Lord Sidmouth or Lord any Body xx send all the yeomanry in the Country they cannot harm us, the Solid Square will resist them, *I was with a Gentleman who scaled the Walls of the Bastile* in France and who, *no doubt would assist us Scale the walls of all the Bastiles in England* – what is the prince *Regent or the King to us*, we want no *King – He is no use to us* – And I say openly I am a Republican. If they will not give us our Liberty let us take it. But gentlemen the rich were always enemies to the poor they despise us, they not only despise us themselves but they teach their Servants to do so, we ask them for assistance, but they as I said before despise us.[15]

Wedderburn is keeping to an extremely simple argument: 'If they will not give us our Liberty let us take it.' At best, Wedderburn is only prepared to accept the appropriation of bourgeois leaders like 'the Great Mr Coke of Norfolk' and he draws the simple lesson that whatever Coke gave to post-Peterloo Manchester had been paid for by taxes on even 'the most humble meal'. The simple brevity of Wedderburn's rhetoric is well fitted to oral discourse: 'three fourths of what he Swallowed was taxed'. It is this simplicity of argument (a simplicity fundamental to Spencean ideas) which Wedderburn bolstered with narratives concerning his personal history. Oral discourse functions in a markedly different way from written text and Wedderburn knew how to reach the audience he had personally admitted to the Hopkins Street loft scarcely an hour before.

For the Hopkins Street audience Wedderburn, the 'stout man of colour', is the carnival presence of misrule, one who is not only visually extraordinary to Regency London (if not to Hopkins Street) but one who also carried the authority of a vividly wide personal and referential history. Wedderburn's speech is laced with sudden and shocking transitions ('if they were under the necessity of having a man of property – of having some one in the back Ground . . . if he decieved You Blow his Brains out') coupled with a defamiliarizing of the domestic: 'if . . . he takes a Bribe . . . Chop of his Head, Any man can chop a Stick and a head is as easy chopped off as a Stick'. Right the way through he keeps to the discourses of contemporary history. Chopping sticks or heads leads him to the key textual sites of the French Revolution, events whose images and principal texts had been more or less distributed *gratis* in the 1790s by the reactionary Association for Preserving Liberty and Property against Republicans and Levellers: *'I was with a Gentleman who scaled the Walls of the Bastile in France and who, no doubt would assist us Scale the walls of all the Bastiles in England –* what is the prince *Regent or the King to us,* we want no *King – He is no use to us'*. The identity of the Bastille scaler is not known but his mysterious existence is stamped and authenticated by the personal visibility and presence of Wedderburn who has already woven his speech with the right credentials. It is highly likely that Wedderburn served, at the very least, his passage from the Caribbean to England in the Royal Navy and that he would have 'learnt to prime and load and Fire the great Gun' and shoot muskets from the 'Top' mast. Some of the Hopkins Street audience could probably do the same and such audiences figured in the Spencean plans to seize field guns from the London Artillery Ground during the Bartholomew Fair of 1817. Above all, Wedderburn draws a simple and logical lesson: civilian 'Military Training' will enable them to 'advance and seize our Rights' and 'defy all the Yeomanry of England' in their siding with the Peterloo magistrates.

Wedderburn's speech digs deeper for its authenticating credibility than events which were universal news. Wedderburn's urging of 'Military Exercises' in order to 'know how to form the Solid Squares [and] from that to extend our Line' takes as its specific historical example 'the Irish at Vinegar Hill'. The Irish camp on Vinegar Hill had been one of the main rebel centres in the bloody rebellion of 1798. The Irish were eventually heavily routed at Vinegar Hill but, remarkably, Wedderburn is giving here a post-colonial history: the initial Irish success when they were able to 'advance in a Body' as a solid phalanx. Taking this outside perspective further, Wedderburn contrasts the Irish success with an English defeat in Holland. The Duke of York (and Wedderburn takes the English common soldier's dangerous perspective) weakened 'our Centre and let the enemy rush through and oblige us to run away'.

Wedderburn was perfectly capable of reaching for the politician's tub-thumping abstractions ('And I say openly I am a Republican. If they will not give us Liberty let us take it') but he also knew how to bring the original debating question back to the cultural sphere of his artisan audience when he said that 'the rich . . . not only despise us themselves but they teach their Servants to do so'. The political indifference of the 'fat swarthy butler' and 'smirking footman' had been condemned by Thomas Preston in his *Life*. Wedderburn knew how to make his observations on the rich register.[16]

But Hopkins Street was not the site of a closed, monolithic political discourse. Anyone who paid their sixpence could have their say. For one young coloured man in the audience, Wedderburn's perambulations to Vinegar Hill and the Bastille lacked immediacy:

> The fourth Speaker a Young black man complained that Gent^m had not confined themselves to the subject, the question before [?] meaning the Question (given on the 1st page) He for his part thought they might come nearer the Question, he publickly declared himself a Republican he avowed the principles, he admired them what did we want with King or Regent without it was to waste in Extravagance the Money of the people.
>
> In the cause of Reform Blood must be shed, but that would be trifling Ministers would soon be obliged to give way.
>
> The question was not put and carried of choosing a Leader from among themselves.[17]

The vigour of this concluding contribution sounds like William Davidson. What is certain is that black men were accepted as ultra-radical leaders in the London of 1819.

Wedderburn's perspective as a 'foreigner' gave him a radical purchase on English politics at the beginning of the nineteenth century. For him, England must have seemed a remarkable place, breathtakingly enchained beside liberty. Chetwode Eustace heard Wedderburn say in August that 'the Slaves in some of the West India Islands . . . fought in some instances for twenty years for "Liberty" ' and he must have been incredulous to find liberty near but far away. A November speech found Wedderburn putting these thoughts with elaboration:

> Wedderburn stated that being a foreigner and having heard before his arrival in this country of the Glorious constitution and humane laws that it was govern'd by; he began the moment he arrived to make enquiries about them and was soon given to understand that it was govern'd by King Lords and Commons and that when an Act was brought before the Commons the people remain'd silent as though their very life depended on it but when it passed the Lords they gasp'd as it were for breath; and when the Royal assent was given they became *petrified*; and thus he soon discover'd that the people had no confidence in their rulers.[18]

Wedderburn is mirroring and mocking his own original disbelief at English passivity and the report captures him at the height of his powers. On that night they were debating a familiar Hopkins Street theme of the autumn of 1819, the politics of the post-Peterloo situation and the necessity for independent radical action. The debate is worth following because it was filed under two separately written reports.

In the tense autumn of 1819, the Hopkins Street debaters saw the dismissal of Earl Fitzwilliam after his expression of liberal misgivings over Peterloo as a 'Crafty Design' by Government to get them to adopt an aristocratic leader and, clearly, their debates show them to have been in no mood to accept the sympathies of either Coke of Norfolk or Earl Fitzwilliam.[19]

The Hopkins Street ultra-radical position was articulated most succinctly and clearly by a man referred to as 'Pinley' in Plush and Mathewson's report: 'Gent^m 'tis not from among the rich that we are to expect to find a friend to Radical Reform, no it is ultimately among ourselves then let us boldly step forward in the cause of liberty and if we should fail Die Gloriously in the Struggle'.[20] Wedderburn's speech shared this view, though expressed in ever more strident and personal terms:

> Ministers have sacrificed the Welfare of the country to enrich themselves and it is now high time we look'd after them – but the Bloody Revolution is near at hand; yes the Bloody Revolution *I say* because some of these Bloody Murdering thieves who would rob us of the Shirt from of our Backs will either be shot or lose their Heads; and to stimulate my sons I take care to show them their degraded situation and call them Cowards !!![21]

Wedderburn's fiery discourse of blood and assassination is couched in the most personal of terms which includes the hint that the audience are cowards.

In the anonymous report of the same speech, the physical force detail is made more specific, at the expense of its political and cultural aspects:

> He assured his hearers of the certainty of the success of their efforts to bring about a Revolution – they had now acquired too much strength to fail – the Army is corrupted – even the Navy tainted – the People manufacturing and learning the use of various description of Weapons, and considerably advanced in the Acts of discipline and war, and are now capable of forming into line and Solid Squares &c. . . . they must give up the idea of petitioning – it is of no use – for his own part tho' he is fifty seven years of Age he expects to kill a few with his own hands in

the progress of the business – Nothing can be done to interrupt the radicals, for the Land is the Strength of the Country and they will shortly possess themselves of that.[22]

As on 6 October, Wedderburn seems to have given particular emphasis to the 'discipline' of war when he maintained that the radicals were 'considerably advanced' and 'now capable of forming into line and Solid squares &c.'. This report is consistent with its other version in stressing the bravado of Wedderburn's intention of personal involvement in an action which had 'the certainty of success'.

By his own account, Wedderburn hoped to have 'the pleasure of shooting' or killing 'a few with his own hands'. There is evidence to suggest that this was not mere boasting. Psychologically, the ultra-radical tendency towards physical force was boosted by a persisting belief in the political fragility of the armed forces ('the Army is corrupted – even the Navy tainted') which must have been based on their own service backgrounds (like Davidson and Wedderburn) as well as from sounding out the discharged servicemen who swelled their social class. Three days earlier someone had pulled a gun at the White Lion in Wych Street just before Watson Snr was due to speak.[23]

It is difficult to know whether these high spirits signify wider scale arming, but weaponry was much discussed. Two days earlier, also at the White Lion, there was a difference of opinion when a man called Hartley was 'expelled the Committee because he asked the question if they were not all to go armed'. The next day (and in the same place), Thistlewood declared 'let them all go armed I know nothing of it' and on 1 November they turned up at the White Lion with a fierce array of weaponry:

Nov 1. White Lion Wych St 10 OClock AM several loading Arms
Hartley a horse Pistol
Briant a Pistol loaded with 2 balls
Chambers a Pistol & Dirk
Hall a Pistol and Dirk
Sold[ier], Harrison – Pistol & Dirk
Harland – the same
a Little man in a black Coat & White Apron a large Pistol in a black Belt
the rest to the amount of 40 all armed & loaded
Thislewood [*sic*] came in & inspected them
. . . Walker Sec[retar]y wore a White hat & [?] Crape
Chambers & Hartley sold the address
Forrester at the Meeting recommended the People to arm
Thislewood the same[24]

This simultaneous overlaying of politics ('the address'), non-verbal communication ('a White hat & [?]Crape') and physical force is typical of this group's employment of a multiplicity of discursive practices.

The physical movement of men was one of the material discourses at the heart of the ultra-radical cause. The 'Mob' had to be attracted with the appropriate signs and the armed forces 'seduced' by political infiltration. Gathering men together as military and political groups served the double purpose of training and of assessing strength. When the post-Peterloo high spirits had waned in November, the Thistlewood group 'Agreed to try their strength by meeting to exercise Sunday Morng next at 7OClock on Primrose hill'.[25] Not surprisingly, a police officer was ordered to the spot that weekend and came across 'several Men mustered' and 'Marching & wheeling in a Military manner in close order and open order on the side of Primrose Hill towards West End Hampstead'. No arms were visible 'but each had a stick, which they shouldered and carried like a Musket' although it is more likely they were drilling ready to receive the pikes they had ordered in the summer. Pikes-from-broomsticks was the subject of a little tract entitled *Every Man His Own Pike Maker* which the Home Office had seized by June 1817.[26] Nevertheless, the numbers who turned out to march up and down Primrose Hill were dismally small (even though they made the excuse of the cold weather) and a couple of hours later they separated towards Marylebone New Church and Jews Harp House. Interestingly, 'one of them a Man of Colour was very active': this is probably William Davidson who had been present the night the drilling was suggested.[27]

The overlaying and infiltration of moderately radical politics by the physical force faction is nowhere better illustrated than in Hunt's procession into London. Hunt's processional entry on 13 September came hard on the heels of consistent attempts by the Thistlewood group to provoke a post-Peterloo metropolitan clash. On 1 September thirty of them had met at the White Lion in Turnmill Street to discuss the large meeting which was due to take place the next day in Covent Garden, Westminster: 'all agreed to go armed' and their core of about fifteen men (including a soldier called Harrison, Thistlewood, Blandford and Davidson) proceeded 'with Flags', 'all armed' to the meeting.[28] Nothing happened. Two days later Thistlewood declared to seventy people that 'nothing would do with the P[rince] R[egent] we must fight for it' while a more sanguine Watson Snr suggested they next meet in the City to ensure a radical London jury if they were arrested.[29] When Hunt entered London on 13 September it was a set-piece of radical culture with the Thistlewood side in coalition with Hunt.

This coalition was too uneasy an alliance to last for long. At that evening's Crown and Anchor celebratory dinner there was a 'violent quarrel' between Hunt and Watson Snr 'respecting the nomination of Sir C[harles] Wolseley to the Chair without his concurrence'.[30] Wolseley was too venerable and too titled a noble radical for the Watson group to stomach: the rejection of non-artisan leaders was an unbreachable tenet and could not be allowed to pass, chariot rides notwithstanding. Once again, the culture was sufficiently resilient to coalesce when toasts and police-baiting, however, reinforced fragmented solidarity. Gale Jones, no doubt shrewdly gauging the new opportunities for veteran speech-makers like himself, had drawn up a list of toasts. Ever ambivalent, Jones's toasts ran the gamut from Huntite entreaties of 'A new Era where public functionaries may hold their Office in trust only for the good of the People', via the briefer 'La Fayette & the Liberties of France', across the weakly revolutionary 'Liberty or Death, & may the wretch who will not subscribe to this, live a Slave and die unlamented –' to the more Watsonite 'May every soldier be a Citizen & every Citizen become a Soldier'. The historical touchstone of the tutelary deity of the 1816 Spa Fields rising was also toasted: 'Wat Tyler and may every Briton that receives a similar outrage follow his heroic example'.[31] Spy-baiting came in the form of 'some busy fool' spotting police officer Birnie in the Crown and Anchor gallery resulting in Hunt subjecting him to a tirade of oratory. Birnie, understandably, left early reporting that it was actually 'a quiet sort of dinner'.[32]

What disappeared, and was to disappear further in the run-up to the Cato Street arrests, was the visibility of the Spencean ideology. There are two reasons for this: the arrests of the Spencean ideologues, Wedderburn and Watson Snr, and the consequent uncounselled rise of the pragmatic revolutionary Arthur Thistlewood.

Iain McCalman has found that Wedderburn was languishing in gaol charged with blasphemous and seditious libel on 16 August, the day of the Peterloo massacre, and the picking off by the authorities of the Spencean revolutionary group might be taken as beginning from that date: Cato Street was only one in a whole line of attempts to seize convincingly and prosecute the major figures.[33] After Peterloo events moved so swiftly that the ultra-radicals were caught with their strategies down and, by this time, they were so autonomous that they were unprepared for the potentially fertile collusion with Hunt. Iowerth Prothero has noted how there was a relatively quick sequence of events at the end of August and the beginning of

September which show the Spenceans to have been politically outflanked.[34]

A Spencean arranged Smithfield meeting on 25 August did not attract the massive support Watson, Thistlewood and Preston wished and neither did it provoke the armed clash that might have led to a revolution or insurrection. Instead, the three made a circuit of Smithfield Market in a hackney carriage 'amid the chorus of a perfect blackguard mob too contemptible to reflect on' who greeted their speeches with 'huzzas'. They had flags with 'the same inscriptions as before' ('Liberty or Death' and a picture of a pike) but now surmounted by 'a piece of black crape' for the Manchester dead.[35] After the meeting a spy who had been with them at Smithfield accompanied Watson and Davidson back to the White Horse in Turnmill Street. It is possible from his account to gauge some of their frustration with that day's events.

The informer went into the 'Skittle Ground' of the pub where he heard 'the report of A Pistol' and Watson Snr admonishing someone for firing it off. An hour later he returned and found 'A Black Man Whose Name . . . was Davidson Standing on A seat in the Skittle Ground'. Entering into conversation with him, Davidson said 'he came their Armed' to Smithfield and had pushed himself to the front 'thinking they was Surrounded by Police Officers'. Davidson said 'he was prepared for' this and would, he implied, have started firing but instead of being the start of a clash, he found that Watson and the rest 'wanted him to speak' to the crowd which he declined 'as he was in his working Cloathes and did not like to Apear'.[36] Of course, it is impossible to know how accurately this spy is reporting a pub-garden conversation but it is significant that Davidson was already known as an orator and was, by his own account, willing and able to come out firing if required. No less extreme than Davidson was a handbill found the previous night near a drunk who was found lying in a Holborn street:

> To a Brave British People
> Britons Arise and take up Arms in Support of Your Lawfull Rights & Privileges . . . the Northern Counties will be as active as You & they Expected London to show them an Example . . . Brave Countrymen Your Leaders have all Sworn to Perish with you or the [sic] bear in Triumph with You the Heads of Castlereagh & Sidmouth the [sic] Temple Bar Gates as a Terror to their Confederates, We will Destroy Machinery Store Houses & Brewhouses but Destroy no Grain nor Liquor . . .[37]

Northern radicalism, Luddism and the moral economy of the breadriot are all here but now in the context of the political assassination urged by Thistlewood. The site of this text, adjacent to a drunk, shows that the revolutionary factions in the metropolis were reaching their (unheeding) Mob audience. The speed and context of the radical handbill is not to be underestimated. A handbill, forwarded with post-Peterloo pamphlets, had obviously been circulating at the Smithfield meeting and it asked 'Philanthropists Of every Denomination' to come forward and bail 'Robert Wedderburn, a Prisoner in Newgate – for what he knows not!' but one 'well known to the World, through his Exertions at Hopkins Street'. By 25 August Wedderburn was already out on bail but the handbill took pains to point out his stand against the 'Tyrant, Bigot, or Hypocrite'.[38]

In August, the net was already closing round marginal discursive activities. Two days before Smithfield, Samuel Waddington appeared briefly before his colleagues to announce that 'he had been just liberated on bail from Union Hall for walking about with a Placard on a Board, & that he was to appear again on Tuesday morning'.[39] That same day the spy Hanley reported from the Jacobs Well in the Barbican that two hundred of the Spencean hard core turned out to hear a number of speakers including 'another *Man of Colour* besides Wedderburn whose Mind seems to have been equally perverted with the revolutionary Doctrines now so unfortunately prevalent'. This must be Davidson again. That night Hanley considered them 'to be very apprehensive of Danger' because 'even Preston advised them to speak in Metaphor – '.[40] Speaking in metaphor was not something they were very good at: about the most sophisticated example would be when, four weeks before the night of Cato Street, Davidson 'said he had taken all the tools (Arms) to his own house'.[41] Preston's apprehension arose from another arrest related to the group's dissemination of information and arming.

E.J. BLANDFORD, REVOLUTIONARY AND SPENCEAN POET

The routine suppression of handbill posters was an established fact of London ultra-radical life by mid-August 1820. Bill stickers were employed on a casual basis. One arrest for the posting of handbills produced by the Spencean printer Thomas Davison made hilarious reading when it appeared in *Medusa* (which he also printed). Two night constables watched two men called Loadsman and Redfern sticking up about one hundred handbills at 2.30 a.m. one August night on the 'corner of St. Martin's Le Grand'. They intervened: ' "We don't *think* you have any right to stick bills up at this time in the morning" ' they said. Redfern and Loadsman replied that they were doing it because sticking up handbills at that hour would deter crime. The night constable promptly confiscated the bills whereupon there was an argument about who owned them. 'Upon our refusing to give up the bills, a scuffle ensued, – and they gave *us* in charge to the watchman, little thinking we were the constituted authorities of the night.' The confusion sorted out, Redfern and Loadsman were clapped in Giltspur Compter, and Dogberry pursued his calling in calling on Thomas Davison. Davison was not there:

> but a woman (whom I supposed to be Mrs. Davison) gave me this here address [i.e. handbill], and said she would give me fifty if I would promise to distribute them among my countrymen (supposing me to be an Irishman by my dialect) as they were calculated to show the importance which every Irishman ought to attach to liberty of conscience, and to free him from the degrading trammels of a vile, borough-mongering, protestant oligarchy.

'I refused to accept of any more than one,' said Dogberry, sheepishly.

But then, from William Shakespeare to Justice Cocklecarrot. The night constable and his man had related all this at the committal hearing where Lord Mayor Atkins was eccentrically kind:

> Lord Mayor: Young men, you have been waiting a long while, will you take a sandwich?
> Loadsman: I thank you, my lord.
> Redfern: I thank you.

Atkins told them that they had better tell him who had ordered the posting of the bills and 'Consider what a dreadful thing a revolution in the country would be; YOU WOULD BE STARVED TO DEATH'.[42] This is a far remove from the harsh conditions of Margarot's trial in 1793 and *Medusa*'s avuncular approach is a reminder of how certain the journal could be in gauging the ironic response of its readership.

The immediate condition for Thomas Preston's anxieties in late August 1819 was not Davison's handbills but ones given over to the responsibility of another Spencean colleague, Edward James Blandford. Blandford is an individual whose progress is worth studying. On 23 August George Edwards (alias 'W——r——') reported that 'Preston is very uneasy at Blandford's having disclosed to the Lord Mayor the name of Harnell who made the pike found on Blandford'.[43] What had happened was that, in the course of an everyday arrest for 200 handbills proclaiming a 'Public Meeting', a man arrested for sticking them had told the authorities that he got them from Blandford in July (Blandford's name was printed on the bills which had been paid for by 'Mrs Watson Wife of Dr Watson'). The handbills would have been an irritating but fairly minor issue, the small change of ultra-radical persecution, but the arrest had gone disastrously wrong for Blandford.

Police constables Thomas Girton and Samuel Fogg were waiting outside Blandford's house to arrest him on 20 August for being the handbills' originator. In order to locate him in sure possession, Girton waited until Blandford was returning to his house, and as 'he was shutting the door I put in my foot.' Using the finest PC Plod tactics, Girton 'laid hold of him' and suddenly discovered that Blandford was carrying 'in his right hand – a pike'. There was a struggle as Girton 'dragged' Blandford out of the door and he called for Fogg who saw 'struggling a door open, a Woman appearantly [sic] fainting'. Fogg 'got her up stairs – Children naked on the floor' where he 'read the Warrant' to Blandford and got him to 'come quietly'. When Blandford was searched in the Compter they found a horn of gunpowder, 'a Bullet', the handbills and a number of reasonably embarrassing letters which they copied. The situation was now more serious and it is no wonder Preston was worried.

Girton and Fogg's deposition is a revealing glimpse into Blandford's domestic arrangements in one of the upstairs flats that poorer people lived in but the deposition also records how Blandford vainly tried to avoid giving anything away. 'One Evening Monday or Tuesday being late a person gave it to me [the pike] I felt it, he said it was for my defence I wished to return it he said keep it'. What interested the authorities was that the pike was a pattern, a prototype from which others could be made. Blandford's story got weaker as he claimed he 'picked it up in Old Street Road' and he eventually gave the name of the person who gave it to him: 'I think his name is Harland', he 'lives somewhere in Shoreditch.'[44]

The authorities soon found Hartland's (or Harland or Harnell's) address and three days later searched his house. One of the spies in the Thistlewood group was there to report that Hartland had told an 11 a.m. meeting at the White Lion that on Saturday night 'his Wife informed him, that 5 Police Officers had just quitted the house having searched it but found nothing'. Hartland 'observed it was very odd how he escaped as all the tools (Pike heads) lay plain to view in different parts of the shop'. Hartland verified that it was Blandford who brought two paper patterns for the manufacture of pikes.[45] It must have been that night, at the Jacobs Well in the Barbican, that Thomas Preston related his fears about Blandford's indiscretion within the hearing of 'W——r——', George Edwards. Preston 'ordered Harnell to put away the Pikes till the day' and there is every reason to think that they were steadily committing themselves to revolutionary action. Blandford was reabsorbed back into the group, a testimony that he came from a long involvement with the Spenceans.

On the day of his arrest Blandford gave his occupation as 'musician' but he also worked as a hairdresser and wrote poetry.[46] His poetry is probably better than Allen Davenport's and he found a ready outlet for it in the journal *Medusa*. *Medusa: or, Penny Politician* was Thomas Davison's decidedly pro-Spencean publication. 'A Spencean Philan-thropist' poet, for example, was given space in *Medusa* to promulgate the basic Spencean tenets such as that it is politically incredible that in the middle of 'bounteous nature' which 'yields such store / . . . man should know distress'. That landlords are 'tygers lurking for their prey / So on the watch they keep, / Lest working men, by any means, / Their labour's fruit should reap.'[47] 'A Spencean Philanthro-pist' also wrote a memorable and significant sequel called 'The Rights of Man, Or, Things as they were intended to be by Divine Providence':

> Thou cursed'st him, whose pride or power
> Should, slily in the dark,
> By any artifice whate'er,
> Remove the old land-mark,
> Join *field to field* or house to house,
> By heathen Pagan sway:
> Forbidden is such wickedness
> From that time to this day.[48]

This poem reveals the fairly sophisticated poetic discourse which the Spencean ideology was receiving after the clumsier efforts of earlier Spenceans. The anonymous poet has compressed the ideology: the removal of 'the old land-mark' acts as a synecdoche for all of grasping landlordism while the comment that this happens 'slily in the dark' is capable of sustaining the metaphor that legal actions are invisible. Politically, there is also some level of sophistication. The power of the 'heathen Pagan sway' is a specific naming and description of the morality of the ruling class, a deconstruction of the alliance of church and state. However, it is the single line 'A country's land's the people's farm' which makes the poem's most succinct Spencean statement, an equation of nation with national productivity and of nationhood stripped of imperial ideology.

The phrase 'the people's farm' is startlingly compact and explicit. It is a syntactic formulation whose origin demonstrably does not reside with its author because Spencean Philanthropy literally signs and authors the poem. Ideologically, England in 1819 is thinking itself out of the industrial revolution and encompassing England as a dominantly agricultural nation where the means of production, the soil, is owned by the people.

For this Spencean poet, husbandry is the foundation of the civic. After differentiating hereditary titles from natural rights, the poem lists the civil divisions and civil labours of the people's farm:

> Thus all the world BELONGS to Man,
> But NOT to kings and lords;
> A country's land's the people's farm,
> And all that it affords;
> For why? divide it how you will,
> 'Tis all the people's still;
> The people's county, parish, town;
> They build, defend, and till.[49]

Politically and syntactically everything is predicated on tillage of the soil. Nearly thirty years earlier, Paine had ridiculed the absurdity of hereditary titles but now the Spencean ideology gives an economic and civil foundation for that redundancy. So ideologically firm was the concept of the people's farm, it enabled leading Spencean ideologues to side-step the potential dissipation of their revolutionary efforts in tackling the issue of what to do with the system of hereditary titles. Thomas Evans, in *Christian Policy the Salvation of Empire* (1816), neatly foresaw the continuance of titles after the revolution for the same reasons. Acute observers and sometime sympathizers like Robert Southey noted that 'kings, lords, and commons, are tolerated in the librarian's [Thomas Evans: librarian of the Society of Spencean Philanthropists] scheme, whereas, according to the original system, "the Spensonian Republic is one and indivisible" '. It was because there was a firmly economic basis to their political reasonings that the veteran campaigner Evans was prepared to run the gun of Southey's ironically assuming that Evans was making 'a trifling concession' to existing laws.[50]

Even 'A Spencean Philanthropist's' apparently throw-away phrase, 'divide it how you will', is ideologically founded. The people's farm, Southey's remarks notwithstanding, is indivisible except for the purposes of civil, regional or linguistic convenience. This rolling back of traditional colonial divisions would have been long argued and pondered in the shadowy United circles of the late 1790s. Its implications for civil nomenclature surface occasionally such as when, in a spy's report on discussions in Thistlewood's group in late 1817, they decided that there would be 'no Distinction of Countries,

150

or Counties, but the People are to be distinguished as Northern Britons, Western Britons, &c. &c.'[51] The impetus to remove national boundaries was intrinsic to the withering away of the State in the earliest versions of the Spencean plan: with nations organized upon tiny parochial units, self-sufficient because of better distribution of wealth, nationhood would be a superfluous desire.

It was for the physical force sympathies of *Medusa* (masthead motto: 'Let's Die like Men, and not be Sold as Slaves') that E.J. Blandford began writing in April 1819. Blandford signed his pieces 'E.J.B.' but, if his identity were not already obvious, George Edwards alias 'W——r——' did his bit in keeping the Home Office informed of the author's name.[52] His first poem for *Medusa*, 'Nature's First, Last, and Only Will! Or a Hint to Mr. Bull', restates the Spencean version of history: the land has been plundered from the people:

> When Nature her pure artless reign began,
> She gave in entail all her stores to man;
> The earth, the waters, eke the air and light,
> And mines and springs, man held in equal right
> For ever; the probate of her will declares
> Her boundless bounty fram'd in equal shares,
> Alike to all, nor more to one or t'other,
> *That man on no pretence shall wrong his brother:*
> Or for encroachments urge exclusive claim,
> But all in her abundance share the same,
> Of what the elements combin'd produce,
> By time and season for man's equal use,
> Thus charging justice to chastise abuse![53]

Blandford's poem is important in restating ultra-radical claims on the word 'Nature'. 'Nature to feed the hungry' the Spa Fields flag had read and Blandford specifically says that 'Nature' is the source of the abundance of the land, an abundance which includes its 'mines and springs' as well as the earth and fields: 'all her stores' belong to man's 'equal use' without anyone's 'exclusive claim'. Malcolm Chase has discussed the extensive implications of a continuing debate within radical circles of the concept of 'nature' and how Spencean and other artisan radicals wished to maintain its social and economic meaning.

As Iain McCalman discovered, there is an important series of articles by Allen Davenport in Carlile's *Republican* discussing his belief in the 'abundance' of nature.[54] Davenport mirrors Blandford's poem because both writers share the same ideological and discursive context:

> The moment a mechanic lays down his tools, every prospect of gain is suspended, all is still and mute, nothing stirs around him, nothing

supplies his absence, to facilitate the conclusion of what he had begun: whilst the man who possesses land, has only to put his grain into the ground and leave it to the creative hand of nature, who will not fail in due time, by mysterious operation, to raise it up and multiply it fifty, or an hundred fold; and this is all performed in the absence of the labourer.[55]

For Davenport, the presence of nature 'supplies' 'the absence of the labourer' and its actions only complete and continue the cultivator's toil, finally yielding the material reward which is nature's 'boundless bounty' (as Blandford puts it). In the same article, Davenport goes on to say that 'The whole of this immence labour is performed by the energies of an invisible hand; by the hand of nature.'[56]

Davenport's (and Blandford's) argument is of enormous significance. It shows how the struggle for the meaning of the word 'nature' could still be framed within a discourse of radicalism two decades into the nineteenth century. The ultra-radical 'nature' was still a concept different from the newly dominating transcendental metaphysic of 'nature' being put into circulation through the reception of the Romantic poets. Davenport's ideas about 'nature' include a metaphysic of its 'mysterious' 'energies' but this metaphysic is a fairly redundant one because it needs no further explanation or elaboration. Indeed, Davenport's conception of 'nature' remained intensely materialistic, sometimes to the point of very crude simplicity. In his collection of poems *The Muses Wreath*, written around 1827, Davenport's poem 'The Globe' repeats his belief in the abundance of 'nature' ('Each earthly blessing that is heap'd on man, / Proceeds from bounteous Nature's glorious plan') to the artless extent that he thinks of the earth as a joint of meat roasting in front of the fire of the sun:

> The 'universal joint upon the spit!'
> And, faithful to the culinary plan,
> The ocean may be term'd the dripping-pan
> . . . .
> Thus Nature, ever bounteous, ever kind,
> Prepares the constant feast for all mankind.[57]

'The Globe', which is no more excessive in its dogged metaphor than many an eighteenth-century poem, cleaves hard to the concept of 'Nature' as a benevolent provider of material welfare. What is important to Allen Davenport is the situation of 'nature' within a materialist and socialist politics.

Both Davenport and Blandford suggest that 'nature' is the surplus value of labour and this is an important Spencean rereading, against the grain, of Locke's argument that labour is property. In his *Republican* debate with Carlile, Davenport crystallizes the point succinctly: 'Nature owns the peasant, and proclaims the assistance she receives at his hands'.[58] 'Nature' 'proclaims' the labourer's 'assistance' by giving up her fruits as the signifier of that help. Everything that grows or is produced by 'nature' is the combined product of their mutual activity.

According to Davenport, 'nature' 'will not fail'. His *Life* shows that he knew hunger at first hand and in the *Republican* Davenport makes it clear that famines and food shortages are the result of political rather than natural forces. To make his point, he refers back to the privations of the year Blake left London:

> And if we look back to the years of 1800, and 1801, we shall see that hundreds of individuals were starved even to death by a dearth of the necessaries of life which was proved afterwards to be only an artificial one: to be a dearth created by the murderous hand of monopoly.[59]

The importance of this Spencean argument is that it resists the process of the naturalization of the political and the historical because of its ideologically simple binaries where the Spencean plan is opposed to borough-mongering politics, productivity to shortage, labour to idleness. The belief in the abundance of 'nature' was the economic base for a social and political ideology. What the Spenceans were doing was making this ideology intervene in contemporary politics.

The most direct examples of this intervention can be found in the politics of Robert Wedderburn. Most of his speeches are garbled by the reporting of spies but he may have used an amanuensis to overcome his illiteracy or semi-literacy in order to transpose the vigour of his Hopkins Street speeches into blunt prose when he exclaimed against the 'wooden-headed gentry' who needed to be told that 'the produce of the land belongs to those who cultivate it'. The equation of God, 'nature' and labourer was expressed in unequivocal terms by Wedderburn: 'Tell the fat parsons, that TRUE RELIGION is to eat our bread with sincere thankfulness to HIM that causeth the earth to bring forth her increase.'[60] Wedderburn's 'HIM', strikingly, is the labourer, the one who provides 'our bread' which the minister redundantly blesses. E.J. Blandford was no less direct. According to the version of history told in his poem 'Nature's First, Last, And Only Will! Or a Hint to Mr. Bull', the natural order was lost when 'despots, rose and seiz'd the fertile land'. Exactly because 'Nature' and the labourer are equated, Blandford could conclude his poem with the cry 'Let Nature rouse!' and justice will 'draw the sword!'; enigmatically, the battle-cry of revolution is the battle-cry of 'Nature'. Those who read only a Romanticist metaphysic of 'Nature' would miss the call to the populace to arm, an injunction Robert Wedderburn was to make more explicit at Hopkins Street that autumn.[61]

In a three-month run from April to June, hardly an issue of the *Medusa* was printed without a Blandford poem. His next poem, 'A REAL DREAM, Or, Another Hint for Mr. Bull!', allowed Blandford the opportunity to offer an expanded return to his former subject. The poem takes the form of a visionary journey. He falls asleep and 'Fancy' takes him:

> First, through some richly verdant fields we stray'd,
> Where sportive plenty ruddy health display'd;
> Where rustic swains and sylvan nymphs appear'd,
> In sweet contentment, by the prospect cheer'd,
> Where fruits and grain abundant round them grew,
> Which all had care each season should renew;
> Where equal toil the fertile soil prepar'd,
> And all the equal gain of produce shar'd;
> Where old and young an equal balance held,
> And each had equal space for his abode,
> With nature's equal laws their only code.[62]

This picture of Spencean happiness, where the 'fertile soil' grows 'abundant' produce 'prepar'd' by 'equal toil' for 'ruddy' nymphs and swains living in their 'equal space', is vividly simple. Blandford is a *bricoleur* using the most conventional of tropes to hand and reinhabiting them with a revolutionary ideology. Blandford's visionary does not stay in this Spencean possible world, for 'soon the scene revers'd' and he returns to his own sublunary present. Here, the 'idle few are fed' by a laborious class and 'Methought insulted nature seemed amaz'd, / That proud profusion round these miscreants blaz'd'.

So far, Blandford's poem is proceeding on a predictable course borne along on conventional late-eighteenth-century tropes of outrage. All this changes, ultra-radically, when Fancy interrupts the visionary with a suggestion:

> 'Could these dumb guards, while they these dens surround,
> Be *moved* to action, and to sense of sound;
> Could these dumb ranks of *iron-railing* speak,
> They'd from their stations start, – their yokes they'd break,
> And cry aloud, that e'en the deaf might hear,
> In FREEDOM'S CAUSE we deprecate [*sic*] delay,
> When COURAGE shall command us, – we'll obey!!

> The tongueless IRON then in accent steady,
> Replied "when wanted you shall find us ready!" '[63]

The use of the iron railing surrounding the houses and estates of the rich was a tactic much recommended at Hopkins Street in the autumn of 1819. One Monday night in mid October, Robert Wedderburn gave a particularly fiery speech saying:

> . . . but if we can't all get Arms, theres them Iron Railing in front of these Big fellows Houses these will supply some with Arms they will make excellent Pikes used by a strong Arm and some will serve to turn into that long Gun we mean to have which will do wonderful execution; but even the very Women calls us Cowards and ask us why we have not begun before. They will assist us as the Women of France did their Husbands they will serve to finish those who may be only half killed.[64]

On another October night the Hopkins Street spy took down the gist of a speech which even more clearly places this particular physical force tactic adjacent to the Spencean ideology:

> 4th Wedderburn – spoke at great length, that there was no Constitution or Liberty in England since William the Conqueror – The day is now drawing near when the landholders must give up to us, and the soldiers will join us – let us be firm and united, there is no fear of success, we shall want Arms at first, but the Streets of London will furnish us with Arms for 200,000 Men, where? Why from the Iron Railings in front of every house, they my friends are excellent Weapons well handled, & let us loose no time in using them. I am ready – Twice warned, half armed therefore let Government beware, their Yeomanry will not save them, but let us rush upon them.[65]

Blandford's poem, in other words, contains an instruction to arm which is buried away within the tropes and pathetic fallacies of 'dumb guards' 'moved to action' and iron railings which 'speak' 'in accent steady' and say ' "when wanted you shall find us ready!" ' Information on Blandford is difficult to come by but it is consistent with his role as bill-poster and armourer to the Thistlewood group in August that his sentiments in the poem should prefigure those expressed later by Wedderburn.

In a quick succession of *Medusa* poems in the spring, Blandford made clear his devotion to physical force: 'Whatever weapons they may wield, / Sure conquest on the action lies . . .', 'soon shall justice strike the ALL-AVENGING BLOW'.[66] At the same time he continued a political analysis, sometimes in a crudely ironic tone ('We've

GLORIOUS FAMINE in each street, / With glorious rags and shoeless feet'), at other times in more elaborate constructions of parody and buffoonery. 'SATAN'S WILL, TESTAMENT, and FINAL CODICIL' was fastidiously laid out and partially printed in Gothic lettering and:

> Made, declared and delivered a few moments prior to his death, which took place at No. 11, Hopkins Street Chapel, near Berwick Street, Soho, on Wednesday evening May 12th, 1819, after a severe struggle, precisely at ten Minutes past ten o'clock, to the great grief of his Pious friends.[67]

This piece of positive infidelity makes Satan the original exploiter and monopolizer of the nation's 'fruits, and stocks, and crops'. It is a safely humorous squib but one which shows that Blandford must have been an early visitor to Hopkins Street which had opened only three or four weeks earlier. It seems to have been too early in Hopkins Street's activities for there to have been a spy or informer present to cover the 12 May debate but a man called William Porden, writing to complain about Hopkins Street Chapel, says that he had seen posted up in the Oxford Street area 'the result of a Question respecting the existence of a Devil, which, I think, was decided in the negative'.[68] It would have been entirely in character for the debate to have deviated into a blunt and outspoken condemnation of the alliance of religion and politics. The passing of the vote (was the 'severe struggle' an unusually vociferous Christian debater?) at 10.10 p.m. correlates, approximately, with the hour Hopkins Street debates were closing in the spring of 1819.

As the spring wore on, Blandford's poems exhibited an increasing frustration at the lack of armed insurrection. At the same time, the *Medusa* continued to prepare the ideological ground by publishing didactic and highly orthodox Spencean poems such as the anonymous 'Man in Prospective, Or Things As They Are to Be' which collects up the succinct slogan 'the people's farm' alongside the Christianized philosophy which was the hallmark of Thomas Evans's *Christian Policy the Salvation of Empire*:

> And are you not all christians,
> Except the pagan lords,
> And members of the church of God,
> All that it affords;
> His policy extends to all,
> Who can deny your claim?
> To hold the land in partnership,
> And all enjoy the same,

> Thus, as the lands and houses do
> Compose the people's farm,
> Each parish sure could let the same,
> Collect without larm, [sic]
> The parish rents, – as now the rates,
> The public dues discharge,
> And what remain'd divide among
> Parishioners at large
>
> Then read and teach, and sing and preach
> Of christian policy,
> For till you do divide the rents,
> You never can be free
> To do as you'd be done unto,
> Is justice from on high,
> No other system will admit
> But christianity.[69]

The description of the dispersal of rents from parochially owned land is straightforward grass-roots Spenceanism but the renewed attempt to graft Spence's ideology over the existing Christian structure reveals the impulse of Thomas Evans. This is why odd things happen to the syntax: 'And are you not all christians, / Except the pagan lords, / And members of the church of God, / All that it affords'. The last line states that church lands, after the Spencean revolution, would be disinvested from the church and re-invested in the people. The strained syntax shows how existing poetic structures are ill-suited to articulate an emergent politics. The more reflective mode introduced to Spencean ideology in this poem is fully marked by the new injunction to 'read and teach' as well as 'sing and preach' Christian policy (the title of Evans's book) in the 'free and easy' club or the seditious chapel.

Some of Blandford's poems continued this didactic line. 'PRIMITIVE TIMES, Or, Wholesome Advice for a Plundered People' gave the all-important history of how the common stock had been wrenched from the people:

> When NATURE first commenced the simple plan . . .
> Then LABOUR its full honest wages had
> For then in idle sloth, no tyrants fed,
> No titled thieves purloined man's hard-earned bread,
> 'Twas LABOUR then that best was fed and clad!

In Blandford's poem, the context of the new noun compound 'working class' helps define a class which is laborious and a class which is idle:

> TOIL, then to PLENTY'S well stored cupboard led . . .
> While PLENTY every where the table spread;
> The EARTH by LABOUR urged abundance gave
> But then no lazy, worthless few could dare,
> To touch the CROPS their hands did not prepare,
> Or take ONE GRAIN whate'er their hearts might crave![70]

The poem hints that a future redistribution of wealth ('Twas LABOUR then that best was fed and clad!') would also entail a redistribution of labour ('no lazy, worthless few could dare, / To touch the CROPS their hands did not prepare'). Blandford's poem is profoundly agricultural in its sympathies because the primary culture is agriculture, the cultivation of the land. The labourer urges the abundance of 'nature' in a close relationship between 'abundance' and 'LABOUR'. The political lesson is straightforward: the common 'well stored cupboard' has been 'plundered' by the 'few'.

Blandford's Spencean views were also Davenport's and the two men similarly shared a growing tendency to urge physical force. Davenport's 'A Song', published in the same issue as 'PRIMITIVE TIMES', cried 'Briton's rise, the time is come' while Blandford had already given 'AN EX POST FACTO HINT, FOR JOHNNY BULL' which referred back to his own 'A Real Dream' published more than a month earlier:

> I dreamed a real dream awake,
> And told those sleepers what to do!
> But they, too DULL to understand,
> Or else their *nerves* too *weak* and *loose*,
> Are with the weapon in the hand,
> Too COWARDLY to try its use.[71]

Blandford's chauvinist taunting is a device common to Wedderburn's Hopkins Street tactics but his 'A Fervent Appeal to the Swinish Multitude!!!' published two weeks later displays a more sustained and exasperated polemic: 'Why, ye ALL POWERFULL MANY, why so tame, / So dull, so spiritless?' How can the people 'rest your weary toil-worn limbs at night / *With PLENTY*, out of reach though full in sight?' His poem shifts from calling for a general armed insurrection to one visualized as led by a more specific 'PATRIOT BAND':

> Are you in callous cowardice so wrapt, . . .
> That when a brave, united, PATRIOT BAND
> Would from OPPRESSION snatch your native land;
> When they in BATTLE'S FRONT shall nobly dare
> Assert their RIGHTS, can you the stigma bear,
> That in the GLORIOUS ACTION you'd no share?[72]

There is much here of the *coup d'état*, a rising led by a vanguard in 'BATTLE'S FRONT' but backed by the populace.

Blandford's *Medusa* poetry ceased in the middle of June. From this point on he seems to have become more and more engaged in the committee of the Thistlewood group. With hindsight, it is possible to see that his poems 'AN EX POST FACTO HINT, FOR JOHNNY BULL' and 'A Fervent Appeal to the Swinish Multitude!!!' figure the people as the outsider, a mass which needs to be led by the sort of insurrectionary cell Thistlewood was building towards. Blandford's sense of the need for physical force was mirrored in the other ultra-radicals. On 13 July Blandford 'was to have the Posting bills out tomorrow' for a meeting, already once postponed, at Smithfield on the 21st. The next day, a 'Man in [a] white hat brought the bills' which had the signature of Blandford and also, ominously, the name of 'Rich. Tidd', one of the Cato Street conspirators to be hanged the following May.[73] In this culture, clothing signified. In October a short-lived journal called *The White Hat* was begun, it was an article of clothing of 'so many steady and decided patriots', a headgear which had been 'battered by the bludgeons of the special constables, slashed by the sabres of the Yeomanry Cavalry' and one 'too honourable to be neglected, and too formidable to be despised'.[74] The spy who noted radical millinery dogged the group right the way through that month and into the next year until the decisive débâcle of Cato Street.

A couple of extracts from the spy's précis for August give the context of Blandford and the ultra-radical activity of his colleagues:

8 Aug Sunday – George East Harding St
Dr Watson Produced Placard – and delivered addresses
Thislewood [sic]
Blandford
Wedderburn – should debate tomorrow 'if any sin to kill a Tyrant'
Gast – very violent
Hartley
Shaw
Preston – nothing but physical force
Harrison – was sure the Soldiers were all ready

9th – Wedderburns Chapel

10th Johnsons – Long Alley – Spencean debate division of land[75]

Although this is one full week pre-Peterloo, sentiments such as the 'very violent' ones expressed by Deptford shipwrights' leader John Gast are already very sanguine. These three consecutive August dates also illustrate the frequency of ultra-radical conference and the drawing together of a wide variety of extreme political and insurrectionary experience. Watson Snr and Preston were, of course, the leading veterans of the 1816 Spa Fields rising who had already been charged with high treason while 'Thislewood' had been under surveillance for about three years. 'Shaw' is almost certainly Dennis Shaw, a long-term Irish activist who, on 15 August, told the spy Banks that he had been 'conspicuous in the Irish Rebellion' of 1798 while James Hartley was bold enough to footpad a man near Regent's Park in an October attempt to find cash for arms. John Harrison was an ex-soldier who, days before, had declared he 'would not be disappointed to Arms to Arms'. After Peterloo he would go on to recommend 'setting fire to the house[s] in Smithfield to affect their escape if attacked by the Military' when they decided to change the venue of their meeting to the more urban-guerilla-congenial Smithfield instead of risking the vulnerability of Kennington Common's open spaces.[76]

The discursive context of these meetings is also important. The 'Spencean debate' on the 'division of land' took place at the Mulberry Tree in Moorfields. Johnson and his wife Mary had Spencean sympathies: they owned the freehold of the Mulberry Tree and were able to maintain a defiant independence despite local pressure from the authorities when their tavern became a regular and much-spied-on Spencean haunt in the post-war years.[77] Two weeks after the Cato Street arrests, the spy James Hanley ruefully reported that 'Political Debates are still carried on at the Mulberry Tree and Language of even a Seditious Nature too frequently used'.[78] Information about Wedderburn's debate 'Can it be murder to kill a Tyrant' came into the Home Office from at least two informer reports. William Porden wrote to the Home Office to say that the 'offspring of an African Slave will open the question' at the 'Temple of Sedition called Hopkins-Street-Chapel', as he irately called it, while the Revd Chetwode Eustace wrote in to complain that he had just visited Hopkins Street himself 'to hear the question discussed whether it was right for the People of England to assassinate their Rulers' 'tho' proposed in other terms'.[79] This double cycle of conspiratorial committee and public debate is what makes this group so fascinating and Wedderburn's position, actively straddling both sections, is tremendously important. Wedderburn's chapel was a double platform because it gave him authority within the inner, secret, committee but also gave him the means with which to judge and gauge their following by his first-hand assessment of the mood and quantity of the Hopkins Street audience.

The Peterloo massacre found the radicals disunited and unprepared even though they were eager to capitalize on the event.[80] Two days after E.J. Blandford told the spy Banks that Arthur Thistlewood was 'the Robispierre of the day', news of Peterloo reached London. Shipwrights' leader John Gast read an account to 200 people assembled at the George in East Harding Street: Blandford was 'very violent', Thistlewood said 'that all should be armed' and Thomas Preston declared he 'would lay down his life'.[81] Two days later at the same place, on the day Blandford was arrested, pike in hand, Watson told them of the *realpolitik* 'Coalition of Burdetts Party & Major Cartw[right]' which threatened to leave the Watson and Thistlewood group high and dry. On 22 August 290 people turned up at the Jacobs Well but Watson collected only £2 from them. Hair-trigger emotions were exemplified by ex-soldier Harrison telling their small secret committee that they should 'make away with all who nark' to the authorities. On the 24th, at the Red Cross in Fore Street, Cripplegate, the dedicated Spencean Robert Moggridge and the infiltrated spy Banks resigned their control of the treasury 'on account of monies been expended in Ammunition' although both continued to attend subsequent meetings.[82] The spy system was also under strain to keep up with the swift transition of events and it may have been the sheer number and myriad direction of political meetings in late August which prevented any decisive anti-radical initiative on the part of the Government which was, in any case, hamstrung by the non-assembly of Parliament and by (Home Office records show) trying to deal with the political fall-out of Peterloo. One informer, filing on 25 August, wrote back exhaustedly to report all sorts of reconciliations between the ultras:

> I have been up all night wat[g] the movements of the disaffected . . . At Johnstons (the Mulberry Tree) last night Preston, Frankland, Savadge &c &c . . . even Old Evans & his Son were strenuous in impressing upon the minds of the Party present [the] necessity of immediate action.[83]

If Thomas Evans had returned to the fold, despite his acrimonious break with Preston's friend Wedderburn over the Hopkins Street debating club, then all sorts of coalitions were possible. For good measure, the spy enclosed a list of 'Vendors selling the Seditious Publications and Notices', a list of suspicious coffee houses and a printed handbill urging 'Universal Civil & Religious Liberty' signed by Secretary Blandford (Middlesex), Dennis Shaw (Southwark) and Samuel Waddington (Surrey).[84]

The parameters of ultra-radical discursivity at this politically critical time are well summed up by these types of small but significant events. At a Crown and Anchor meeting at the end of August John

Gale Jones also turned up to address a diverse assembly of ultras: 'he hoped the time would soon come when their Prince would not be making Excurtions by Land and Water when his subjects where suffering under the hands of Murderers and Tyrants'. Perhaps this carefully phrased hope was too milk-and-water for 'Davidson the Black' who next rose to speak and 'Stated to the Company that he was alwaies ready to go any leanths with the Friends of Reform'.[85] Only days before, Davidson had attended the Smithfield meeting armed and had expected to be involved in a clash with the authorities so there can be little doubt to what 'leanths' he would be prepared to go. As it was, Gale Jones's appearance was a flash in the pan: a piece of would-be hijackery. He must have judged the violent mood of the assembly and gauged the impact of the rise of people like Wedderburn and Davidson because he did not turn up the next day. The spy James Hanley reported that Thistlewood's group 'are Angry with G Jones and Wooler for not attending their call'.[86]

While the ultras were increasingly able to sort out their own differences, their fundamentally male artisan base gave little opportunity for the female support and alliance on which, ultimately, all political actions of their devising would depend. While the Thistlewood group were more than eager to cement and further relationships and correspondence with northern groups, the visit of a 'Female from Manchester' to a meeting held in the 'covered Skittle Ground' at the White Horse in Turnmill Street on 29 August may have proved too intimidating a conference to be conducted in anything other than a conversational mode. The spy Hanley was there to report that 'This Lady (who was placed near the Chairman [Watson]) was Invited by Preston to Speak but She did not gratify their expectations on this ocasion'. That night there were 'about 60' present including Thistlewood, Wedderburn, Dennis Shaw and Hartley. Ultra-radical discourse was simply too dominated by its artisan male base. It readily accepted and forwarded coloured men like Wedderburn and Davidson but women were still unable to have a place which put them on an equal footing: the male tavern culture was ill-suited to their presence. Women had been in the forefront of the Peterloo massacre when over a hundred of them had been injured and there can be little doubt that this unnamed 'Female from Manchester' was a timely piece of fraternity and an opportune moment for the female cause.[87]

If ultra-radical awareness of the possibilities of sexual political equality was dismal, the boys in the back room of the pub got on with chairing their endless meetings but were now outflanked by Hunt's massively successful return to London to face the silly charge of high treason for his mild low profile at Peterloo. Halfway through the month, on 14 September, there was the touchy quarrel between Hunt and Watson at the White Lion dinner over who could or could not chair the meeting. There were also attempts to form a 'London Union formed after the Manchester plan' proposed by a Mancunian activist called Tetlow who had come down to London on 16 September and was changing his lodgings nightly under the alias of Westwood or Wedgewood. Tetlow proposed decentralized sections of twelve with each member paying a penny a week subscription, and this seemed to work. Typically, the night he proposed this at the Crown and Anchor, King Street in Seven Dials, 'several' of the number were 'armed with Pistols & spring Bayonets'.[88] The autumn and winter of 1819 to 1820 found the ultra-radicals becoming more and more prone to carry weapons. By the end of the year the Hopkins Street debating club was working in full conjunction with the physical force activists as the views of one reflected the views of the other.

CHAPTER SIX

Hopkins Street to Cato Street: Surveillance and Resistance, 1819–20

THE 'TEMPLE OF SEDITION' AT HOPKINS STREET

One of the Manchester-style sections, based at Wedderburn's Hopkins Street Chapel, Hopkins Street, became the scene of an unusually vivid and vibrant ultra-radical articulacy. Wedderburn decisively broke with Thomas Evans's Archer Street Chapel which they had jointly licensed in early 1818 when Wedderburn set up a more extreme group on his own in April 1819. As McCalman writes, Wedderburn did it 'in typical style; he took the benches with him'.[1] There was acrimony which Wedderburn turned to good use by publishing two handbills. The first was a single-sided flier containing an advertisement for 'Hopkin-Street Chapel, near Berwick-Street' at the bottom of a sharp little poem satirizing both Thomas Evans and his wife, Janet:

A FEW LINES FOR A Double-Faced Politician

Evans, my apostate son, was once a pleasant child,
But, Ephraim like, a half baked cake, by ignorance is beguiled;
But when in wisdom, he doth see his folly and his crime,
Forgiveness he will early seek, and worship at the shrine;
Then *Wedderburn* to him will say, 'Confession humbly make,
For Spence's God doth me command, to turn the half bak'd cake,'
His brandy fac'd Dulcina cried – 'I'll turn the cake myself,
As long as I the breeches wear, I will have all the pelf;
And he that would my husband turn, would find an arduous task,
Though he's a hypocrite in grain, he wears a patriot's mask.'[2]

165

The blatant sexism of the poem is as good an indication as any of the Spenceans' catastrophic failure to adequately engage women with their cause, even though they had been tacitly included in Spence's original plan. As McCalman notes, 'A Few Lines . . .' might be the Wedderburn faction's riposte to Evans for specifically welcoming women to Archer Street, *gratis*.[3] Only one copy of 'A Few Lines for a Double-Faced Politician' seems to have survived and only because it was methodically forwarded to the Home Office by a spy. It is by 'R.W.' but its true composer is unlikely to have been Wedderburn.

The informer 'A', James Hanley, promptly told the Home Office that 'The Spenceans have broken up their meeting in Archer Street' and 'Wedderburn took away clandestinely some of the Benches'. He enclosed a handbill called 'A few PLAIN QUESTIONS FOR AN APOSTATE' which Wedderburn (who signed himself 'Spencean') published and printed and which describes how Evans had 'charged him with Felony' at Marlborough Street police station and then led three 'banditti' who 'seized' him in the street 'exciting' the attention of a 'mob of hundreds'. Evans forced his way into Wedderburn's house 'forcibly taking away a stool, in spite of all the resistance my wife could make to the contrary'. For good measure, Wedderburn reprinted the first six lines of 'A FEW LINES FOR A Double-Faced Politician'.[4]

As Iain McCalman has discovered, in addition to the benches, Robert Wedderburn successfully Pied-Pipered many of Evans's Archer Street congregation across to Hopkins Street. Wedderburn was so outspoken at Hopkins Street that he was gaoled and bailed in August and appeared to face a charge of blasphemy and sedition in September 1819. It was only after his acquittal on the 21st that he was able with certainty to pledge Hopkins Street to Watson's and Thistlewood's post-Peterloo cause after he had triumphantly claimed 'the true and infallible genius of prophetic skill' when he told the court he had predicted blood would be spilt in England. In September the awful Manchester example was too contemporary for a jury to miss the point of these 'sleepy visions'.[5] Within days Wedderburn was back in the swing of debate at his Carnaby Market 'Temple of Sedition'.

Hopkins Street is a fierce forum for capturing, at one remove, the speech and articulacy of a lost culture. As he said on 18 October, because 'his name had gone abroad as a strange curious sort of fellow and their might be there [some] who would wish to hear him say something . . . he should offer a few remarks'.[6] Bravely, Wedderburn pitched in after his acquittal with the taunting riposte of the debating topic 'Is the Bible the Word of God?' with an audience of 'upwards of

60 Persons': 'Wedderburn quoted the books of Moses, Daniel, Saul and [he] called Moses a Whoremonger and compared him to the P[rince]. R[egent]. David a murderer – like the Manchester Magistrates & the Ministers.' Wedderburn's comments are direct, immediate and highly political. With the voice of the outsider they carved through the country's religious, political and social system: 'we should think none greater than ourselves & follow the example of the Asiatic States – if their leader offend then cut their heads off'. Wedderburn's occasional colleague Samuel Waddington spoke in similar vein when he 'quoted several Passages' from the Bible calling for 'blood for blood' and went on: 'If the right hand offend thee cut it off – The PR is the right hand of the people, he has offended thee & waged war against us.'[7] Nor did it stop there: that Wednesday they went to the Mulberry Tree to debate the question (a little belatedly) 'Is the Revolution commenced at Manchester or not?' A week later Wedderburn was 'very violent against the Ministers & the PR – said they were all bloody Tyrants & should be cut off, because the Princes ancestors were brought over & made King did they suppose the family was to enjoy it for ever, no, serve him as Charles the firsts Soldiers did, spit in his face & cut him off, therefore arm & be ready, the day is near at hand.' Hartley, who was then in charge of Thistlewood's armoury of pike-heads, spoke next and, perhaps a little hopefully, offered himself as the necessary leader.[8] The pace was breathless and exuberant. His example may have prompted the debating question of four days later 'ought the public Society to reject all persons of property and their Leaders and Choose from among themselves the men of ability to manage the business of Reform'.[9] Although Hopkins Street was dominated by Wedderburn, an important function of his chapel was that it provided a platform for both other veteran activists and newcomers.

Allen Davenport has left a unique autobiographical account of how he first came to make a speech in a post-war Spencean debating club. Davenport had been a committed Spencean since 1805 but he seems not to have come across any Spencean organization until after their attempted suppression in 1817 and the subsequent imprisonment of the two Evanses in Horsemonger Lane gaol under a Suspension of Habeas Corpus.[10] They were not released until January 1818 and it was then, when they went to Archer Street 'to carry on discussions upon the same principles, but by another name', as Davenport recalled it, that he came across them quite by accident:

And I shall never forget the joy I felt, when going down Newcastle Street, Strand, on seeing a bill in Mr. Evans's window, directing the public to their place of meeting, and inviting people of all classes, to take a part in their discussions. On receiving this information, not knowing Mr. Evans, or any other Spencean at that time, I flew away with all speed to the place named in the bill, in order to make sure of the place to which the bill directed, that I might easily find it on the next discussion night, to which I was firmly resolved to go, and to unite myself to the men, whose principles I had so long approved of, and advocated among my friends and acqaintances.[11]

What Davenport is describing here is a life-changing experience, an event which had the vitality of when he first came across Spence's plan some fifteen years earlier. It is important to set Davenport's *Life* in the context of nineteenth-century working-class autobiography. Writing these recollections in 1845, Davenport is validating his experiences for himself and on behalf of his class. Davenport was one marginal and subsistence-level mechanic making a breakthrough contact with his common ideological community. The Spencean handbill, once again, had reached its audience. The audience was not expected to remain passive but 'people of all classes' were invited to 'take a part in their discussions'. Allen Davenport went to Archer Street with the specific intention of speaking. He was going there 'to hear what the Spenceans had to say' but, equally, 'to deliver' 'and express' his own views 'on the subject of agrarian reform'.[12]

When Davenport got there he heard two or three 'clever' speeches including one by John Wright, a professional orator and respectable radical. A casual call by a spy at the (usually Spencean) Mulberry Tree in December 1817 found nearly a hundred 'very respectable Men' and when 'an avowed Atheist' spoke 'he was called to order' and 'Mr. Wright cautioned the Company lest they should be apprehended.'[13] Davenport thought Archer Street 'rather too tame':

> I seized the first opportunity, to deliver myself of the mass of thought, and Spencean ideas, that had been accumulating since 1805, in my mind. I plunged into the discussion, with all the warmth and zeal of an enthusiast; indeed, I was too warm to be correct; and my maiden speech consisted of fiery and ungovernable declamations, and invectives against the present administration of landed property in England, and all other civilized nations in the world. But I was listened to with patience, and gained some applause, as the reward of my zeal; it certainly could not be for either the splendour of my eloquence, or the correctness of my logical deductions.[14]

This is a vivid recollection by a Spencean activist of Archer Street Chapel in 1818. It pictures the isolation, even in the metropolis, of an artisan who worked and struggled and whose spare time from 1813 was already occupied with being a representative of 'the fifth division of women's men', a fourteen division shoemakers' union which met at the York Arms, Holborn.[15] If Davenport had not before had opportunity to express in speech 'the mass of thought, and Spencean ideas' which had accumulated over twelve years, the 'patience' and 'applause' with which he was received must have consolidated his own sense of having arrived at a welcoming discursive community and he returned 'and spoke occasionally' until it 'broke up' when Wedderburn left.[16]

In 1819 Davenport 'became acquainted with' Hunt, Thistlewood, Watson Snr and Preston and 'all the out and out radicals of that radical period'. By the latter half of that year, there was a dual structure of Spencean-based ultra-radicalism in London. On the nights that Hopkins Street debated, Thistlewood's secret committee held parallel meetings elsewhere: there was close organizational proximity between them which was a type of autonomous inter-dependence. On Sunday 10 October, for example, while Wedderburn was at Hopkins Street, the Thistlewood group met at Watson Snr's house off Fleet Street and then at the White Lion before going on to Pitts Place, Drury Lane.

That evening Thistlewood reported back on his journeys to Derby, Nottingham and Leicester while 'fresh Union meetings' or sections, on Tetlow's Manchester model, were 'announced' including ones at Cripplegate, Marylebone, St Pancras, Battlebridge and Fleet Market. The Cripplegate Union sent a fraternal, if not conspiratorial, 'Deputation'.[17] Meanwhile, over in Carnaby Market the Hopkins Street Chapel was well under way with London Irish leader Dennis Shaw starting off the evening's debate with rumours of mercenaries to be used to quell the English radicals.[18] The fear of foreign mercenaries was pervasive because the ultras had an almost traditional confidence that their own soldiery would come over to their side in the event of a rising.

The second Hopkins Street speaker that night was the house painter William Carr, a long-standing friend of Thomas Evans:

> 2nd *Speaker Carr* – said he was only a poor mechanic who labored late & early but could not obtain food for his family; there was no time to be lost talking there, and that it was only by vigorous preparation we could succeed in attacking our Enemies, before they could receive any aid from Foreign Troops.[19]

Carr's speech is only a circumspect call to arms but his social identity and precarious economic circumstances would have been typical of many of the speakers at Hopkins Street. Carr's speech, with its sense of urgency and immediacy, illustrates the economic and social basis of his mentality.[20]

Hopkins Street was in high gear. The next day, Monday, they discussed the question 'Which of the Characters are most dangerously situated. The Prince who has lost the Confidence & affection of his People, or the Subject who has gained it – ?' Perhaps the subject was a little too abstract or politically elliptical for the audience because the debate veered towards more immediate subjects:

> Principal Speaker was Wedderburn, who dwelt chiefly on the late Affairs at Manchester; that the bloody Revolution had begun in blood there, & it must now end in blood – That the Prince had lost the Confidence of & affection of his People, but being supported by the army & surrounded by his vile Ministers, nothing short of the People taking arms in their own defence, could bring about a Reform & prevent the same bloody scenes taking place at the next Smithfield Meeting, as had taken place at Manchester, for his own Part old as he was, he was learning his exercise as a Soldier & could be on[e?] if he fell in the cause, for he had rather die like Cashman, if he could but have the satisfaction of plunging a Dagger in the heart of a Tyrant. That the next Meeting on 1 Nov would be such a General Meeting throughout the Country as well as London that then only was the time *'therefore all come armed or its of no use and be sure you bring plenty of Ammunition with you'*.[21]

That the Prince Regent was badly advised by his 'vile Ministers' was an article of policy if not of faith amongst the ultra-radicals. In a defiant letter to Lord Sidmouth composed in Tothill Fields prison during the Cato Street round-up, Thomas Preston defended the Brunswick family who were 'as much insulted as the people by a proud and cruel holligarchy' while Watson Snr, more shrewdly, had proposed a radical flag 'motto'ed *The Prince & the People against the Borough Mongers* this he said would have a great weight with the Public'.[22]

Wedderburn's announcement of a national meeting at Smithfield on 1 November had been decided in secret committee only three days before. Indeed, on this very Hopkins Street night, the committee's conversations about the national meeting were being spied upon as they gathered in Watson Snr's house.[23] The visualization of an 1816 Spa Fields rising scenario is explicit in Wedderburn's reference to Cashman who was executed for his raid on a gunshop during the rising. Wedderburn's bravado collects up the heroic memory of Cashman who yelled from the scaffold 'Hurra, my hearties in the cause! success! cheer up!'[24] An armed clash in the close kennels of Smithfield, abetted by risings elsewhere in the country, was the ultra-radical utopia.

The next day the secret committee met at the White Lion and proposed 'forming the Continual Philanthropic Radical Union', perhaps an attempt to universalize their movement under a mild-sounding banner. It is a significant aspect of their attempt to think on the wider national basis which was to culminate in the projected national rising of November.[25] On the 18th the subject of imported Russian troops or mercenaries was discussed again. Fear of the Russians was activated by bitter memories of the three-day sacking of Warsaw by what Allen Davenport called a 'monster' of a Russian general in the 1790s.[26] The debate is worth following because it reveals an artisan version of cultural and political history:

> The first speaker commenced by saying it was a question which he could enter on with pleasure though all the Spies and Informerers [sic], tho' all the Officers of Marlborough S^t together with all the magistrates in London were in the Room as he felt confident their was nothing in the question which was possible for them to catch at . . . because we must naturaly suppose that a British army would never suffer a Horde of Barbarians or hired Mercenaries to come among them, for on refering to History we find that Englishmen were always directly opposite to such a system; for when they sent over for Wm the Dutchman to come to govern them they were even compell'd him to send his Dutch guards Back again to Holland.[27]

This speaker is unidentified but his words reveal that everyone knew 'Spies and Informerers' were likely to be in the room because information had already been collected against Wedderburn who was there once again. Why this braggadocio? Even Thistlewood's secret committee knew, by the end of 1819, that they had probably been infiltrated by one or more spies, so why did they continue? The speech of this unidentified Hopkins Street debater gives some clues.

As far as he was concerned, he was safe because 'notwithstanding the Soldiers were estranged from the People', a political crisis would 'unite all factions' and the army especially. Wedderburn, the fourth speaker, makes the point more clearly:

> we'll have none of your Ugly cut throat Russians here a British Army will never join them or if they do we have a Disbanded Militia who have suffer'd with us and know the use of Arms we have a disbanded Volunteer force too who also know the use of arms they are discharging men from the Army because they wont give them [an] extra penny a

Day agreeable to Mr Windhams Act, they become disatisfied, they enlist poor half starved devils half of them unfit for soldiers and these they have to train before they are fit for service so much the better, now one poor fellow who had been discharged we made a subscription for in this room and they shall all have subscriptions that come to this place – now who knows but this Disbanded Militia this Disbanded Volunteer force may join the jacobin Mob and most of them have arms but what shall we do for Officers why there are many who have Borne commissions Discharged.[28]

Radicals since Despard's time had sought and received the support of elements in the armed forces and Wedderburn's remarks here show that Hopkins Street, as a part of its philanthropic base, was assisting individual distressed soldiers and considering what they could 'do for Officers' who had been discharged. Apart from the discharged regulars, another problem had developed for the authorities. As recent work has shown, the local volunteer militias put together during the French war were considered to be highly unstable because they allowed and necessitated a lower-class armed soldiery who were partially trained but who also, because of their volunteer status, could disregard any and all orders from superior officers.[29] These militias had been expected to be sufficiently responsive to national politics to defend their country while remaining disenfranchised. Post-war depression must have hardened this contradiction. As Wedderburn said that night, 'who knows but this Disbanded Militia this Disbanded Volunteer force may joint the jacobin Mob and most of them have arms'.

Allen Davenport was one of the speakers that night. It is a remarkable opportunity to be able to take this snapshot of Davenport's ultra-radical activities. By his own account, Davenport became a 'desperate politician' in the 'perilous years of 1818 and 1819' and it is a measure of his perception of the danger of the times that he adopted the alias 'Ferguson' at Hopkins Street. Unknown to him, this disguised nomenclature had already been penetrated by the spies who wrote him in as '2nd Speaker Ferguson' '(Davenport alias)'.[30] Davenport gave a polished and wide-ranging speech beginning that 'it was his oppinion that in no spot in the known World were questions proposed and argued of that magnitude that there were in that room'. Davenport's statement of the importance of Hopkins Street correlates with the Archer Street impressions related in the *Life*. Hopkins Street was a unique forum: 'It gave him infinite pleasure when he thought of it', he said, 'as he hoped ere long the World would see that they had not been Idle; and tyrannical and Despotic Ministers would face the Vengeance of an injured People.'

Davenport warmed to his theme and he turned next to attempts to curtail the freedom of the press:

> they might convict Mr Carlile and imprison him for publishing Paine's Age of Reason, but they could not tear it from his bosom; it was there and he would hug it as he would the dearest friend he had got. what was Lord Castlereagh Lord Sidmouth or Lord any body else more than he was they were but men and they like him must Die and become Dust as others – but the time has come when we will be no more dazzled by the sound of a Name or glitter of an Object – what was the use of all these Lords & Dukes and Princes without it was to buy and sell you as they did living stock.[31]

Davenport's *Life* makes clear his youthful determination to become literate, and the value he placed upon the freedom of reading, writing and speaking is implicit in all that he did and said. He returned to this theme in his speech at Hopkins Street ten days later when he declared that 'every journeyman Mechanic should become a Politician.' They were now able to do this because of the subversive effects of reading: 'the fools through their charitable Institutions were teaching all Classes to read the Bible in hopes that they would Fear God and Honor the King and become passively obedient to their oppressors but they forgot that when they could read the Bible they could read Paine's Age of Reason or M[r] Carlile's Republican'.[32] Davenport's speech reveals the unrespectable use of respectability.

In 1819 Davenport was heavily committed to sedition. 'Every man should study Politics', said Davenport, 'for my part I study them all Day I write on them I dream of them at Night, I stand here twice a week preaching Blasphemy and Sedition (as they call it) and will continue to do it unless they rob [me] of my liberty which I know they are likely enough to do.'[33] Some of the vigour of Davenport's oratory has survived the mangling of the Hopkins Street spy. He was every bit as violent as Wedderburn. The time for humbly petitioning corrupt authority was over:

> war as I observed on a former evening has already been declared against us why then should we hesitate, for my own part I am ready now, – but let us wait 'till Parliament meets is [the] cry of some few but what will they meet for? why to pass a Bill of Indemnity for those murderers the Magistrates and Yeomanry of Manchester, the adjourning of a Coroners Inquest at Oldham was sufficient to tell them that; it was evident they decided it going further but they jury should return a verdict of Wilfull Murder; what would be the Regents Vote of thanks, they yeomanry had murdered our fellow Countrymen but had we even in our Defence shot one or two of them it would have been called

Murder and Rebellion, but we will put up with it no longer I compare
the present time [to] the crisis of [the] French Revolution, we must arm
ourselves as they did and in the open day too and though we may loose
a few lives in the onset yet what is the army compared to the Mass of
the Country who are labouring under the yoke of Despotism.[34]

Moderation was never much on the agenda at Hopkins Street and the
aftermath of Peterloo had brought its own lessons. Satirized by
Davenport here is the Prince Regent's ill-timed and insensitive letter
of thanks to Manchester's magistrates and military's 'prompt,
decisive, and efficient measures for the preservation of the public
peace'.[35]

Hopkins Street regulars were never backward in coming forward.
'Why then should we hesitate, for my own part I am ready now,'
cried Davenport. Personal pledges were well received and were
probably considered a necessary part of the ultra-radical portfolio of
credentials. Additionally, because this is speech and not writing, the
immediate effect of this self-dedication delivered to the audience in
the full presence of the speaker must have been an extraordinary
representation of the validity of utterance. At the same time as this
transgressivity, steadier forces were at work, ones which built up a
background of a distinct political history relevant to these artisans.

Ten days later Davenport put together 1688 and 1789 to make a new
point about 1819:

if we can only bring over two Regiments to our cause good bye to the
Poor Russians good bye to your state Religion good bye to Castlereagh
and your Paper Government, the sound of our little Victory would
bring the whole British Army over to us, they like the Soldiers of France
would fight for us, there would be a Bloody Revolution!!! not like your
Milk and Water Revolution of 1688, were they swore one thing one
Day, trampled it under foot and swore to the contrary the next No, No,
that was a Revolution very different to what ours will be.[36]

Continual references were made at Hopkins Street to a political
history relevant to the culture of its audience. As well as France and
1688, the historical reach of Wedderburn went further back and was
enough to encompass the history of state and religion across two
reigns:

The priests of Oliver Cromwell preached sermons upon Charles the
first losing his head, they said it was all right it was the will of God as a
punishment for the Distress he had brought upon [the] land – then only

mind the turn coat rascals when they restored Charles the second; he was their legitimate King the Lords annointed, he was, the Vice [?regent] of God; Gods Vicar on earth !!! (touch not the Lords annointed) oh! these deceitful rascals.[37]

Here the history of the collusion of priests and their opportune hypocrisy extends Spencean infidelity by displaying how religious authority is an arbitrary historical whim. On the same night that Dennis Shaw and Carr addressed the Hopkins Street crowd, Wedderburn 'spoke at great length, that there was no Constitution or Liberty in England since William the Conqueror' and put this assertion in the context of the Spencean ideology:

> The day is now drawing near when the landholders must give up to us, and the soldiers will join us – let us be firm and united, there is no fear of success, we shall want Arms at first, but the Streets of London will furnish us with Arms for 200,000 Men, where? Why from the Iron Railings in front of every house, they my friends are excellent Weapons well handled, & let us loose no time in using them. I am ready – Twice warned, half armed therefore let Government beware, their Yeomanry will not save them, but let us rush upon them –[38]

The day 'when the landholders must give up to us' would be the day when 'the Streets of London' furnished 'Arms for 200,000 Men'. The Thistlewood group's preoccupation with the pike as the weapon of urban revolutionary warfare is a constant theme and Wedderburn was prepared to back such extreme assertions by pledging his own involvement, being 'Twice warned, half armed'.

Unknown to Wedderburn, even his conversations in the street were being overheard and reported. The informer J. Brittain, who wrote a sequence of suspiciously colourful reports in late 1819 and early 1820, told of how he went to Hopkins Street, heard him utter 'Blasphemy upon Our Saviour' and then waited until 'he had left the Chapel' and heard him talking to 'two or three friends that was with him, as they appeared to be'. Brittain's reports have enough familiarity with the culture of ultra-radical London to make it probable that he knew a little about what he was writing:

> If the soldiers should make or offer to make an attac [sic] upon the People of London, we have some good friends beside the Gass & Railing – their is a Great number of Bakers Ovens that runs under the street which can be easy Blown up, & the best of all the Bakers are almost to a Man Radicals or & Spenceans London stands upon nothing,

it has foundations but Vaults, Shores, Ovens, Pipes, Cesspools So that
One shock whould fall like unto the tower of Bable.[39]

Brittain's allusion to the 'Gass & Railing' echoes Government fears
which were taunted into a Hopkins Street debating topic which asked
why 'his Majesty's Ministers' have 'taken down the Iron Pallisading
throughout the Empire . . . to destroy the Gas-works, to prevent the
Radicals making use of them in case of Civil War?'[40] Whether Brittain
was right in saying that the ultras were turning the gaze of the
bricoleur onto 'Bakers Ovens' is uncertain, but the 'great many'
persons who met at the Fox and Goose, Pooley Street, back in early
1818 were 'chiefly Bakers' and their main topic of conversation had
been how to assassinate Lords Sidmouth and Ellenborough in the
Houses of Parliament.[41] Like other of Brittain's reports, he weakly
stressed the danger he was in when he said that he remained 'in the
Public Street' 'till my Company seemed not by any means desirable
[when] they all gave me a Contemptable look & went away.'[42]

Whatever the veracity of Brittain's reports, it really did look as if
'London stands upon nothing', it has 'no foundations but Vaults,
Shores, Ovens, Pipes, Cesspools So that One shock whould fall like
unto the tower of Bable'.[43] Allen Davenport ended his Hopkins Street
speech on 27 October by declaring 'let us prepare to knock down this
system of tyranny to rush upon the Cannons Mouth and if we should
not succeed Die Gloriously in the Struggle.'[44] 1 November 1819 had
been designated as the day of a national rising.[45] It did not take place
but the idea of it, along with Spencean ideas, had gone the rounds of
the whole country.

On 20 October the Revd J. Monteath of Paisley wrote two careful,
courteous but alarmed letters to the Home Office about local unrest.
His principal fear was the turbulent discussion of an 'agrarian law':

> The Spirit of Revolt, and Revolution, apparent to me, from everything I
> can see, and from every Quarter that I can learn, [seems] to have taken
> root, and to be spreading daily wider and wider. An agrarian law is
> openly talked over among vast numbers of People, in the [??]itiest and
> most extra-urgent terms – virulent hatred and contempt of all the
> higher ranks of Society, and even of the middling ranks, appear
> universally to prevail, and this hatred has, of late, been particularly
> manifested against the ministers of Religion – the minds of the People
> are poisoned by atheistical and deistical, and revolutionary publications
> continually conveyed to them from London, industriously conveyed to
> them, and often gratuitiously bestowed, or furnished at a very low
> price, and carried about by Hawkers, from door to door . . . Every
> pretence is laid hold of for large publick meetings; even the most

opposite things, a marriage, or a funeral; a fair, or a field preacher, may be made equally a pretence to assemble; and then discuss the affairs of the Nation and revile the government – Even women, forgetting the honourable station which the British constitution has placed them in, are forward in all these meetings, and if a peace officer but happen to lay his hand on their shoulder, or say 'stand by, and let me pass in the crowd' the cry and yell of murder! is instantly vociferated by the females.[46]

There is a wide sweep of subject and anxiety in Monteath's letter. 'An agrarian law' is 'talked over' by 'vast numbers of People', 'atheistical . . . deistical, and revolutionary publications' from London are widespread. More significantly, there is every indication here of the resourcefulness of another ultra-radical culture, a culture where the traditional social assemblies of marriages, funerals, fairs and impromptu chapels are turned towards a resistant politics capable of involving 'Even women'.

On the day Monteath wrote his letter, the metropolitans were already backtracking. A Government spy on that Wednesday morning met Robert Wedderburn who told him 'it was no use to rise on 1 Novb, there were not above 2000 persons and not all armed.' Meeting up in the White Lion that evening, Watson Snr and Thistlewood were 'of the same oppinion'.[47] Word had come to London by the 19th that the Manchester radicals would also hold a public meeting on 1 November which, in the context of Peterloo, might have insurrectionary potential. As the day approached, Harris and Hartley (who came tooled up on the day with 'a horse Pistol') attended Thistlewood's secret committee as an official deputation from the 'New Round Court Society', one of the new Manchester-model sections. They came 'to know how they were to act on Monday' (1 November). 'Dr Watson replied, they were left to their own Choice whether they would live in Chains or break their fetters. They both replied we Understand you –'.[48] This must have been face-saving on Watson Snr's part because the next day Edmonds, editor of the *Democratic Recorder and Reformer's Guide*, 'reported to the meeting that he had heard that Hartley & black Davidson had been collecting money on account of the Meeting [on 1 November] – on which Hartley was called in and questioned'. Hartley was already selling pike-heads at 1s 3d each and funding for this arming must have been the 'Private purpose' Hartley admitted to under questioning. Dramatically, 'Mr Hartley said . . . it was for – here Dr Watson stopt him, saying it was for a private use and it was all very well & Hartley was ordered to retire.'[49] It was probably the unofficial siphoning of money which Edmonds objected to rather than its end-use: only three weeks before his *Democratic Recorder* had declared not only that 'A soldier in England is an armed citizen' but also that the country needed 'citizens with arms'.[50]

When 1 November arrived, forty ultras 'armed & loaded' themselves at the White Lion in Wych Street, whereupon 'Thistlewood came in & inspected them' and after Forrester and Thistlewood 'recommended the People to arm', they dispersed. They met up again that evening when 'D[r] [Watson] thanked them for their attendance, hoped they would always be ready to lay down their lives in the cause of freedom' and arranged another mass public meeting for the 15th. It must have been a depressing night. For the 15th, Watson Snr 'hoped all would be prepared, but trusted the Ministers would grant what they asked without a Revolution.'[51]

While the private room of the White Lion was the gloomy meeting place for the ultra core of Watson Snr, Preston, Hartley, Thistlewood and several others, things were livelier that Monday evening over at Hopkins Street Chapel. Wedderburn had done his bit. On 27 October, speaking after Davenport to a 'flagging' audience with, rarely, 'no speaker coming forward', he had cried 'then let us rise and destroy these tyrants who have so long opposed us – they may take my liberty from me immure me in a Dungeon (I don't expect to have it long) but while I have it I will speak'. It is possible that William Plush and Matthew Mathewson got Wedderburn's sense wrong. He might have been saying that he did not expect to be in a dungeon for very long because he expected to be freed when the people 'rise'. The proposed freeing of the two Evanses at the time of Bartholomew Fair 1817 would have been a similar priority he could have relied on. On the night of 1 November, Wedderburn gave a particularly blasphemous speech which, with others, formed the basis of his arrest in December 1819 and successful prosecution and imprisonment in May 1820.

HOPKINS STREET AND ULTRA-RADICAL CULTURE

Hopkins Street Chapel was a forum in which the discourse of the emergent could be grafted over the discourse of the dominant. Wedderburn told the Hopkins Street audience that Jesus Christ had taught men to 'call no man Master'. 'Theres a Reformer for you; theres a leveler for you; be your own Masters' Wedderburn said on 27 October. He repeated this view on 1 November when he 'again refer'd to Christ saying acknowledge no Lord acknowledge no Master acknowledge no Priest acknowledge no superior.'[52] Religion could be read as an allegory of politics. Christ's entry into Jerusalem, Wedderburn declared, was like Hunt's entry into London on 13 September 1819. Wedderburn elaborated this allegory into a condemnation of the spy system:

> he again spoke of Christ's riding to Jerusalem with a Mob after him as big as Hunts Mob crying out Huzza !!! (for Hosanna means nothing else) but the Jews where afraid of losing their places the same as our great Men an[d] had planted an old artfull Jew among them a sort of spy; who told him he might not suffer it but he thought he was all right as God told his Grandfather David, (in private for nobody heard him beside himself) that out of his loins should come all the Kings of Israel. now here you see he believed himself the son of Joseph though he had been gammoning the People that he was the Son of the Holy Ghost but the old artfull spy this Jew knew better he went and give Information [to the] Priests and Governors and they had him Apprehended; No, No, it would not do for them to wink at that for his doctrine was too much upon equality for them.[53]

As well as likening the London 'Mob' to early Christians, Wedderburn's transposition of contemporary politics to biblical Jerusalem includes the making of Judas into an exemplary spy-figure whose giving of 'Information' was comparable to the contemporary spy system. Wedderburn's rereading of the Bible was a convention of contemporary radicalism. In *Sherwin's Political Register* back in 1818, Allen Davenport had written: 'There is no book in the English language, which, if properly understood, is more diametrically opposed to the present order of things than the Bible. The Clergy must be *mad* to promote the circulation of such a book.'[54]

Wedderburn also made an analogy between Christ and the situation of colonial Ireland. Ireland was the vanguard and the blueprint for the English revolutionary faction. Wedderburn had had an analogous colonial background and he could see that Christ announcing himself king of the Jews in an occupied territory of the Roman Empire was similar to someone declaring himself king of Ireland.[55] Wedderburn tried to use this outsider's perspective in his defence at his blasphemy trial in 1820. On that occasion, Wedderburn had a learned defence (probably composed by George Cannon) read out to the court. He told them that having received no education, and 'being fascinated with the reports of Christianity, he thought, when at home [in Jamaica], that if he could once get to a Christian country, he should be happy'. On arrival in England, however, 'he found the number of sects so great, that his mind was distracted with doubts raised by the various conflicting opinions which were entertained'. In other words, having come to England as a would-be convert, he found the 'Christian country' riven with sectarian 'doubts' and 'conflicting opinions'. He 'mixed' 'first . . . with the Arminians; then with the Calvinists, and afterwards he fell in the Unitarian persuasion'. This satire was lost on the jury. He got two years despite the jury's recommendation of mercy 'in consequence of his not having the benefit of parental care': which is a politely inadequate comment on Wedderburn's slave-owning father.[56]

On at least one occasion Wedderburn brought to Hopkins Street 'two west Indian blacks' to discuss the influence of Wesleyan ministers in the 'West Indies'. The Wesleyans were imperialists, 'vipers' who 'preach the Gospel to poor [black] devils and passive obedience to the planters there marsters'. Noticeably, Wedderburn's attack is aimed at the political role for all races of Christianity. Methodism is an agent of state control for the slaves but also for 'there marsters' because 'the Missionaries . . . was sent from London by the Secretary of State for the Home Department.'[57] Wedderburn's strength as a speaker was that he was able to incorporate into his speeches a rich diversity of subjects and treatments. But however much he discussed the near and the far, the familiar and the unfamiliar, the political and the religious, his discourse was always centred around a distinct and revolutionary Spencean ideology.

Perhaps the clearest example of Wedderburn's combination of infidel and anti-colonial arguments is a speech reported by John Eshelby at the end of November 1819. Eshelby had written an outraged letter to the Home Office after he called in at Hopkins Street one November Sunday, perhaps thinking it was a proper chapel. He found 'the language and blasphemy' and Wedderburn's 'ridiculing the Scripture . . . most shocking'. The audience 'consisted of mostly young Men: who kept their Hats on and applauded any thing that he indicated in the Scriptures most violent the same as shewing their approbation at a Theatre'.[58] It is quite likely the Home Office urged him to return and write a voluntary report for their files.

Two Sundays later Eshelby found a similar picture. Once again, '200 Young Men' 'kept their hats on and applauded every thing that he said most violent'. Wedderburn, whose 'language was shameful':

> began his discourse about Blacks in Jamaica said that a black who had a chapel at Kingston who preached to the slaves that all men were Christians ought to be set free they pulled down his Chapel and put him in prison and sent to know whether he was free his master did set him free at sixteen then they said that it was not lawful to be set free

before twenty and one however he got out of prison and being determined to preach no one would allow him ground to build a Chapel upon but a Jew who did not believe in him and said that as their Government was sanctioned by the Princes and his ministers they ought to be made away with but xxxx he says I dont say who xxxx for it is said in scripture that he that stealeth a man and selleth him ought to be put to death and that the missionaries dare not preach that and another sentence in Jamaica Do not own yourselves masters and that he did not think on him so much his enemy as Government who were looking at him open mouthed ready to devour him or emprison him as they did Richard Brothers who had preached for years but when he began to launch out against the Government they had him confined as a madman.[59]

Wedderburn's story about the Jamaican chapel pulled down by the slave-masters plays upon feelings of outrage and his infidel audience's residual feelings of sacrilege. His story also shows how the Jewish outsider (who thinks 'the Princes and his ministers . . . ought to be made away with') provided the land for the black man's chapel even though he 'did not believe in him' (i.e. in Christ). But this liberalism is not all. Wedderburn also points out that the plantation owners' law was biased and retrospective in rescinding the freedom of the slave and that the planters' religion is biased in refusing to preach the apposite lesson 'Do not own yourselves masters'. Although Eshelby's report is imperfectly written, the Jewish bene-factor also seems able to quote scripture to the effect that stealing people is wrong. If these various narratives within narratives were not already clear, Wedderburn ended with an effective conclusion: religion was an arm of the State's power ('and that he did not think on him so much his enemy as Government').

Wedderburn's swingeing attack on contemporary government also runs as another thread in the speech from the opening reference to Richard Carlile's trial right through to his vivid comment at the end of the speech that government crouched 'open mouthed ready to devour him or emprison him'. He also made a particularly effective point by mixing contemporary politics with religion: 'as for Jesus being able to forgive sins it was a lie for if none but Herod could at that time forgive sins and that none but King George and the Prince regent can forgive him or if he is Drunk or sleepy as he is generally He authorizes lord Sidmouth in his stead'. Wedderburn's point here, although once again mangled by Eshelby's reportage, is extremely vivid: forgiveness is not vested in religion but in politics; and politics, figured in the 'Drunk or sleepy' Prince Regent and his lackey Sidmouth, is exercised in a condition of stupefaction. Wedderburn's speech is a highly effective compression of an easily assimilable and vigorously stated critique of politics and religion.

But Hopkins Street could do more than give revolutionary debates the charisma of self-presence, it could unfold a whole and separate cultural history.

Some of the longer speeches at Hopkins Street are full of the fraternal expression of a culture known and shared by those present. On a November night which debated the question of whether 'Religion is necessary for the preservation of Christianity and good in Society – or a crafty design of the Ministers and Priests to preach up passive obedience to the people with a view the more easy to enslave them', one unidentified speaker (but perhaps George Cannon) gave a speech whose quiet dignity and ordered harmonies have survived the spy's notes:

> there was a time when I was in Business and kept a House a parish officer called on me for what he called Church Dues; I told him I was not a Member of that Church and he answer'd I might if I chose the Church Door were open to me and consequently I must pay this tax or tythe . . . when I told him that I had to contribute to the support of another establishment (that of a catholic) he said he had nothing to do with that he must have the money, I paid him, at [the] same time telling him I considered the merry Andrew who erected his Booth at Bartholomewfair for the purpose [of] tumbling or juggling was a honest Man compared with him; he did not come and demand money of me because his Booth was in the neighbourhood of my house and tell me that his Booth was open and I might have come and see his tricks if I liked no, he only took money of those who thought proper to witness his performances and consequently was by far more honest than the man who would come and exact money from one who had never enter'd his Booth or Church nor ever wished to do so.[60]

This is a carefully structured little story: the unexpected caller, the debate, the demand, the dramatic pause to know whether the parish officer was paid, the detailed comparison with a specific 'merry Andrew' at 'Bartholomewfair' and a final ending with the striking juxtaposition equating 'Booth or Church'. The speech reveals a panoply of cultural difference. The main point is to liken the Church of England to the 'performances' of a fair-ground juggler, an optional side-show where the parish church is like 'merry Andrew's' booth. The tithe collector's call at the speaker's (public?) house gives rise to a rapid debate about the cultural and economic meaning of religious freedom. The liberalism of the Church of England extends to the assumption that all within range of its church doors must be tithepayers because all are potential church-goers. The unestablished 'catholic' church is devoid of such a status. This speaker ended by agreeing that religion was a 'crafty design' to 'preach up passive obedience': he had made his point by showing that the Church founded its economic power on the assumption of the passivity of religious belief and expression.

If this speaker could dress up political points in parables, Robert Wedderburn could follow him by compressing his speech into three main principles before launching into another story saturated with his own charisma. Wedderburn had developed a technique of slight self-deprecation before becoming the star turn he knew himself to be:

> Wedderburn followed but stating that unfortunately for him the subject had been pretty well handled before he began but he thought he could throw a *little* light on the subject if he had any sence at all for be it known to you there is no true religion in the world whatever – if you want to know what religion is I'll tell you – it is common sense – reason – and rights of Man – now I'm going to give them a blowing up altogether but not the Priests, for they have got an Act of Parliament that we must not blow them up or else *they* will be throwing me into the spiritual Court for Blasphemy (for they are a Bloody set of Villians [*sic*] for they have got sermons for every Day in the year and for every subject.[61]

Wedderburn's Enlightenment trio of 'common sense – reason – and rights of Man' is a raw ideological statement, a new version of 'what religion is', but his speech closely supports the first speaker by saying that he will not 'give them a blowing up altogether' precisely because of the protective 'Act of Parliament' which establishes the Church of England. If this 'Bloody set of Villians' had the cultural equipment to blanket the populace with a sermon 'for every Day in the year and for every subject', Wedderburn countered them with his own stories about their doings:

> the poorer part of the clergy have an envious method of endeavouring to excell each other in the hope of obtaining one of there big livings, for when I was in the House of Correction Cold Bath fields (I suppose you all know I was there) there was a chaplain wanted and there was a poor uncouth Welchman applied for it and poor fellow he labour'd and strove with all his might – but his language was not fine enough. then next Sunday there came [a] fine [?] dressed man powder'd and of polish'd language I knew he would get it because he could tell us poor devils a pack of Damn'd lies for we are not allowed to be the Judges of who should preach to us no; it must be magistrates for they sat and heard it all and [it] was a doctrine suited to their purpose, he told us

what a blessing it was that we were confined in that place with nothing but Bread & Water to live on and have the benefit of hearing the gospel preached to us as he called it, but even tho some of them had [been] robbing all over the country what mercy it was that we were there, for those whom God loveth he Chasteneth then he [?] melted it down again !! then he made the Magistrates smile consequently he got the place and we were obliged to sit and hear all this, and he was compell'd to get done before 11. OClock that he might go and hold forth somewhere else for they will grasp at as many places as they can get at.[62]

This tale of Wedderburn's plays upon his own reputation for committed notoriety: it is not known when or why he was in Cold Bath Fields prison but it was a splendid radical credential, having been the particularly harsh prison used to incarcerate Colonel Despard under the Suspension of Habeas Corpus back in 1798 and subsequently the subject of a Government inquiry. Wedderburn follows the thread of the previous speaker in paralleling a personal anecdote but, in a broader sense, he is significantly continuing the theme of using his prisoner's tale to examine the passive obedience exacted by the Church on a captive but would-be restless congregation.

The November debates at Wedderburn's Hopkins Street Chapel seem to have kept the conspirators engaged in their own radical culture and politics even as hopes for a rising dwindled. Wedderburn's chapel spawned imitators: an informant wrote from Lambeth that a room had been taken for 'Mock Worship' in Pratt Street and he feared that passer-by Sunday school children would read the handbills posted outside.[63] The indefatigable Samuel Waddington must also have cheered flagging spirits with his contributions. Waddington sometimes played two-handed with Wedderburn at Hopkins Street Chapel. He could be serious, as when he told the Hopkins Street audience in early November that 'the Bloody Revolution must come and was not far distant; their was a great similitude between the present times, and those that brought about the Revolution of France' and that 'Lord Castlereagh would not rest until the Radicals had brought his head to the Block'.[64] But he could also be outrageous: as when he announced that Balaam's spiritual voices were 'some artful Ventriloquist most likely Balaam himself for he was a conjurer' and that the Witch of Endor sent Saul a 'parcel of smoke' or some 'sort of trick'. On that night Allen Davenport rose to say that 'the Scriptures had been well handled'.[65]

Waddington was an inveterate intervener who ran a serious risk of prosecution. At the Smithfield meeting of 25 August Waddington,

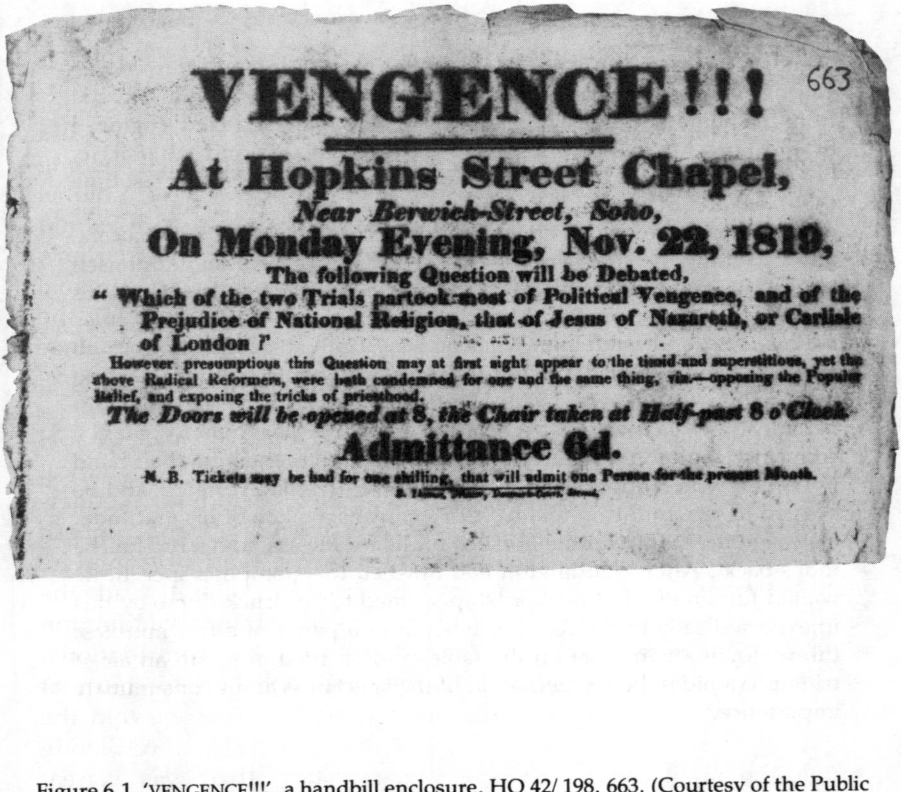

VENGENCE!!! 663

At Hopkins Street Chapel,
Near Berwick-Street, Soho,
On Monday Evening, Nov. 22, 1819,
The following Question will be Debated,
" Which of the two Trials partook most of Political Vengence, and of the
Prejudice of National Religion, that of Jesus of Nazareth, or Carlisle
of London ?'
However, presumptious this Question may at first sight appear to the timid and superstitious, yet the
above Radical Reformers, were both condemned for one and the same thing, viz—opposing the Popular
Belief, and exposing the tricks of priesthood.
The Doors will be opened at 8, the Chair taken at Half-past 8 o'Clock.
Admittance 6d.
N. B. Tickets may be had for one shilling, that will admit one Person for the present Month.

Figure 6.1 'VENGENCE!!!', a handbill enclosure, HO 42/ 198. 663. (Courtesy of the Public Record Office)

who gave his profession as printer and shoemaker 'in a one pair of stairs back room' in Long acre, had been arrested for 'unlawfully publishing a certain seditious handbill' tacked to the top of a pole which he was marching around Kennington Common. The authorities deemed that this was intended to 'excite, stir up, and provoke tumult, riot, sedition and disaffection'.[66] In the autumn he seems to have been acquitted of this charge but the 'little diminutive fellow' turned up at the Mansion House to comically hijack the legal proceedings and bait the Lord Mayor. On being 'spoken to rather sharply' by a marshal, Waddington 'stuck his hands in his side, and cocking his white hat with a menacing air, asked him, "If he knew who he was talking to?"' Waddington's white hat was his badge of radicalism and he was not to be so easily dismissed. At the end of that day's business he returned:

> Waddington, who is about 4 feet 2 inches high, . . . [and] dressed in a suit of black, got upon the railings of the bar to elevate himself, but from the alteration in his appearance, was not immediately recognized by the Lord Mayor, who had first seen him in rags and tatters. He, however, addressed his Lordship; and said, that since he had last time the pleasure of seeing him, he had been tried by a Jury of his countrymen, who had given the lie to the calumnies of his prosecutors, and had flung the charge in their teeth. He, however, thought himself bound in gratitude to come and personally return thanks to his Lordship for having raised him by a prosecution to his present *proud pre-eminence*, and made him what he was. He had published his trial, and dedicated it to his Lordship, as a specimen of his abilities and good conduct as a Magistrate; to Mr. Trotter, the Chairman of the Quarter Sessions, as a mark of respect for his zealous endeavours to obtain a conviction; and to the Court lawyers, as a lesson to them on their blind imbecility, when opposed to common sense, in whatever garb; and he begged to present his Lordship with a copy as a token of his gratitude. He called it, 'a whip for the horse, a bridle for the ass, and a rod for the fool's back'. After Waddington had finished this pompous speech, he waited for a reply; but his Lordship seemed to be struck dumb by this unexpected sally of the Radical, who, after a pause of a few minutes, threw down a pamphlet on the table, and strutted out with an air of triumph, amidst the consternation of the spectators at his consummate impudence.[67]

While there is no mistaking the presence of a studiously literary *Times* copy-writer (who finished his piece with the Lord Mayor pictured feebly castigating the court officers for their inefficiency), the event must have taken some degree of nerve on Waddington's part. Ten days later Waddington rented a shop in Holborn opposite Gray's Inn Lane 'for the sale of Pamphlets & Pike heads'. A spy reported that 'he intends to attract notice by having up in his Shop – 3 Halters suspended with the Labels for LS[idmouth] LC[astlereagh] & LL[iverpool]'.[68] Waddington's satirical turns were always edged with the serious stuff of 'Pamphlets & Pike heads'.

THE CATO STREET CONSPIRACY AS ULTRA-RADICAL
CULTURE

In the revolutionary party, after the embarrassing stand-down of 1 November, there was a gloom in the White Lion which only the ardent Thistlewood attempted to dispel: 'the D^r [Watson] dispaired of being able to do any thing – thistlewood – don't despair, we are sure of gaining our point or dying in the cause –'.[69] On 5 November, Watson warned that the newspapers had reported 'more drilling at Wedderburns Chapel' but they had now 'moved their quarters' to avoid surveillance. Four days later the mass meeting projected for 15 November was put back to the 24th and their attempts to assess their strength with an early Sunday morning arms drill on Primrose Hill drew a dismal response. By 19 November, Watson Snr was advising 'no Resistance to the civil power' at the Smithfield meeting on the 24th 'But Thislewood Hartley Harland and others swore they would go armed & fight'. After the meeting there was a disaster: Watson Snr was arrested for debts incurred at the last Smithfield meeting and he was carted off to prison.[70]

The political consequences of Watson Snr's arrest and that of Robert Wedderburn a week or so later cannot be overestimated. What went out of circulation with them was the ideological framework of Spenceanism. What was left was a revolutionary group of conspirators headed by Thistlewood aided by Preston. Except at Hopkins Street, the Spencean national incorporation of land had been seldom discussed but, reportedly, it may have continued to figure in planning. On 11 November, the Revd Chetwode Eustace had written to tell the authorities 'I have been assured of the existence of a Committee in London, the Members of which are now (& have been for some weeks past) busily engaged in ascertaining the extent of the different Estates in every party of the united Kingdom'.[71] On 30 November several of them met at Preston's lodgings and 'resolved to put themselves under the Banner of Preston' who was a Spencean of long standing.[72] Communication was maintained while Watson Snr was in prison; a spy went to see him in gaol on the 28th, while on 5 December Thistlewood read a letter from him to fifty men assembled at the White Lion. Watson Snr's letter recommended 'Union as the time was come when a blow must be struck'. At its close Preston gave 'a long speach to the same effect' before leaving to further the cause at an unknown ultra-radical appointment over in the Borough.[73]

Even without the veteran politicking of Wedderburn and Watson Snr, the radical culture was strong enough to maintain its stability. Metropolitan ultra-radicalism was deeply rooted and not dependent on individuals. One informer reported going into an unidentified tavern 'parlour about 7 in the Evening but there was nobody there, but the Landlady and a Friend, I was Ask'd to take a seat by the fire, I call'd for a glass of Radical and entered into Conversation with the Landlady's Friend'. 'Radical' was a beverage drunk as an alternative to heavily taxed tea, coffee and alcohol: to order and drink a 'glass of Radical' was to take part in an economic boycott. Like a white hat, it was a badge recognized by others: the spy in the pub struck up a conversation with a 'Journeyman Mechanic' who 'Came in a[nd]' also 'call'd for a glass of Radical'. 'This is the way to serve them,' said the mechanical:

> The conversation turning upon the Prince [Regent] going to the House, the landladys friend said I dare say he will be hissed as he was last time I hear they have Order'd all the Stones & Rubbish in the [road] to be cleared Away, Ah says, the Other its no matter if they had broke his Neck.[74]

Elsewhere, the occasional surfacing of fugitive literature reveals the depth of ideological commitment to the philosophy that the labouring poor had been disinherited from the plenty of the land. Thomas Hazard, a crippled man who 'kept a day school for Boys 33 years', was thought to have given 'lessons in Politics' for the ultra-radical Marylebone Union Society. Hazard's occupation and radical politics might suggest that he had Irish roots and came from the tradition of teacher-activists in that country with a strongly agrarianist stance. He was eventually arrested for allowing his house off the Edgware Road to be used as one of the assembly points for the Cato Street conspirators.[75] Hazard had written and printed a poem of Spencean sympathies which has survived because a copy of it was packed off to the Home Office in the course of the assembling of information about the conspiracy. Hazard's *A True Picture of Society, As Displayed By Certain Rich Characters Towards Their Poor Neighbours, A Poem* quoted as its epigraph a pithy verse from Isaiah: 'Ye have eaten up the vineyard; the spoil of the poor is in your houses'. Hazard's poem does not, in fact, specify any particular 'Rich Characters' but his Spencean outlook is clear ('You say the land is all your own, / And that a vulgar crew / Was only made to work and groan, / And passive be to you') and expressed in the language of class difference. The rich are a 'pamper'd host' of 'Tyrants' who 'do not work at all, / But live in sinful pride'. Hazard's poem is empowered by the new noun phrases of the idle and the laborious classes: 'You never labour, never toil, / But you can eat and drink'. In the Spencean politics of *A True Picture*, the rich 'never cultivate the soil' to increase the earth's plenty, the 'blessings God bestows / So bountiful for all'. Natural abundance usurped by the conquest of a few comprises the poem's central economic and political ideas: 'God opens wide his liberal hand, / His creatures to supply, / But, O! it is a cruel band, / His bounty doth deny'.[76] Hazard's poem was an important means of self-expression even though it must have circulated in extremely marginal circumstances. When he was arrested and put in Tothill Fields prison in March 1820, Hazard wrote a bitter letter: 'I petitioned L. Sidmouth for the free use of pen ink & paper. I have obtained what he calls the free use [in] that what I write is looked at before it is sent to you'. Hazard's letter was impounded and never reached its destination. The Government's surveillance and suppression of Hazard's discourse makes his hackeneyed poem important to us and to him. In prison, Hazard all but identified himself as a political prisoner by comparing his lot with the 'Common depradators [sic]': 'what liberty they have in being Jovial with each other and I not permited to speak to any'.[77]

By the beginning of December 1819, Wedderburn and Watson Snr's absences were resuplied by the enthusiasms of the black man William Davidson. Davidson's rise to prominence in the conspiratorial group led by Thistlewood can be quite fully charted in the winter of 1819–20. His secretaryship of the New Union of Shoemakers, reported on 14 November, was only one aspect of his activities as he became increasingly more violent and organized. Four days later Davidson came across one of the (incognito) Government spies in Castle Street and related that he had '450 stand of Arms & about 2700 Rounds of Ball Cartridges', that he was now 'buying more Powder to make Cartridges' and that 'all the Gunsmiths shops were marked for the day of the meeting' at Smithfield.[78] The meeting was inconclusive at best. On 30 November 'Black Davison' began to emerge as a speaker whose views, judging by the hasty notes of the spy, increasingly express the exasperation of the group. No doubt using experience gained at Hopkins Street, Davidson said 'That something Must be Done immediately he said that he was come to hear What was Ment to be Don'. Davidson wanted a London rising, one to set an example for the rest of the country:

the Bl^k said would it not be a Great Slur on the Londoners if they let the Country begin by themselves Thi^w said so it must be the Blk said Much about army ammunition Ball cartridge Grenades Drilling on primrose hill &c he said that Night would be the best time.[79]

Davidson became more vociferous. On 3 December he declared 'something must be done or why go to such expence' in the gaining of arms and ammunition.[80] But Davidson also gained the respect and

THE COMBINATION

Figure 6.2 From *The Queen in the Moon*, G. Cruikshank [Mar.] 1820, woodcut. (Courtesy of the British Museum: Department of Prints and Drawings)

recognition of his peers and, on 7 December, the spy reported 'Black Davison in the Chair'.[81] This was the day after he had sworn that 'if no one else he would go by himself' when Thistlewood 'proposed they should all go in a body to the P.R.'. Only twelve had volunteered at a show of hands whereupon 'Preston said he was for swearing on the T[a]ble for all to quit their home & conquer or die & that all who swore & did not attend – he would take away their lives'.[82] Davidson, in contrast to Preston, combined equal degrees of rhetoric and violence.

When Davidson acted as Chairman, the meeting revolved around him. The spy's report captures the mood of the moment:

> Black Davison spoke at a Great Length urging them to fight & expressing a fear that Many of them would Rather Joke & Laugh than fight (cries of no we will fight) for My part said he I may not live till to Morrow night it is therefore proper to be serious When a Man is so near his last as this for I mean to fight to Morrow and I wish to know if I am to Die alone for fight I will and if I am to be opposed to a Life Guard Man by Myself so it shall be (Cries of no Davison you shant be alone While I am living Resounded from several Persons) I have not had the honour to wear the Red jacket But have fought in a Blue One it would be Gratifying to Me in My Last Moments to see My fellow creatures fighting in the same cause for which I am Bleeding but should I in my Last moments When My Eyes are closing behold my self forsaken & the cause abandoned this Would Give Me More pain than My Enemies could inflict.[83]

Davidson was shrewd too. A week later, at a midday meeting at Preston's house, he went spy hunting when 'Davidson asked B. what they should do if they caught a Spy amongst them – [B.] replyd why hang him – suspects they meant him'. Davidson had dogged his man: the day before he had personally escorted Williamson to a meeting at the Rose in Wild Street, Drury Lane as a part of an elaborate plot to secure secrecy.[84] Tempers were getting frayed at the frustration caused by the clear lack of popular support.

Five days before Christmas at the White Lion 'B', Williamson, took Banks, the writer of the précis, aside and 'said he would speak to me he said I must take care of myself as they intended doing me a mischief'. Williamson took his own advice and boarded for the Cape, he had seen too much danger:

> did you observe hartley tap me on the head & ask if I was coming, they took me into a house in a Court in the Strand there were about 30 all armed – they chose 5 on a Committee of Secrecy – he believes Chambers, Sykes Edwards & 2 others.

This was highly dangerous espionage work because Banks was already being omitted from some meetings because he was suspected. Banks was doubly in the dark since neither he nor Williamson appears to have known that 'Edwards' was the Government's 'W——r——'. 'Keep away from them – Thislewood is at the head of it', Williamson warned.[85] The plan was to 'Rush into the houses of

Parliament & take the lives of those they have marked' and Banks met a journeyman baker on 26 December who told him he 'has had no Rest all night . . . expects every horn he hears to be the signal for the General rise'.[86] Hartley was attending the meetings armed with 'a Pistol' while London Irish leader Dennis Shaw was avidly collecting 'from the Irish in Surry'. On 29 December there was a dramatic event. Banks went 'to Davidsons house by his desire' and there Robert George 'fired a piece off almost to Banks head – loaded with ball supposed intended for him'. Banks's nerve must have held and proved his mettle: 'Thislewood said B[anks] you had a narrow escape but passed it off in a joke' and Banks's cover must have seemed cast-iron when 'Preston told Informant he was sure if he was wanted he would be at his post' and, for good measure, 'asked me if I knew where the Cabinet Dinners were to be'.[87]

The possibility of ambushing and murdering the entire Cabinet while they were at dinner was the plan which the Government eventually hoaxed back at the conspirators by inserting an advertisement in the *New Times* giving details of a Cabinet dinner to be held at Lord Harrowby's house on 22 February 1820. The details of the Government counter-ambush and the swift arrests do not need to be retold.[88] For the revolutionists' part, the Cabinet assassination plan was merely an extension of a scheme to commit political murder which had been floated as long ago as June 1817 but its planning may have had some impetus from William Davidson. At his trial, Davidson claimed that 'he had nothing to do with the plot of assassination' but he also told the court and its 'nearly empty' galleries that 'he knew Lord Harrowby for years' because he had 'worked at his house in Staffordshire'.[89] It may be that Davidson knew the layout of Harrowby's London home and that this accelerated the Cato Street plot. From the point of view of assessing Cato Street as a rational event, there were also other forces operative: a suspicion of infiltration but also the fraternal reassurance of an active culture.

On 21 January 1820 Banks went to Preston's house and underwent an experience which was to show that he was still treated with enormous suspicion. There were several conspirators at Preston's, all heavily armed: Davidson had a 'Bayonet Pistol & firelock', Robert George a 'firelock Pistol & Dirk', a man called Wilson carried a 'Carbine and Pistol' while another man, Sykes, was armed with a 'stick Broad Sword & Pistol'. Suddenly, Banks wrote, 'Davidson clapped a Pistol to my head'. Banks 'struck it away & presented a loaded Pistol at his head saying no tricks'. This was a moment of high drama and then climbdown when the company 'passed it off as a joke to try my spirits'. Banks must have been severely shaken at this second violent test of his sincerity in three weeks but it proved a watershed in testing Banks's nerve and all was friendly camaraderie. Robert 'George then said why you were denounced as a Spy – but now we dont believe [it]' and the linchpin Preston told Banks 'I only wish I had a hundred like B[anks]'.[90] In the absence of Watson Snr and Wedderburn, Preston must have been their ideological leader at this time. Six days later they met again at his house, which had become the main venue for their meetings. This time, with Davidson 'in high spirits' because he had just been 'relieved by the Parish', 'all declared themselves ready to act with Preston' who 'said he would die in the attempt'. 'Butcher' Ings, voicing the group's infidelity, 'said he would have nothing to do with any Man who feared God or the Devil'.[91] It is possible that at this point, with people like Davidson and Ings coming forward, the more thoughtful leaders decided to go onto back-burner: on 29 January Banks went to see Watson Snr in prison and heard him express the sentiment that he was 'very sorry Thislewood keeps such Company'. Two days later, again at Preston's house, ex-soldier Harrison 'said he would sink his life to Crown the P.R. with an Axe'.[92]

On 13 February, hardly more than a week before the attempt, a dinner was held at Davidson's house. Considering the poverty of their situation and Davidson's being on the parish, the most remarkable thing about this last supper was that it showed how their ultra-radical culture, now specifically dedicated to the impending use of physical force, included the domestic sphere of the family: Davidson's wife, Sarah, and their two children were present, Preston brought his three daughters, Robert George his two-year-old, and they 'all dined together'. During the dinner Wilson 'was in & out' while Manchester delegate Walker 'came & drank a draft of porter & read out' aloud to them.[93] On 22 February, when they were to have all assembled at Cato Street, Preston turned up late and missed the police swoop. This is why he could not be convincingly indicted on the charge of high treason on which he was arrested.

The conspirators were kept under rigorous conditions. School-master Thomas Hazard in Tothill Fields prison 'slept for 4 nights locked up in a Cell & the hoar frost beating in on me that I was in a Constant shiver'. He wrote that he felt like 'a harmless hare among a pack of –' when interrogated before the Privy Council, '3 or 4 speaking to me, asking me questions, & 5 or 6 writing what I said'. His impounded letter proclaimed it a 'Grand falsehood' that he 'let out my school to traitors conspirator': 'it is as likely for a pipe of Tobacco to set fire to the dome of St Pauls, or a husk of Chaff to

Contend with a Whirlwind'.[94] Enigmatically, Hazard's reference to 'Chaff' captures the name of someone who informed on Davidson, while setting fire to the dome of St Paul's might encrypt a message to rise.[95]

Thomas Preston, under charge of high treason, took the opportunity of writing an elaborate and pugnacious riposte to Lord Sidmouth, perhaps with an eye to publication. Twisting from image to image, Preston thanked Sidmouth for allowing him 'to perform so great a part on the Horizon of Political Life' by being:

> the traveller that having found in the interior of a wood the flower that would have bloomed, blossomed and decayed had it not have been brought forth and given to the florist whose skilful judgments have preserved the seed and rendered it delightfull and charming with a fragrance enchanting to mankind . . .

Preston, in his half-hearted persona of a flower, charged Sidmouth with being either misled or in the power of 'blood money men'. Preston's cheeky nerve was founded on the Government's frustration at not having found him *in flagrante* at Cato Street on 22 February. He claimed he had had 'the good fortune to read most of the Lawyers of antiquity and as well the most eminent lawyers of my Country' including Lord Blackstone, Justice Foster and Lord Hale. The 'inimitable constitution' had been his 'darling Cleopatra' and his 'Polar Star'. He was bent on 'restoring to its Primitive State that beautiful Edifice as pure as our Anglo Saxon fore fathers intended Britons should enjoy it' and he pledged his 'aid towards transmitting to the rising generation this most sacred deposit of our great Alfred'. If Anglo-Saxon constitutionalism was Preston's touchstone ('that Illustrious Alfred the great that intended the british subject should be as free as his own thoughts'), he also paraphrased Blackstone to the effect that 'resistance to oppression is obedience to our god'. Preston finished his letter, however, on a Spencean note: 'the people are starving for want in all parts of the country . . . as though providence had . . . afflicted the nation with famine whilst the lazy borough mongers is rioting and feasting on the plunder of the people.' Preston's letter is a fascinating document for its daring tone and its ideological consistency even if he did manage to get his meaning the wrong way round in declaring 'therefore my Lord I think you have mistaken treason for patriotism'.[96]

Ideological commitment was also manifested while the Cato Street defendants were confined in the Tower. John Brunt wrote two poems on 'the Walls in the Room' in which he and Ings were confined 'before they were tried'. The Home Office methodically 'Copied' them down in their attempts to gain some understanding of these men:

> Written And Composed by J T Brunt
>
> Tho in A Cell im Close Confind
> No fears Alarm the Noble mind
> Tho Death itself Appears in View
> Daunts not the Soul Sincerely true
>
> Let Sidmouth And his base Colleagues
> Cajole And Plot their Dark intrigues
> Still each Brittons Last Words Shall be
> Oh Give me Death or Liberty[97]

This poem reveals that although they felt themselves to be victims of a 'Plot', a piece of theatrical politics, they also had a counter-rhetoric of 'Death or Liberty' and a Romantic belief in a 'Noble mind' 'Sincerely true' to their ideological cause.

Brunt's declaration of authorship is interesting and probably an attempt to circulate his thoughts to a wider audience after his execution and subsequent to some Home Office leakage.[98] His other prison poem is a bitter combination of irony and ideological declaration:

> Written in the tower by J T Brunt
>
> The home Departments Secretaire
> His Orders they would make you Stare
> An hour A Day Consigned to Walk
> But mind they Neither Wink nor talk
>
> For these Are Gifts of human reason
> And they Are Adepts At high Treason
> No biger rogues on earth they be on
> For so Saith edwards the espion
>
> You may Let them eat drink And sleep
> But Knives And forks must from them keep
> or theyll Comit Assasination
> The rogues would Overturn the nation
>
> for Modes of faith Let Graceless zealots fight
> his cant be wrong whose Life is in the right
> Lifes But A jest And All they shew it
> i thought so once But now I know it[99]

Brunt's infidelity is clear in this poem but his 'Life in the right' is as much a commitment to an ideological as to a moral cause. Brunt's poem also highlights the role of 'edwards the espion'.

Just as Colonel Despard had been circumspectly interrogated by the prison chaplain, Arthur Thistlewood and the rest of the Cato Street conspirators were interviewed by chaplain the Revd Ruell. Thistlewood was more than a match for him. Attempting ingratiation, Ruell tried to impress Thistlewood by telling him that he had bought a copy of Paine's *Age of Reason* before one of Carlile's trials 'with a view to ascertain what could be advocated against Xtianity'. Thistlewood's reply was quick: 'I wonder you were not convinced!'[100] Ruell's polite interrogations reveal a very different sort of conspirator from those represented in the popular press.

Ruell described 'Butcher' Ings (executed) as 'a most desperate & turbulent character & a political enthusiast of the first order'. Nearly all of them had read the Enlightenment infidel authors. Brunt (executed) told Ruell that 'he had read much, especially the books of Voltaire, Paine, Volney &c.' Wilson (transported) 'Had been led to embrace infidelity by reading Paine, Voltaire, Volney & similar writers'. Like Spence's tutelage under his father and Allen Davenport's discussions with his shoemaker colleagues, radical discussion for the Cato Street conspirators had centred on the workplace. The tailor Wilson told Ruell that 'himself & others of the same trade had been in the habit of reading such books at their leisure time & afterwards discussing their principles & merits during their working hours'. William 'Black' Davidson (executed) had also 'been in the habit of reading Paine & other infidel publications', Monument (transported) though 'not . . . so hardened in infidelity' 'confirms that he had read Paine & Voltaire'. Strange (transported) was also 'a disciple of the same writers' and told Ruell that 'Voltaire had given him much clearer views of the Deity & religion than the Bible!' Ruell concluded his report on 'these deluded men' by noting that 'it appears quite clear that by reading infidel writings they were induced to cast off the fear of God & were thus fully prepared for the commission of any crime.'[101] The State's surveillance was subverted by writing, talking and the circulation of radical texts.

The *Black Dwarf* proved a solid friend in recording the horror of their executions but it also did much to diminish the significance of the radical political culture of the conspirators. In particular, less than a week after the arrests the *Black Dwarf* initiated what was to become a powerfully influential theatrical tropology to explain Cato Street. There were two plots and two sets of plotters: the Thistlewood Theatre Company and the Sidmouth Theatre Company with George Edwards understudying for both.

If it had not been for the bloodshed of the arrest (when Thistlewood ran a runner through with his sword), the *Black Dwarf* argued that 'it would have proved as burlesque a conspiracy as the attempt to take London, with a military chest of 27s. and a half pound of powder, tied carefully up in the foot of an old stocking.' The pantomime ineptitude of the conspirators and the Government's evil designing were heavily emphasized by the *Black Dwarf*. The *Black Dwarf* knew enough about the history of Thistlewood's group to link them with the richly opportune comedy of the 'Bartholomew Fair intended insurrection, when all the ginger-bread soldiers were expected to march to the attack of the bank, the tower, and the head quarters of the Commander in Chief' but this farce, it said, was now paralleled by a Government which realizes that 'it may suit them to affect a terror, which they do not feel.' Warming to the theme, the *Black Dwarf* wrote:

> The ministers of this country seem to copy the practice of a tragedian here. His name is John Kemble; and he was so studious of giving proper effect to his appearance, that he rarely entered upon the stage, without a flourish of trumpet, to announce something great was forthcoming . . .[102]

The *Black Dwarf*'s line was that the Government had been scare-mongering on the 'eve of an election', unable to resist the 'theatrical effect of seizing upon [the conspirators] in consultation, with the machinery of the performance about them.'[103]

When it came to the trial at the end of April and the swiftly executed executions, the *Black Dwarf* was more prepared to allow the conspirators the dignity of their own intelligence. Brunt's prison poem with its reference to petty rules and the denial of their 'Gifts of human reason' suggests that this favour was long overdue. Of the speeches from the dock, Brunt's was probably the most effective. Thistlewood declared that 'Brutus and Cassius were extolled to the skies for the murder of one tyrant' but he was interrupted by Lord Chief Justice Abbott who said 'we cannot allow a person even in your situation to attempt to justify assassination'.[104] This was typical of the to-and-fro of English justice and ultra-radicals:

> Thistlewood resumed . . . his remarks on his majesty's ministers and mentioned that, when men set themselves above the laws, insurrection was a duty. (He was again interrupted by the Court) . . . His object was to free his country, which, he regretted, was still in the hands of despots . . . he declared his mangled body would, he knew, soon be consigned to its native soil; but he was sorry it should be a soil for slaves, cowards and despots.[105]

Thistlewood had nothing to lose because sentence had already been passed, but the court was only too ready to interfere and regulate the discourse of the condemned prisoner. James Ings spoke in much the same vein and concluded his short speech with a paraphrase of one of their own flags: 'He would rather die like a man than live like a slave. He would say no more.'[106]

Cell wall poet John Brunt had more to say. 'He had intended to have written the observations which he should make, but he had not had the benefit of ink and paper':

> He cared not for his life . . . when in liberty's cause . . . he was no traitor to his country . . . he was no traitor to his King . . . but he was an enemy to the borough mongering faction, which equally enslaved both the King and the people. When he could earn 3l. or 4l. per week, he never meddled with politics, but when those earnings were reduced to 10s. he began to inquire the cause. He thought nothing too bad for men who had caused the dreadful outrage at Manchester. He would die a martyr in liberty's cause, for the good of his country . . . If it had fallen to his lot to kill Lord Castlereagh or Lord Sidmouth, he would have done it, and would have resisted the police officers to the utmost of his power: but he would not have resisted the soldiers because they had sworn allegiance to their Sovereign; but, for the others, he would have opposed them whilst his arm had nerve.[107]

Economic determinants and 'liberty's cause' sustained Brunt through the execution and there was little sign that the conspirators were filled with regret for what they had attempted.

The execution proved to be a bloody and extraordinary affair. The 'ordinary' scaffold had to be enlarged 'to such a size as would admit the performance of the most awful part of the ceremony, that of decapitating the criminals', the 'loud strikes of the carpenters'' hammers attracted the attention of passers-by near Newgate prison. On the morning of the execution 'four boards to elevate placards on were brought within the rail which enclosed the gallows. Large bills were nailed to them containing the following words: – "The riot act has been read, disperse immediately" '. Foot guards were posted opposite Newgate with a further detachment towards the City while, according to the *Black Dwarf*, 'helmets, bayonets, and falchions, gleamed on every side'. 'Divisions of military, horse, foot, and cannon' were in position and the crowd was 'repeatedly driven from their stations' and vantage points. When James Brunt came out of the prison, he 'was so struck with this military parade, that he exclaimed – "What! soldiers! What do they here? I see nothing but a military government will do for this country, unless there are a good many such as we here!" '[108]

As Thistlewood 'advanced to the block to have the shackles which bound his legs struck off', something extraordinary happened. A borough Alderman called Wood stopped the execution from proceeding by demanding of Thistlewood ' "when he first became acquainted with Edwards?" ' The trial had generated enormous disquiet at the role of George Edwards and the local authorities were hastily making their own attempt at getting to the bottom of the situation. There was consternation from the officials on the scaffold:

> Mr. Sheriff Rothwell, in a mild and complacent tone, expressed his surprise that a man like the worthy Alderman should thus interrupt the awful proceedings that were going on. Mr. Alderman Wood still persisted in his endeavour to interrogate Thistlewood, and produced a written paper, on which, he said, were three questions which he wished to put to him.

Rothwell protested that 'the unhappy man' (Thistlewood) 'was in fact dead in law, and this attempt to extract from him any particular declarations, was highly improper'. Wood persisted and Thistlewood told him that he first met Edwards in June 1819. Wood then moved to his second question, asking where they had first met. This led to an amazing piece of non-communication:

> Thistlewood replied in an indistinct tone, and in rather an agitated manner, 'At Preston's.' He was at first understood to mean the town of Preston, in Lancashire, but, on being asked to explain, he said 'No, not Preston in Lancashire: Preston's the shoemaker.'[109]

Wood's third question was about whether Edwards had supplied him with money but Sheriff Rothwell insisted there be no further questioning. Like a ghostly rerun of Despard's execution in 1803, the state's insistence on its powers of interruption and interrogation continued unabated: the condemned man was first and last a subject.

'Prepare thyself for a deed of blood', wrote the *Black Dwarf*. 'Exactly half an hour after they had been turned off, the order was given to cut the bodies down'. Thistlewood's coat and waistcoat were forced down over his shoulders and 'a person wearing a black mask, which extended to his mouth, over which a coloured handkerchief was tied, and his head was slouched down so as to conceal part of the mask' came to the scaffold with 'a large knife' similar to those used 'by surgeons in amputation': 'when the crowd perceived the knife applied to the throat of Thistlewood, they raised a shout, in which exclamations of horror and reproach were mingled'. This 'tumult seemed to disconcert' the executioner but he handed Thistlewood's head to the assistant executioner who 'immediately exhibited the head from the side of the scaffold nearest Newgate-street'. Prompted by a man named Shark who dictated the words, the assistant executioner went through the prescribed ritual declamation: 'This is the head of Arthur Thistlewood – a traitor!'. 'A thrilling sensation was produced on the spectators, by the display of this ghastly object, and hisses and hootings of a part of the mob were vehemently renewed.'[110]

When Richard Tidd was decapitated, there were 'cries of "Shoot that murderer" – "Bring out Edward[s]" '. Davidson's head, the *Black Dwarf* put it, 'remained in death, exactly what it had been while he lived'. Blood fell from it 'profusely' and the 'hisses and groans of the crowd were repeated'. With some sense of radical history, the *Black Dwarf* claimed that 'the person who wore the mask, and who performed the decollation, is the same person who beheaded Despard and his associates'.[111]

The executions all but choked the physical force movement but the radical culture continued. In early June an alleged gang of eighty sent a letter to the Government threatening that:

> Thomas Keneadey and Compy Declare that they will take the first opperturnety to Put an End to Lord sidmouth Lord Castlerea and the King as they are a Damnable set of Raskels Thomas Keneadey and Co Declare that they can prove that Lord Sidmouth and Lord Castlerea Gave Edwards there Damnable Spy Twenty pounds a peice for the Life of thislewood and wee have about Eighty of us in the gang we are well Loaded of Pistols Powder and shot and we Declare that the first opperunity that there is we will do the Job as we dont mind dying as wee can die but once
> So Beware of your Gard as we are in strict watch For you all
> Thom Andrue Boyc Sect[112]

Decapitating 'conspirators' was one thing, dismantling a whole culture was something else.

Conclusion

On 13 September 1819, the bailed reformist leader Henry 'Orator' Hunt triumphantly entered London en route to face trial for high treason for his part in the public meeting at St Peter's Fields, Manchester, which resulted in the Peterloo massacre. Hunt's procession was a set piece of radical culture with bands of music, flags, horses and people marching on foot. Somewhere amongst the tens of thousands of people lining the route was the poet John Keats. 'It would take me a whole day and a quire of paper to give you any thing like detail . . . The whole distance from the Angel Islington to the Crown and anchor [Strand] was lined with Multitudes', John Keats wrote five days later.[1] If he was standing on the streets witnessing the procession, as his letter implies, John Keats would have seen James Watson Snr, Arthur Thistlewood and Thomas Preston.

In a post-Peterloo attempt to unify the capital's radical leadership, the Spenceans had joined forces with the more moderate reformers (although they quarrelled irrevocably that night). Hunt's place was in the eighth row of the procession preceded by a pro-Irish green silk flag bearing the inscription 'Universal Civil and Religious Liberty' 'Borne and supported by Six Irishmen' as well as a flag modestly inscribed 'Hunt the Honest Champion of Liberty'. In the fifteenth row, behind Hunt but in front of 'persons connected with the public Press Wooler, Carlile, Sherwin &C.' came a 'Chariot' containing the three Spenceans. By this date, two out of the three had already been charged with high treason while the third, Thistlewood, would be convicted and hanged for the same crime six months later. In a letter written to his friend Charles Dilke in March 1820, Keats doodled and joked back about Dilke's handwritten formation of 'Thistlewood'.

Thistlewood, evidently in Keats's thoughts at that time, was then in prison awaiting trial.[2]

Six days after witnessing Hunt's procession, Keats took a Sunday walk in Winchester on a day of 'temperate sharpness' beneath 'Dian skies'. That autumn's harvest, whose successful abundance depleted stirrings for a national rising, had just been taken in. 'I never lik'd stubble fields so much as now – Aye better than the chilly green of the spring. Somehow a stubble plain looks warm', Keats wrote to John Hamilton Reynolds. 'I composed upon it', Keats confided.[3]

Keats's 'To Autumn' is an apotheosis of contemporary Spencean articles of faith about English natural abundance and fertility, ideas circulated in post-war 'free and easies' and in the 1819 poems of E.J. Blandford and Thomas Hazard. It is an ode ripped from the natural assembly of *Endymion* where, in 'garments white', and 'Leading the way, young damsels danced along' in an orderly version of a Spencean iconography of Spa Fields or Bartholomew Fair. *Endymion*'s 'Hymn to Pan' Wordsworth called 'a Very pretty piece of Paganism', an infidelity in vogue in ultra-radical circles as much as with Keats's acquaintances. The dangerous depths of the 'Cockney Poets' were peopled by East London literary aspirants like Allen Davenport while Keats shared a dubious professional vocation with the 'apothecary' 'Dr.' James Watson Snr.

'To Autumn' is saturated with the common ideology of its contemporary ultra-radical culture:

> Season of mists and mellow fruitfulness!
> Close bosom-friend of the maturing sun;
> Conspiring with him how to load and bless
> With fruit the vines that round the thatch-eaves run;
> To bend with apples the moss'd cottage-trees,
> And fill all fruit with ripeness to the core;
> To swell the gourd, and plump the hazel shells
> With a sweet kernel; to set budding more,
> And still more, later flowers for the bees,
> Until they think warm days will never cease,
> For Summer has o'er-brimm'd their clammy cells.

Nowhere was a poem of 1819 more redolent of the natural, 'conspiring' and unappropriated fertility of England's land. As Robert Wedderburn declared to the Hopkins Street audience six weeks later, 'the Land is the Strength of the Country and they will shortly possess themselves of that'.[4]

Notes

References in these notes to Home Office, Foreign Office, Treasury Solicitor's and Privy Council files have been abbreviated to HO, FO, TS and PC.

INTRODUCTION

1. 4 July 1818, HO 42/168. 283. The circumstances of the Evanses' arrests are given in J. Ann Hone, *For the Cause of Truth: Radicalism in London, 1796–1821*, Oxford: Clarendon Press, 1988, pp. 272–5.
2. 22 November 1819, HO 42/199. 160.
3. 4 July 1818, HO 42/168. 283.
4. For an introduction to Spencean ideas, see Malcolm Chase, '*The People's Farm': English Radical Agrarianism. 1775–1840*, Oxford: Clarendon Press, 1988.
5. N.D. [November 1816], HO 40/3 (4). 925.
6. E.P. Thompson, *The Making of the English Working Class*, Harmondsworth: Penguin, 1963/1980, p. 768.
7. Spencean criminality is studied in Iain McCalman, *Radical Underworld: Prophets, Revolutionaries and Pornographers in London, 1795–1840*, Cambridge: Cambridge University Press, 1988.
8. For a good introduction, see Robert Brendan McDowell, *Ireland in the Age of Imperialism and Revolution, 1760–1801*, Oxford: Oxford University Press, 1979, chapters 14–17. More specifically, see Tom Garvin, 'Defenders, Ribbonmen and Others: Underground Political Networks in Pre-Famine Ireland', and M.R. Beames, 'The Ribbon Societies: Lower-Class Nationalism in Pre-Famine Ireland' in *Nationalism and Popular Protest in Ireland*, ed. C.H.E. Philpin, Cambridge: Cambridge University Press, 1987, pp. 219–44, 245–63; E.W. Roberts, 'Caravats and Shanavests: Whiteboyism and Faction Fighting in East Munster, 1802–11' in

Irish Peasants: Violence & Political Unrest, 1780–1914, eds Samuel Clark and James S. Donnelly, Jr, Manchester: Manchester University Press, 1983, pp. 64–101.

9. An account is given in Richard Holmes, *Shelley: The Pursuit*, London: Quartet, 1976, pp. 136–9, 158–60.
10. 18 September 1812, HO 42/127. 424.
11. William Hone, *The Political House That Jack Built*, London: W. Hone [Dec.] 1819.
12. 18 April 1817, HO 42/168. 326.
13. B.C. 28 November 1819, HO 42/199. 406.

CHAPTER ONE: SEDITION AND ARTICULACY IN THE 1790s

1. BM Add. Ms. 27808, William Hone to Francis Place, 23 September 1830; details of Royal Proclamations are in Albert Goodwin, *The Friends of Liberty: the English Democratic Movement in the Age of the French Revolution*, London: Hutchinson, 1979.
2. Details of Spence's own experiences are from Thomas Spence, *The Case of Thomas Spence*, London: np, 1793. This is a second edition subsequent to the first edition which was apparently published in the last few days of 1792.
3. Thompson, (1963/1980), p. 134.
4. BM Add. Ms. 27808; for discharges on technicalities, including a brief reference to Spence, see Clive Emsley, 'An aspect of Pitt's "Terror": prosecutions for sedition during the 1790s', *Social History*, vol.6, no.2 (May 1981), p. 169.
5. *The Trial of Joseph Gerrald . . . For Sedition*, Edinburgh: 1794, pp. 10–11. Gerrald also thought he had a packed jury: he objected to William Creech, an Edinburgh bookseller, because 'I understand he has repeatedly declared, in private conversation, that he would condemn any member of the British convention, if he should be called to pass upon their assize . . .' p. 117.
6. Gerrald (1794), p. 13.
7. *Ibid.*, p. 240.
8. Thompson (1963/1980), p. 141.
9. Arthur Kidder, January 1813, HO 42/136. 691; 'Particulars as stated by Kidder relative to Margarot', n.d. HO 42/136. 703ff. For Margarot's and Thistlewood's association with Spenceans around 1810–11, see McCalman (1988), p. 23. For a discussion of the place of Kidder's reports, see Hone (1982), pp. 230–4.
10. Quoted in Nicholas Roe, *Wordsworth and Coleridge: The Radical Years*, Oxford: Oxford University Press, 1988, pp. 213–15.
11. *Sherwin's Political Register*, 28 November 1818, pp. 62–4, a copy is at HO 42/182. 663.

12. Clive Emsley, 'An aspect of Pitt's "Terror": prosecutions for sedition during the 1790s', *Social History*, vol.6, no.2 (May 1981), pp. 155–84. Emsley's study is systematically reliable only for sedition cases in provincial England.

13. BM Add. Ms. 27808. fol.249.

14. Ford to 'Notary' 21 December 1801, FO 95/615. 6.

15. Clive Emsley, 'The Home Office and its sources of information and investigation 1791–1801', *English Historical Review*, XCIV (1979), pp. 532–61. See p. 539 and its note.

16. Jane Austen, *Northanger Abbey* (1818), chapter 23, Harmondsworth: Penguin, pp. 190–1. See Robert Hopkins, 'General Tilney and Affairs of State: The Political Gothic of *Northanger Abbey*', *Philological Quarterly*, 57 (1978), pp. 213–24.

17. John Reeves held some Government sinecures, however. See Austin Mitchell, 'The Association Movement of 1792–3', *The Historical Journal*, IV, I (1961), pp. 56–77.

18. All subsequent references are to 'Mr. Reeves's Report on Sedition &c.' 29 April 1794, TS 11/3510 A (2).

19. A detailed account is given in Albert Goodwin, *The Friends of Liberty: The English Democratic Movement in the Age of the French Revolution*, London: Hutchinson, 1979, especially chapter 9, pp. 307–58.

20. See P.M. Ashraf, *The Life and Times of Thomas Spence*, Newcastle: Frank Graham, 1983, pp. 60–1.

21. The pike is the fundamental weapon of English insurrectionary planning. It had proved highly effective during the French Revolution as well as in the English Civil War. Broom handles could be fashioned into pike shafts and the iron pike-heads manufactured rapidly (within thirty-six hours, one English pamphleteer wrote in 1800) and then buried or hidden. They became an extremely effective weapon when used by insurgents in the 1798 Irish rebellion. See David V. Erdman, *Commerce des Lumières: John Oswald and the British in Paris. 1790–1793*, Columbia: University of Missouri Press, 1986, pp. 171–84, 239–40; Thomas Pakenham, *The Year of Liberty: The Story of the Great Irish Rebellion of 1798*, London: Hodder and Stoughton, 1969; *Every Man His Own Pike Maker* c.1817, HO 40/10. 185 shows how to make pikes from broomsticks. Another enclosure tells *How to Arm*, c.1817, HO 40/10. 206.

22. Examination of Frederick Pollydore Nodder 22 May 1794, PC 2/140. 168–9.

23. Examination of George Sanders 22 May 1794, PC 2/140. 169–71.

24. PC 2/140. 177–8; also apparently in PC 1/22 A 36–7.

25. The events may be followed in Goodwin (1979), pp. 340ff.

26. For the date of Spence's hearing, see Ashraf (1983), p. 60.

27. For Masaniello, see Rosario Villari, 'Masaniello: Contemporary and Recent Interpretations', *Past and Present*, 108 (1985), pp. 117–32; Peter Burke, 'The Virgin of the Carmine and the Revolt of Masaniello', *Past and Present*, 99 (1983), pp. 3–21; T.B., *The Rebellion of Naples, or the Tragedy*

of Massenello, Commonly So Called but Rightly Tomaso Aniello di Malfa, Generall of the Neapolitans. Written by a Gentleman who was an Eye-Witness where this was Really Acted upon that Bloudy Stage, the Streets of Naples, anno Domini MDCXLVII, London, 1649. The connection between England and Naples, from the right-wing point of view, was made by a political medal, *c*. 1658, which put Masaniello and Oliver Cromwell as obverse and reverse. See Villari (1985) and Burke (1983), above.

28. *Pigs' Meat* vol. II, p. 14.
29. Hone to Place 23 September 1830, BM Add. Ms. 27808.
30. See Goodwin (1979), pp. 361–4.
31. *Ibid.*, pp. 106, 122, 127, 361–2.
32. See *Gentleman's Magazine*, September 1796, pp. 752–4; April 1797, pp. 267–70.
33. Examples of Spence's tokens, including some discussed below, are conveniently reproduced in David Bindman, *The Shadow of the Guillotine: Britain and the French Revolution*, London: British Museum Publications, 1989.
34. See Allen Davenport's speech on the National Debt at Hopkins Street Chapel, 27 October 1819, HO 42/197. 773–5.
35. Report of 'C' 5 September 1817, HO 40/7 (1). 9.
36. See R.H. Thompson, 'The Dies of Thomas Spence (1750–1814)', *British Numismatic Journal*, vol. XXXVIII (1969–70), pp. 126–62; Christopher Brunel and Peter M. Jackson, 'Notes on Tokens as a Source of Information on the History of the Labour and Radical Movement, Part I', *Bulletin of the Society for the Study of Labour History*, vol. 13 (Autumn 1966), pp. 26–40; Bindman (1989), pp. 54–8, 198–203.
37. Thomas Spence, *The Coin-Collector's Companion; being a Descriptive Alphabetical List of the Modern Provincial and Other Copper Coins*, 1795, Item no. 398. Pitt had said to Wilberforce in November 1795: 'My head would be off in six months, were I to resign'; see Thompson (1969–70), p. 142.
38. M. Volney, *The Ruins: or, a Survey of the Revolutions of Empires*, 'translated from the French', London: Thomas Tegg, 1826, p. 109.
39. See Goodwin (1979), pp. 407–11 and Roger Wells, *Insurrection: The British Experience 1795–1803*, Gloucester: Alan Sutton, 1983, chapter 5 and pp. 95–7.
40. *Pigs' Meat* (3rd edn) vol. I, p. 59.
41. Sir William Jones's 'Ode in Imitation of Alcaeus' is identified as the source of Spence's token in Thompson (1969–70), p. 133.
42. Hopkins Street Chapel, 15 November 1819, HO 42/198. 77. On Government uneasiness about arming lower-class militia and volunteers, see J.E. Cookson, 'The English Volunteer Movement of the French Wars, 1793–1815: Some Contexts', *The Historical Journal*, 32, 4 (1989), pp. 867–91.
43. Thompson (1969–70), p. 139.
44. On the United organizations, see Hone (1982), pp. 48–54, 86–95; on Wolfe Tone, see Elliott (1989).

45. PC/142 A 144 and PC/141 A 138.
46. Wells (1983), pp. 121–7; Goodwin (1979), p. 445; Chase (1988), pp. 70–1. See also 2 March 1801, HO 42/61. 187–8, report on Thomas Evans's release from prison.
47. 26 September 1817, HO 40/7 (1). 29.
48. *The Rights of Infants: Or, The Imprescriptable Right of Mothers to Such a Share of Element as is sufficient to enable them to suckle and bring up their Young*, the Author London: 1797, pp. 8–9. My italics.
49. Spence (1797), p. 8.
50. *Ibid.*
51. See 18 October 1819, HO 42/197. 36–7.
52. Spence (1797), p. 6.
53. *Ibid.*, p. 15.
54. *Ibid.*, p. 8.
55. Thomas Spence, *The End of Oppression: . . . Being a Dialogue . . .*, London: T. Spence (?1795a), p. 3.
56. Spence (?1795a), p. 4.
57. *Ibid.*, p. 8.
58. *Ibid.*
59. Thomas Spence, *Spence's Recantation of the End of Oppression*, T. Spence (1796), p. 3.
60. See Roe (1988), pp. 146–50.
61. On Panton Street, and other clubs, see Mary Thale, 'London Debating Societies in the 1790s', *The Historical Journal*, 32, I (1989), pp. 57–86.
62. 'Sans Culotte': 'breeches-less, a term of abuse adopted as a title of honour; during 1792 it acquired political, social, even moral, significance', notes Gwyn A. Williams, *Artisans and Sans-Culottes: Popular Movements in France and Britain during the French Revolution* (1968), London: Libris, 2nd edn, 1989, p. 121 n.1. Thelwall's Lecture at Panton Street, 25 October 1795, HO 42/37. 414.
63. Thale (1989), p. 58 n.9.
64. Stafford 25 March 1820, HO 44/5. 407; HO 42/197. 506.
65. Panton Street 10 November 1795, HO 42/37. 462.
66. Panton Street 17 November 1795, HO 42/37. 427.
67. 17 November 1795, *Star* repr. in Samuel Taylor Coleridge, *Lectures 1795 On Politics and Religion*, London: RKP, 1971, pp. 359–64.
68. Panton Street 25 November 1795, HO 42/37. 449.
69. Panton Street 9 December 1795, HO 42/37. 432.
70. 'R.W.', *Theological Comet*, 6 November 1819, p. 123.
71. Panton Street 25 November 1795, HO 42/37. 449; see also J. Epstein, 'The Constitutional Idiom: Radical Reasoning, Rhetoric and Action in Early Nineteenth Century England', *Journal of Social History*, 23 (Spring), 1990, pp. 554–74.
72. For the effects on other debating clubs of the Two Bills, see Thale (1989), especially pp. 72–4.

Notes

73. Panton Street 10 December 1795, HO 42/37. 436. Jones, it should be stressed, was to suffer repeated imprisonment in the first decades of the nineteenth century. The longer term view of his career can be followed in Hone (1982).
74. Panton Street 16 November 1795, HO 42/37. 421.
75. Assembly Rooms, Brewer Street 18 December 1795, HO 42/37. 449.
76. Panton Street 19 December 1795, HO 42/37. 456.
77. *Ibid.*, HO 42/37. 457.

CHAPTER TWO: RESISTANCE AND THE CONDITIONS OF DISCOURSE IN THE EARLY 1800s

1. The day-to-day events are outlined in Wells (1983), chapter 9.
2. *The Complete Poetry and Prose of William Blake*, ed. David V. Erdman, New York: Anchor Press/Doubleday, 1982 (hereafter E), E709.
3. *The Four Zoas* (hereafter *FZ*) IX.135: 4–9, E403.
4. Enclosure, HO 42/51. 137.
5. Coombe to Portland 15 September 1800, HO 42/51. 163.
6. Coombe to Portland 17 September 1800, HO 42/51. 198; 17 September 1800, HO 42/51. 205.
7. Coombe to Portland, enclosure 17 September 1800, HO 42/52. 208.
8. Blake to Flaxman, 21 September 1800, E710; Blake to Butts, 23 September 1800, E711, Blake to Hayley, 16 September 1800, E709.
9. 17 September 1800, HO 42/51. 225.
10. Coombe to Portland 18 September 1800, HO 42/51. 234.
11. *FZ* III. 41:10, E328; *Jerusalem* (hereafter *J*), 15:10, E159.
12. Blake to Butts 23 September 1800, E711.
13. *FZ* IX. 135:3, E403.
14. *FZ* IX. 135:4–9, E403.
15. Coombe to Portland, enclosure 18 September 1800, HO 42/51. 236.
16. *FZ* IX. 138:1–3, E406.
17. *FZ* IX. 117:19, E387; *FZ* IX 125:9–10, E394.
18. *FZ* IX. 117:23, E387.
19. 19 September 1800, HO 42/51. 282.
20. Spence (1807), p. 10.
21. *Ibid.*, p. 9.
22. *Ibid.*, p. 11.
23. [Robert Southey], *Quarterly Review*, October 1816 [i.e. February 1817], p. 267.
24. 2nd report of the House of Lords Committee on Secrecy, 15 May 1810, in *Parliamentary History of England from the Earliest Period to the Year 1803* (1819 edn) xxxv., 1307, cited in Chase (1988), p. 70.
25. Thomas Spence (1807), p. 8.
26. Thomas Spence (1807), annotated by George Cullen, BL Shelfmark 900. h. 24 (i).
27. Spence (1807), pp. 9–10.

28. Cited in John Stevens, *England's Last Revolution: Pentrich 1817*, Buxton: Moorland Publishing, 1977, p. 94.
29. Thompson (1963/1980), pp. 732–3.
30. Spence (1807), pp. 8–9.
31. *Ibid.*, pp. 58–9.
32. Report of John Eshelby, Hopkins Street Chapel, 29 November 1819, HO 42/199. 414.
33. For Pastorini, see o Tuahaigh (1990), pp. 67–8 and Connelly (1982), pp. 13, 109–10.
34. See Robert D. Storch, '"Please to Remember The Fifth Of November": Conflict, Solidarity And Public Order In Southern England, 1815–1900' in *Popular Culture and Custom in Nineteenth-Century England*, ed. Robert D. Storch, London: Croom Helm, 1982, pp. 71–99; 28 October 1817, HO 42/170. 450; Shegog, 30 October 1817, HO 42/170. 75.
35. *Quarterly Review*, October 1816 [i.e. February 1817], pp. 225–78.
36. *Ibid.*, pp. 267–8.
37. *Ibid.*, p. 266.
38. *Ibid.*, p. 263.
39. *Ibid.*, pp. 267, 271.
40. *Ibid.*, p. 271.
41. *Ibid.*
42. For the context of the Evanses' arrest, see Hone (1982), pp. 272–5.
43. *Quarterly Review*, October 1816 [i.e. February 1817], p. 266.
44. HO 42/168. 338.
45. Thompson (1963/1980), pp. 188–92 was the first to identify the centrality of Despard to the history of revolutionary politics. Other authorities are Marianne Elliott, 'The "Despard Conspiracy" Reconsidered', *Past and Present*, 75 (1977), pp. 46–61 and Hone (1982) pp. 103–37. My account is culled from reports in *The Times*, from printed trial transcripts and from Home Office files.
46. Quoted in Roger Wells, *Insurrection: The British Experience 1795–1803*, Gloucester: Alan Sutton, 1983, p. 238.
47. *The Trial of Edward Marcus Despard, Esquire. For High Treason* (1803), pp. 59–60, 69.
48. Wells (1983), pp. 29–38.
49. HO 40/8. 52.
50. 6 August 1819, HO 42/197. 500.
51. In addition to the authorities cited above, see Wells (1983), pp. 38, 123–7, 166–70, 237–50.
52. *The Times* 22 February 1803. The second version is in *State Trials at Large (Taken in Short Hand), The Whole Proceedings on the Trials of Col. Despard, and the Other State Prisoners . . . With an APPENDIX, containing the Behaviour of the Convicts and a particular Account of their Execution*, 4th edn (n.d.), p. 78. See also printed handbill, n.d., HO 42/70. 191.
53. Quoted in Wells (1983), p. 248.

54. Robert Southey, *Letters from England: by Don Manuel Alvarez Espriella. Translated from the Spanish*, London, 1807, edited by Jack Simmons (1951), Gloucester: Alan Sutton, 1984, p. 379.
55. Thompson (1963/1980), p. 515.
56. From *The Times* 22 February 1803 and *State Trials at Large (Taken in Short Hand), The Whole Proceedings on the Trials of Col. Despard, and the Other State Prisoners . . . With an APPENDIX, containing the Behaviour of the Convicts and a particular Account of their Execution*, 4th edn (n.d.), p. 79.
57. See Wells (1983), pp. 246–7; Hone (1982), pp. 103–19.
58. *The Trial of Edward Marcus Despard, Esquire. For High Treason* (1803), p. 61.
59. 'The Independence of Great Britain and Ireland. The Equalization of Civil, Political and Religious Rights. An ample Provision for the Families of the Heroes who shall fall in the Contest . . .', quoted in Wells (1983), p. 221.
60. See Emsley, 'Repression, "terror" and the rule of law in England during the decade of the French Revolution', *The English Historical Review*, vol. c (1985), pp. 801–25.
61. *The Trial of Edward Marcus Despard, Esquire. For High Treason* (1803), p. 69.
62. *Ibid.*, p. 70.
63. *Ibid.*, p. 70.
64. *Ibid.*, p. 95.
65. *Ibid.*, p. 117.
66. *Ibid.*, p. 98.
67. *Ibid.*, p. 73.
68. *Ibid.*, p. 96.
69. *Ibid.*, p. 88.
70. *Ibid.*
71. *Ibid.*, p. 89.
72. *State Trials at Large (Taken in Short Hand), The Whole Proceedings on the Trials of Col. Despard, and the Other State Prisoners . . . With an APPENDIX, containing the Behaviour of the Convicts and a particular Account of their Execution*, 4th edn (n.d.), pp. 43, 45.
73. 15 February 1803, HO 42/70. 77.
74. W. Wirkworth 19 February 1803, HO 42/70. 118.
75. 20 February 1803, HO 42/70. 117.
76. *The Times*, 15 and 16 February 1803.
77. W. Wirkworth 21 February 1803, HO 42/70. 211–17.
78. *The Times*, 22 February 1803.
79. Ford to Moody 23 February 1803, FO 95/615. 25.
80. Dorothy George, *Catalogue of Political and Personal Satires Preserved in the Department of Prints and Drawings in the British Museum* (1935–54), No. 9969.
81. See BM Add. Ms. 2808. 322, R. Wedderburn to F. Place, 22 March 1831.
82. See McCalman (1988), p. 116.
83. C.F. Mortimer, *A Christian Effort To Exalt The Goodness Of The Divine Majesty, Even In A Momento, On Edward Marcus Despard, Esq. And Six*

Notes

Other Citizens, Undoubtedly now with God in Glory. An Heroic Poem: in Six Parts, n.d. (1803?), Part III.
84. Mortimer (1803?), Part I.
85. *Ibid.*, Part V.
86. Quoted in Wells (1983), p. 249.
87. For Despard's exemplary martyrdom, see Hone (1982), pp. 103–16.
88. Blake to Butts 16 August 1803, E732 and 'Blake's Memorandum', E735.
89. G.E. Bentley, Jr, *Blake Records Supplement*, Oxford: Clarendon Press, 1988, p. 25.
90. Blake to Butts 16 August 1803, E732.
91. Emsley (1981), p. 156. Emsley's study is valid up to 1801 for the English provinces only.
92. For the extent of radical infiltration of the navy at this time, see Wells (1983), chapter 5.
93. Blake to Butts 16 August 1803, E733.
94. Emsley (1981), Appendices A and B.
95. Emsley (1981), pp. 162, 172.
96. Quoted in Emsley (1981), pp. 159–60.
97. Blake to Butts 16 August 1803, E732–3.
98. Emsley (1981), pp. 161–2 and Appendices A and B.
99. 'Blake's Memorandum', E735.
100. David V. Erdman, *Blake: Prophet Against Empire* (1954), 3rd edn, Princeton: Princeton University Press, 1977, p. 36; 23 August 1803, HO 42/72. 232.
101. 8 August 1803, HO 42/72. 397.
102. Enclosure 9 August 1803, HO 42/72. 380.
103. 14 August 1803, HO 42/72.
104. 22 September 1803, HO 42/73. 462.
105. 18 December 1803, HO 42/74. 132.
106. Erdman (1954/1977), pp. 35–6, 159.
107. T.B. and T.J. Howell (eds), *State Trials*, London, 1813–20, vol. 25 contains the trial of Horne Tooke.
108. Thomas Martyn's *Plates to Illustrate Linnaeus's System of Vegetables* would be a typical example of his work. Dodd's Ms. *History of English Engravers* refers to Nodder as 'an accomplished naturalist, probably of German origin'. BM Add. Ms. 33403. fo. 134.
109. 'Mr: Nodder's' 30 April 1794, TS. 11.953. 3497.
110. 'F.P.N. (Sedition) to Evan Nepean' 2 June 1794, TS. 11.953. 3497.
111. *Ibid.*
112. See Clive Emsley, 'The Home Office and its sources of information and investigation', *English Historical Review*, XCIV (1979), p. 559; Nodder to Sidney, 5 August 1794, TS. 11.953. 3497.
113. Thomas Spence, *A Letter from Ralph Hodge, To His Cousin Thomas Bull*, London, c. 1795, pp. 1–2.
114. *The Trial of James Watson for High Treason . . . taken in short hand by W.B. Gurney*, 1817, vol.2, pp. 503, 583.

115. Erdman (1954/1977), pp. 409, 409 n.40.
116. E735.
117. G.E. Bentley, Jr, *Blake Records*, Oxford: Clarendon Press, 1977, p. 124.
118. Alison G. Olson, *The Radical Duke: The Career and Correspondence of Charles Lennox, Third Duke of Richmond*, Oxford: Oxford University Press, 1961, p. 93.
119. Bentley (1977), p. 145.
120. For the psychological effects of the 1803 trial on Blake's work, see Paul Youngquist, *Madness and Blake's Myth*, Pennsylvania: Pennsylvania State University Press, 1989, *passim*.
121. See the dated entries in Bentley (1977).
122. For justices 'Peachey', 'Kwantok', 'Guantok', 'Gwantok', 'Breretun', see J5:25, E147; J19:18, E164; J32[36]:16–17, E178; J46[32]:11, E195; J71:28–30,32, E225.

CHAPTER THREE: 'A FREE AND EASY SOCIETY TO OVERTHROW THE GOVERNMENT': POST-WAR SPENCEANS

1. Spence (1807), p. 56.
2. *Ibid.*, p. 59.
3. Thomas Evans, 'Inventory Book', HO 42/168. 338; Robert Essick, *William Blake's Commercial Book Illustrations: A Catalogue and Study of the Plates Engraved by Blake after Designs by Other Artists*, Oxford: Clarendon Press, 1991, pp. 19–20.
4. William Hone to Francis Place 23 September 1830, BM Add. Ms. 27808; 'Mr. Reeves's Report on Sedition &c.' 29 April 1794, TS 11/3510 A (2).
5. The fullest account of these 'quiet' years is in Hone (1982), chapter 4.
6. Thomas Preston, *The Life and Opinions of Thomas Preston, Patriot and Shoemaker*, London: 1817, pp. 18–19.
7. Preston (1817), p. 19.
8. *Ibid.*, pp. 4, 5, 9, 13, 16, 20–1.
9. *Ibid.*, pp. 22–3.
10. Examination of T. Preston 4 December 1816, HO 40/10. 303.
11. George Wiggins HO 40/3 (3). 21.
12. Examination of T. Preston 4 December 1816, HO 40/10. 303.
13. George Wiggins HO 40/3 (3). 21; Preston (1817), pp. 31–3.
14. Allen Davenport, *The Life And Literary Pursuits of Allen Davenport*, London: G. Hancock, 1845, pp. 8–11, 14.
15. *Ibid.*, p. 38.
16. *Ibid.*, p. 30.
17. *Ibid.*, p. 34.
18. *Ibid.*, p. 41.
19. *Ibid.*, pp. 41–2.
20. T.J. Evans to F. Place, BM Add. Ms. 27808. 229.
21. Davenport (1845), pp. 41–2.

Notes

22. See, for example, 'The Topic', *Sherwin's Political Register*, 3 January 1818, p. 96.
23. Davenport (1845), pp. 44–5.
24. *Ibid.*, p. 45.
25. *Ibid.*, pp. 45–6.
26. *Sherwin's Political Register*, 5 September 1818, p. 284.
27. Davenport (1845), p. 56.
28. *Ibid.*, pp. 45–6.
29. Allen Davenport, *The Kings, or Legitimacy Unmasked, A Satirical Poem*, London: 1819, p. 10. A copy of *The Kings* is in HO 42/202.
30. *Sherwin's Political Register*, 15 August 1818, p. 236.
31. The condition of publishing can be pieced together from information in Hone (1982), *passim*, while a commentary and fully annotated list on this press can be found in McCalman (1988).
32. Allen Davenport, *The Muses Wreath: Composed of Original Poetry*, London: n.d. [1827], p. 35.
33. *Sherwin's Political Register*, 17 October 1818, p. 376.
34. See Hone (1982), pp. 272–3.
35. Davenport (1845), pp. 44–5.
36. *Sherwin's Political Register*, 25 July 1818, p. 192.
37. 18 October 1819, HO 42/197. 36.
38. For Davenport's development, see Chase (1988), pp. 88–91, 127–30, 160–2.
39. Davenport (1827), p. 56.
40. Davenport (1845), p. 41.
41. *Theological Comet*, 23 October 1819, 6 November 1819.
42. Davenport (1845), p. 46.
43. *Ibid.*
44. *The Trial of Edmund Marcus Despard, Esquire, For High Treason* (1803), p. 120.
45. Iain McCalman, 'Ultra-radicalism and Convivial Debating-clubs in London, 1795–1838', *English Historical Review*, 102 (April 1987), pp. 309–33.
46. *The Trial of Edmund Marcus Despard, Esquire, For High Treason* (1803), p. 120.
47. On the vicissitudes of Reid's career, see Iain McCalman, 'The Infidel as Prophet: William Reid and Blakean Radicalism' in *Historicizing Blake*, eds Steve Clark and David Worrall, London: Macmillan, forthcoming.
48. William Hamilton Reid, *The Rise and Dissolution of the Infidel Societies in this Metropolis* (1800), p. 8.
49. Reid (1800), p. 14.
50. *Ibid.*, p. 32.
51. *Ibid.*, p. 16.
52. *Ibid.*, p. 109.
53. *Ibid.*
54. See Thompson (1963/1980), p. 306.

55. HO 42/172.
56. Thomas Evans, *A Humorous Catalogue of SPENCE'S SONGS*, Part II, ?1811.
57. ?1817, HO 42/172. 176.
58. 'C' 30 September 1817, HO 40/8. 44.
59. See Penelope J. Corfield, 'Dress for deference and dissent: hats and the decline of hat honour', *Costume*, 23 (1989), pp. 64–79.
60. R. Chaff March 1820, HO 44/5. 494. Davidson's exercise book is HO 44/5. 493.
61. Davenport (1845), p. 46.
62. For a list of places see HO 40/3 (3). 906.
63. 4 February 1817, HO 40/3 (3). 906.
64. *Ibid*.
65. 13 November 1817, HO 40/7 (3). 17.

CHAPTER FOUR: ARTICULACY AND ACTION

1. The following account is principally pieced together from *The Trial of James Watson for High Treason . . . taken in short hand by W.B. Gurney*, London: M. Gurney 1817, 2 vols; and from the two copies of the Spa Fields speeches, 'A Narrative of the Proceedings at the Spa Fields Meeting on 2 Dec 1816', filed at HO 40/3 (3), 28ff. and HO 40/3 (3) 895ff.
2. The time of arrival of the waggon, the Watsons and Thomas Preston is given by Thistlewood, 2 October 1817, HO 40/8. 52.
3. *The Trial of James Watson for High Treason . . . taken in short hand by W.B. Gurney*, 1817, vol.1, pp. 180, 182.
4. 'The wind blew the contrary way, and I could not make out the words', Charles Sheerman, the Elder, witness, *The Trial of James Watson for High Treason . . . taken in short hand by W.B. Gurney*, 1817, vol.1, p. 198.
5. 2 October 1817, HO 40/8. 52.
6. *Ibid*.; McCabe's presence is identified by Iain McCalman; private communication.
7. *The Trial of James Watson for High Treason . . . taken in short hand by W.B. Gurney*, 1817, vol.1, p. 163.
8. Iain McCalman notes that Dowling was unaffectionately known as 'the spectacled spy' and may have had a radical past in the LCS. In the 1820s, he became editor of *Bells Weekly*; private communication.
9. *The Trial of James Watson for High Treason . . . taken in short hand by W.B. Gurney*, 1817, vol.1, pp. 136, 157, 164, 203ff.
10. Reappropriated, Nelson's famous Trafalgar order had been re-addressing Londoners from Spencean handbills since October:

    ENGLAND EXPECTS EVERY MAN TO DO HIS DUTY

    Four Million in Distress!!!
    Four Million in Embarrassment!!!

> One Million and half fear Distress!!!
> Half a Million live in Splendid Luxury!!!
> Our Brothers in Ireland are in a worse state The Climax
> of Misery is complete It can go no further
> [Copy of handbill, HO 40/3 (3). 27].

11. George Wiggins, n.d. but *c.* October 1816, HO 40/3 (3). 21.
12. Penelope J. Corfield, 'Class by name and number in eighteenth-century Britain', in *Language, History, Class*, ed. Penelope J. Corfield, Oxford: Basil Blackwell, 1991, pp. 101–30.
13. *The Trial of James Watson for High Treason . . . taken in short hand by W.B. Gurney*, 1817, vol.1, p. 144.
14. The Cock, Grafton Street 15 January 1817, HO 42/158. 229.
15. *The Trial of James Watson for High Treason . . . taken in short hand by W.B. Gurney*, 1817, vol.2, p. 40.
16. *Ibid.*, vol.1, p. 203.
17. 'A Narrative of the Proceedings at the Spa Fields Meeting on 2 Dec 1816', HO 40/3 (3). 28; also at HO 40/3 (3). 895.
18. *The Trial of James Watson for High Treason . . . taken in short hand by W.B. Gurney*, 1817, vol.1, p. 203.
19. *Ibid.*, vol.1, pp. 203–4.
20. *Ibid.*, vol.1, p. 222.
21. *Ibid.*, vol.2, p. 33.
22. *Ibid.*, vol.1, p. 153, vol.2, p. 312.
23. Accounts of the events at Spa Fields can be found in Thompson (1963/ 1980), pp. 693–6; Hone (1982), pp. 263–4; and John Stevenson, *Popular Disturbances in England, 1700–1870*, London: Longman, 1979, pp. 193ff. The Spencean context of Spa Fields is given in Chase (1988), pp. 97–104, 189.
24. *The Trial of James Watson for High Treason . . . taken in short hand by W.B. Gurney*, 1817, vol.1, p. 217.
25. Mr. Clarke n.d., ?February 1817, HO 40/3 (4). 925.
26. 30 October 1816, HO 40/3 (3). 24.
27. Thomas Storer 14 November 1816, HO 40/3 (3). 911.
28. *The Trial of James Watson for High Treason . . . taken in short hand by W.B. Gurney*, 1817, vol.1, p. 358.
29. *Ibid.*, vol.1, pp. 358–9.
30. 30 April 1817, HO 40/10. 155. For Moggridge's links with Watson Jnr, see McCalman (1988), p. 111.
31. Williamson 24 September 1817, HO 40/8. 33.
32. McCalman (1988), p. 106.
33. Thomas Storer 14 November 1816, HO 40/3 (3). 909ff.
34. *The Trial of James Watson for High Treason . . . taken in short hand by W.B. Gurney*, 1817, vol.2, p. 456.
35. Thomas Storer 14 November 1816, HO 40/3 (3). 909ff.
36. Thomas Storer 27 November 1816, HO 40/3 (4). 919.

Notes

37. *The Trial of James Watson for High Treason . . . taken in short hand by W.B. Gurney*, 1817, vol.2, pp. 370ff.
38. *Ibid.*, vol.2, pp. 518–24.
39. Castle's toast was well known and usually continued 'By the guts of the last of Priests'; *The Trial of James Watson for High Treason . . . taken in short hand by W.B. Gurney*, 1817, vol.2, pp. 258–75.
40. For an account of Seale's activities, see Chase (1988), pp. 71–2, 92–4, 100–8.
41. *The Trial of James Watson for High Treason . . . taken in short hand by W.B. Gurney*, 1817, vol.1, p. 101.
42. For Seale's role as Spence's printer, see Chase (1989), pp. 49 and 49 n.8.
43. *The Trial of James Watson for High Treason . . . taken in short hand by W.B. Gurney*, 1817, vol.1, p. 102.
44. *Ibid.*
45. 'B', 30 June 1817, HO 40/7 (1). 2.
46. *The Trial of James Watson for High Treason . . . taken in short hand by W.B. Gurney*, 1817, vol.1, pp. 97–8.
47. Ford to Moody 16 January 1803, FO 95/615. 22.
48. 7 February 1817, HO 40/3 (4). 927.
49. 20 September 1817, HO 40/7 (2). 39.
50. See Emsley (1979), pp. 502–61.
51. G. Gurney and W.B. Gurney, *The Trial of Edward Marcus Despard, Esquire. For High Treason*, 1803, p. 176.
52. 'B' is identified by McCalman (1988), p. 264 n.66.
53. 'B' 30 June 1817, HO 40/7 (1); 'B', 30 June 1817, HO 40/8. 5.
54. 'B' 30 June 1817, HO 40/8. 5.
55. As cited in Chase (1988), p. 104.
56. 'B' 30 June 1817, HO 40/8. 5; 'B' 30 June 1817, HO 40/7 (1). 2.
57. 'B' 8 July 1817, HO 40/7 (1). 5A.
58. 25 October 1817, HO 42/170. 402.
59. 'B' 8 July 1817, HO 40/7 (1). 5A.
60. 8 July 1817, HO 40/8. 11.
61. 'B' 8 July 1817, HO 40/7 (1). 5A.
62. The identities of 'B' and 'C' are given in McCalman (1988), p. 264 n.66.
63. 4 October 1817, HO 42/170. 64; n.d., HO 42/170. 475.
64. 'C' 5 September 1817, HO 40/7 (1). 9.
65. 'B' 5 September 1817, HO 40/8. 15; 'C' 6 September 1817, HO 40/7 (1). 12.
66. 'C' 6 September 1817, HO 40/7 (1). 12.
67. 'B' 30 June 1817, HO 40/7 (1). 2. See also 2 October 1817, HO 40/8. 52.
68. 6 September 1817, HO 40/7 (1). 16.
69. 8 September 1817, HO 40/7 (1). 20; 9 September 1817, HO 40/7 (1). 20.
70. 8 September 1817, HO 42/170. 455.
71. September 1817, HO 40/8. 20.
72. 'A' 9 September 1817, HO 40/7 (1). 20A.
73. 'A' 9 September 1817, HO 40/7 (1). 20.
74. 23 November 1802, FO 95/615. 19.

216

75. 'A' 9 September 1817, HO 40/7 (1). 20.
76. *Ibid.*
77. Shegog 18 September 1817, HO 42/170. 270.
78. 2 October 1817, HO 40/8. 52.
79. Shegog 18 September 1817, HO 42/170. 270.
80. Shegog 20 September 1817, HO 40/7 (1). 34.
81. Williamson 24 September 1817, HO 40/7 (1). 26.
82. Shegog 26 September 1817, HO 40/7 (1). 29.
83. Shegog 9 October 1817, HO 42/170. 483.
84. Shegog 9 October 1817, HO 42/170. 484.
85. Champion 9 October 1817, HO 42/170. 486.
86. See chapter 5, 'The Naval Mutinies of 1797', in Wells (1983), pp. 79–109.
87. Champion 9 October 1817, HO 42/170. 486.
88. Shegog 9 October 1917, HO 42/170. 79.
89. 11 October 1817, HO 42/170. 481.
90. Wells (1983), p. 71.
91. Shegog 13 October 1817, HO 42/170. 470.
92. Williamson 20 October 1817, HO 40/7 (2). 43.
93. Shegog 27 October 1817, HO 42/170.
94. Shegog 30 October 1817, HO 42/170. 75.
95. Shegog 30 June 1817, HO 40/7 (1). 2.
96. 28 October 1817, HO 42/170. 450.
97. 5 January 1818, HO 40/7 (4). 21–5.
98. 13 January 1818, HO 40/7 (4). 27.
99. 'A General Officer' 27 January 1818, HO 40/8. 167.
100. 'W——r——' 31 January 1818, HO 40/8. 168.
101. 'W——r——' 31 January 1818, HO 40/7 (4). 39.
102. James Watson, *More Plots, More Treason, More Green Bags: A Letter to Viscount Sidmouth*, London: 1818, pp. 2–3.
103. Watson to Thistlewood 24 July 1818, HO 42/178. 107.
104. 'W——r——' 31 January 1818, HO 40/8. 168.
105. *The Axe Laid to the Root, Or, a Fatal Blow to Oppressors, Being an Address to the Planters and Negroes of the Island of Jamaica* [1817], p. 90.

CHAPTER FIVE: SOME ULTRA-RADICALS

1. 13 January 1817, HO 42/158. 708.
2. Thompson (1969/70), p. 131.
3. 15 January 1817, HO 42/158. 229.
4. McCalman (1988), pp. 132–51.
5. *Ibid.*, pp. 128–33.
6. 15 March 1819, HO 42/190. 82.
7. Stafford 15 October 1818, HO 42/181. 306.
8. Chetwode Eustace 10 August 1819, HO 42/191. 18.
9. Richard Dalton 10 November 1819, HO 42/198. 196.
10. *Ibid.*

11. See the list of jurors, *The Trial of James Watson . . . for High Treason*, 1817, p. 33; W. Porden 10 August 1819, HO 42/199. 61.
12. Lea and Plush 6 October 1819, HO 42/196. 175.
13. *Ibid*.
14. *Ibid*.
15. *Ibid*.
16. *Ibid*.
17. *Ibid*.
18. Chetwode Eustace 10 August 1819, HO 42/191. 18; Plush and Mathewson 3 November 1819, HO 42/198. 422.
19. See Thompson (1963/1980), p. 735.
20. Plush and Mathewson 3 November 1819, HO 42/198. 422.
21. *Ibid*.
22. 3 November 1819, HO 42/198. 428.
23. 31 October 1819, HO 42/197. 255.
24. 1 November 1819, HO 42/197. 500.
25. 14 November 1819, HO 42/197. 500.
26. HO 40/10. 185.
27. John Davies 21 November 1819, HO 42/199. 134; 14 November 1819, HO 42/197. 500.
28. 1, 2 September 1819, HO 42/197. 500.
29. 5 September 1819, HO 42/197. 500.
30. 13 September 1819, HO 42/194. 20.
31. *Ibid*.
32. Birnie 13 September 1819, HO 42/194. 156.
33. McCalman (1988), p. 134.
34. Prothero (1979), pp. 116–18.
35. John King 25 August 1819, HO 42/193. 467.
36. 25 August 1819, HO 42/193. 198.
37. 25 August 1819, HO 42/193. 196.
38. Handbill 25 August 1819, HO 42/193. 490.
39. 23 August 1819, HO 42/193. 108, 132.
40. Hanley 23 August 1819, HO 42/193. 97.
41. 11 January 1820, HO42/197. 500.
42. *Medusa*, 14 August 1819.
43. 'W——r——' 23 August 1819, HO 42/193. 3.
44. Depositions of Hall, Fogg and Girton 20 August 1819, HO 42/194. 2.
45. 23 August 1819, HO 42/193. 295; 23 August 1819, HO 42/197. 500.
46. Committal of E.J. Blandford 20 August 1819, HO 42/193. 92.
47. 'The Wrongs of Man, Or, Things as they Are', *Medusa*, 6 March 1819.
48. 'The Rights of Man, Or, Things as they were intended to be by Divine Providence', *Medusa*, 13 March 1819.
49. *Medusa*, 13 March 1819.
50. [Robert Southey], *Quarterly Review*, October 1816 [i.e. February 1817], p. 271.
51. 26 September 1817, HO 42. 7 (1). 29.

52. 14 July 1819, HO 42/190. 40.
53. *Medusa*, 10 April 1819.
54. See, primarily, Iain McCalman, 'Popular Radicalism and Freethought in Early Nineteenth-Century England: A Study of Richard Carlile and his Followers, 1815–32', unpublished MA thesis, Australian National University, 1975. A further discussion is available in Chase (1988), pp. 127–30.
55. Allen Davenport, *The Republican*, X, October 1824, p. 404.
56. *Ibid.*
57. Davenport (1827), p. 36.
58. Allen Davenport, *The Republican*, X, October 1824, p. 396.
59. *Ibid.*, pp. 410–11.
60. Letter, 'R.W.', *The Theological Comet*, 6 November 1819, p. 124.
61. *Medusa*, 10 April 1819.
62. *Medusa*, 17 April 1819.
63. *Ibid.*
64. 18 October 1819, HO 42/197. 36.
65. 10 October 1819, HO 42/197. 394.
66. *Medusa*, 24 April, 15 May 1819.
67. *Medusa*, 22 May 1819.
68. W. Porden 10 August 1819, HO 42/199. 61.
69. *Medusa*, 12 June 1819.
70. *Medusa*, 5 June 1819.
71. *Medusa*, 29 May 1819.
72. *Medusa*, 12 June 1819.
73. 13, 14 July 1819, HO 42/197. 500.
74. *The White Hat*, 16 October 1819, p. 6.
75. 8–10 August 1819, HO 42/197. 500.
76. See Iowerth Prothero's *Artisans and Politics in Early Nineteenth Century London: John Gast and his Times*, Folkestone: Dawson 1979; 15 August 1819, HO 42/197. 500; McCalman (1988), p. 136; 5 August 1819, HO 42/197. 500; 19 August 1819, HO 42/197. 500.
77. On the Johnsons, see McCalman (1988), pp. 20, 22, 115, 121, 125, 128.
78. Hanley 2 March 1820, HO 40/5. 43.
79. W. Porden 10 August 1819, HO 42/199. 61; Chetwode Eustace 10 August 1819, HO 42/191. 18.
80. See Prothero (1979), pp. 116ff.
81. 16, 18 August 1819, HO 42/197. 500.
82. 20, 22, 24 August 1819, HO 42/197. 500.
83. ?JB 25 August 1819, HO 42/193. 216.
84. *Ibid.*
85. 30 August 1819, HO 42/193. 341.
86. Hanley 31 August 1819, HO 42/193. 375.
87. See the account in Thompson (1963/1980), pp. 752–5.
88. 16, 26 September 1819, HO 42/197. 500; see also Prothero (1979), p. 121 and McCalman (1988), pp. 135–6.

Notes

CHAPTER SIX: HOPKINS STREET TO CATO STREET:
SURVEILLANCE AND RESISTANCE, 1819–20

1. McCalman (1988), pp. 128–33.
2. HO 42/202. 6.
3. McCalman (1988), p. 131.
4. 'A' 15 April 1819, HO 42/190. 72; handbill, HO 42/190. 73.
5. *The Times*, 22 September 1819.
6. 18 October 1819, HO 42/197. 36.
7. 27 September 1819, HO 42/195.
8. 2 October 1819, HO 42/196. 379; 20 September 1819, HO 42/197. 500.
9. 6 October 1819, HO 42/196. 175.
10. Davenport (1845), pp. 41–2; for an account of the Evanses' imprisonment, see Hone (1982), pp. 272–5.
11. Davenport (1845), p. 47.
12. *Ibid*.
13. 16 December 1817, HO 40/7 (4). 16.
14. Davenport (1845), pp. 47–8.
15. *Ibid*., p. 49.
16. *Ibid*., p. 48.
17. 10 October 1819, HO 42/197. 500.
18. 10 October 1819, HO 42/197. 394.
19. *Ibid*.
20. On William Carr, see McCalman (1988), pp. 20, 111, 131–2, 196.
21. 11 October 1819, HO 42/197. 384.
22. Thomas Preston March 1820, HO 40/5. 457; 21 October 1819, HO 42/197. 393.
23. 8, 11 October 1819, HO 42/197. 500.
24. For Cashman and this quotation, see Thompson (1963/1980), pp. 665–6.
25. 14 October 1819, HO 42/197. 500.
26. *Sherwin's Political Register*, 17 October 1818, p. 377.
27. 18 October 1819, HO 4/197. 36.
28. *Ibid*.
29. See J.E. Cookson, 'The English Volunteer Movement of the French Wars, 1793–1815: Some Contexts', *The Historical Journal*, 32, 4 (1989), pp. 867–91.
30. Davenport (1845), pp. 44, 45.
31. 18 October 1819, HO 42/197. 36.
32. 27 October 1819, HO 42/197. 773.
33. *Ibid*.
34. 18 October 1819, HO 42/197. 36.
35. Cited in Thompson (1963/1980), p. 750.
36. 27 October 1819, HO 42/197. 773.
37. 9 November 1819, HO 42/198. 329.
38. 10 October 1819, HO 42/197. 394.
39. 29 October 1819, HO 42/199. 482.

40. Handbill HO 42/199. 422.
41. 9 February 1818, HO 40/9. 615.
42. 29 October 1819, HO 42/199. 482.
43. *Ibid.*
44. 27 October 1819, HO 42/197. 773.
45. Prothero (1979), p. 123.
46. 20 October 1819, HO 42/197. 216.
47. 20 October 1819, HO 42/197. 500.
48. 1 November 1819, HO 42/197. 500; 28 October 1819, HO 42/197. 399.
49. Prothero (1979), pp. 119, 123; 29 October 1819, HO 42/197. 400.
50. *Democratic Recorder*, 11 October 1819.
51. 1 November 1819, HO 42/197. 500.
52. 27 October 1819, HO 42/197. 773.
53. 1 November 1819, HO 42/198. 490.
54. *Sherwin's Political Register*, 19 September 1818.
55. 1 November 1819, HO 42/198. 490.
56. *The Trial of the Rev. Robt. Wedderburn . . . For Blasphemy*, ed. Erasmus Perkins [i.e. George Cannon], London: E. Perkins, 1820, pp. 7–8.
57. 10 November 1819, HO 42/198. 196.
58. 14 November 1819, HO 42/198. 161.
59. 29 November 1819, HO 42/199. 414.
60. 9 November 1819, HO 42/198. 329. Iain McCalman (private communication) has noted that 'Merry Andrew' was George Cannon's trademark.
61. 9 November 1819, HO 42/198. 329.
62. *Ibid.*
63. 19 November 1819, HO 42. 200.
64. 3 November 1819, HO 42/198. 422.
65. 31 October 1819, HO 42/197. 255.
66. *The Times*, 26 August 1819.
67. *The Times*, 6 October 1819.
68. 16 October 1819, HO 42/197. 387.
69. 3 November 1819, HO 42/197. 500.
70. 5, 9, 14, 19, 24 November 1819, HO 42/197. 500.
71. 11 November 1819, HO 42/198. 202.
72. 30 November 1819, HO 42/197. 500.
73. 28 November, 5 December 1819, HO 42/197. 500.
74. 22 November 1819, HO 42/199. 162.
75. HO 44/5. 64; 17 May 1820, HO 44/5. 374; Prothero (1979), pp. 129–30.
76. Thomas Hazard, *A True Picture of Society, As Displayed by Certain Rich Characters Towards Their Poor Neighbours. A Poem*, London: 1819, copy in HO 44/5.
77. Thomas Hazard 25 March 1820, HO 44/5. 405.
78. 14, 18 November 1819, HO 42/197. 500.
79. 30 November 1819, HO 42/199. 535.
80. 3 December 1819, HO 42/197. 500.
81. 7 December 1819, HO 42/199. 545.

82. 6 December 1819, HO 42/197. 500.
83. 7 December 1819, HO 42/199. 545.
84. 13, 14 December 1819, HO 42/197. 500.
85. 19 December 1819, HO 42/197. 500.
86. 19, 26 December 1819, HO 42/197. 500.
87. 29 December 1819, HO 42/197. 500.
88. Prothero (1979), pp. 129–31.
89. *The Trials of Arthur Thistlewood. . .*, Leeds: John Barr, 1820, pp. 83, 87.
90. 21 January 1820, HO 42/197. 500.
91. *Ibid.*
92. 29, 31 January 1820, HO 42/197. 500.
93. 13 February 1820, HO 42/197. 500.
94. Thomas Hazard 25 March 1820, HO 44/5. 405.
95. See R. Chaff March 1820, HO 44/5. 494.
96. Preston to Sidmouth March 1820, HO 40/5. 457.
97. HO 44/6. 338.
98. The poems were printed in the semi-journalistic book-of-the-plot, G.T. Wilkinson, *The Cato-Street Conspiracy*, London: T. Kelly, 1820.
99. HO 44/6. 338.
100. Ruell to Home Office 27 March 1820, HO 44/5. 425.
101. *Ibid.*
102. *Black Dwarf*, 1 March 1820, pp. 273–7.
103. *Ibid.*, p. 277.
104. *Black Dwarf*, 3 May 1820, pp. 609–10.
105. *Ibid.*, p. 610.
106. *Ibid.*, p. 611.
107. *Ibid.*, pp. 611–12.
108. *Ibid.*, pp. 599–603.
109. *Ibid.*, pp. 604–5.
110. *Ibid.*, p. 605.
111. *Ibid.*, pp. 605–7.
112. 6 June 1820, HO 44/6. 289.

CONCLUSION

1. John Keats to George and Georgiana Keats, 18 September 1819, John Keats, *The Oxford Authors: John Keats*, ed. Elizabeth Cook, Oxford: Oxford University Press, 1990, p. 508.
2. John Keats to Charles Wentworth Dilke, 4 March 1820, John Keats, *The Oxford Authors: John Keats*, ed. Elizabeth Cook, Oxford: Oxford University Press, 1990, p. 526.
3. John Keats to J.H. Reynolds, 21 September 1819, John Keats, *The Oxford Authors: John Keats*, ed. Elizabeth Cook, Oxford: Oxford University Press, 1990, p. 493.
4. 3 November 1819, HO 42/198. 428.

Bibliography

MANUSCRIPT SOURCES

Public Record Office

The bulk of this book has been gleaned from Home Office records, and to a lesser extent from Foreign Office, Privy Council and Treasury Solicitor's Papers held at the Public Record Offices at Chancery Lane and Kew (which are eventually to be amalgamated). For the uninitiated researcher, the following hard-won comments may be of some help.

Files of papers are usually stored in chronologically ordered file numbers, but there are exceptions to this rule. I have principally used files in the series from HO 40 and 42. With respect to Home Office sources, the letters designate the archive (e.g. HO), the first set of numbers the class, the second set of numbers the piece, the third set the folio. The folio number is the most useful because the papers within any file will not be stored in chronological order but grouped together geographically; that is, by address or locality. The folio number will be a crucial piece of information for anyone cross-checking my work because dates and names are often missing or illegible. Sometimes folios have two or more sequential numbers: I have provided whichever number appears to be the dominant one in the series within that piece.

Pieces for the Home Office may cover periods of one or two months, or less, depending on the internal political climate of the time and the rate of correspondence. Correspondence from Yorkshire, for example, may be grouped together but may have the occasional insertion from London or elsewhere which interrupts the geographical sequence. Items such as petitions for pensions and queries to the Royal College of Arms are interspersed throughout. Some papers appear to be duplicated in different pieces. There may also have been a Home Office scribe who transcribed items into a more legible Department hand, to the loss of the original. At Chancery

Lane, which has the Treasury Solicitor's and Privy Council papers, files can be found, with difficulty, via the handbooks which give the name of the person indicted at trial. The materials gathered for the evidence of the Crown's prosecutions (the 1794 treason trials and LCS papers being a prime example) can be found here. Pamphlets, newspapers and other printed sources forwarded to the Home Office give a good idea of what local authorities considered to be dangerous and seditious. There appears to be some duplication of materials across the different archives. In the Public Record Office at Kew there is a handlist which provides a very brief description of some of the Cato Street conspiracy correspondence but there is very little other descriptive information on the contents. Papers associated with Arthur Thistlewood and his circle often have the handwritten mark 'Thistlewood Papers' on the folio and betray some past systematic attempt to identify all matters relative to him back to at least 1817. This is a useful, but not definitive, guide. In short, the archives for this important period of British history are pretty well unindexed and remain in an erratic state.

Other Manuscript Sources

British Museum Add. Ms. 27808 (containing LCS member Francis Place's notes, letters and cuttings gathered for his unwritten biography of Thomas Spence).

Dodd's *History of English Engravers*, British Museum Add. Ms. 33403.

Cullen, George, annotations (Spence, 1807). British Library Shelfmark 900. h. 24 (i).

CONTEMPORARY PRINTED SOURCES

The place of publication is London, unless otherwise stated.

Austen Jane (1818), *Northanger Abbey*, Harmondsworth: Penguin.

The Axe Laid to the Root, Or, a Fatal Blow to Oppressors, Being an Address to the Planters and Negroes of the Island of Jamaica (1817).

Black Dwarf (1820).

Davenport, Allen (1819), *The Kings, or Legitimacy Unmasked, A Satirical Poem*, copy in HO 42/202.

Davenport, Allen (1845), *The Life and Literary Pursuits of Allen Davenport, Author of the 'Muses Wreath', 'Life of Spense [sic]', &c., Written by Himself*. Aldermanbury: G. Hancock.

Davenport, Allen (1827), *The Muses Wreath: Composed of Original Poetry*, the Author.

Democratic Recorder (1818–19).

The Trial of Edward Marcus Despard, Esquire, For High Treason (1803), M. Gurney.

Bibliography

State Trials at Large (Taken in Short Hand), The Whole Proceedings on the Trials of Col. Despard, and the Other State Prisoners . . . With an APPENDIX, containing the Behaviour of the Convicts and a particular Account of their Execution (1803), R. Bent and John Mudie, 4th edn.

Evans, Thomas (?1811), *A Humorous Catalogue of SPENCE'S SONGS: Part the First, Part the Second, Part the Third.*

Evans, Thomas (1816), *Christian Policy, the Salvation of Empire,* 2nd edn, the Author.

Gentleman's Magazine (1796, 1797).

The Trial of Joseph Gerrald . . . For Sedition (1794), Edinburgh: J. Robertson; London: D.I. Eaton.

Hazard, Thomas (1819), *A True Picture of Society, As Displayed By Certain Rich Characters Towards Their Poor Neighbours. A Poem.* Copy in HO 44/5.

Hone, William (1819), *The Political House that Jack Built,* W. Hone.

Medusa (1819).

Mortimer, C.F. (?1803), *A Christian Effort To Exalt The Goodness Of The Divine Majesty, Even In A Momento, On Edward Marcus Despard, Esq. And Six Other Citizens, Undoubtedly now with God in Glory. An Heroic Poem: in Six Parts:* the Author, C.F. Mortimer, no.2, Temple-place, Blackfriars-road, Surrey.

Preston, Thomas (1817), *The Life and Opinions of Thomas Preston, Patriot and Shoemaker,* printed for the author by A. Seale.

Quarterly Review [October 1816]; that is (February 1817).

Reid, William Hamilton (1800), *The Rise and Dissolution of the Infidel Societies in this Metropolis,* J. Hatchard.

Republican (1824).

Sherwin's Political Register (1818).

Spence, Thomas (1793), *The Case of Thomas Spence, bookseller, The Corner of Chancery Lane, London: who was Committed to Clerkenwell Prison, on Monday the 10th of December, 1792, for Selling the Second Part of Paine's Rights of Man.*

Spence, Thomas (1793–95), *Pigs' Meat.*

Spence, Thomas (1795a), *The End of Oppression: or a Quartern Loaf for Twopence: Being a Dialogue between an Old Mechanic and a Young One, Concerning the Establishment of the Rights of Man.* T. Spence, 1st and 2nd edn.

Spence, Thomas (1795b), *A Letter from Ralph Hodge, To His Cousin Thomas Bull.*

Spence, Thomas (?1795c), *The Coin-Collector's Companion, being a Descriptive List of the Modern Provincial Political and Other Copper Coins,* T. Spence.

Spence, Thomas (1796), *Spence's Recantation of the Age of Oppression,* T. Spence.

Spence, Thomas (1797), *The Rights of Infants: Or, The Imprescriptable rights of Mothers to Such a Share of Elements as is sufficient to enable them to suckle and bring up their Young. In a Dialogue between the Aristocracy and a Mother of Children. To which are Added by Way of a Preface and Appendix, Strictures on Paine's Agrarian Justice,* the Author.

Spence, Thomas (1807), *The Important Trial of Thomas Spence for a Political Pamphlet Entitled 'The Restorer of Society to its Natural State', on May 27th, 1801, at Westminster Hall before Lord Kenyon and a Special Jury,* printed by A. Seale, 1st edn phonetic 1803; 2nd edn in English.

Theological Comet (1819).
The Trials of Arthur Thistlewood . . . (1820), Leeds: John Barr.
The Times.
Tooke, John Horne (1813–20), *State Trials*, vol. 25, eds T.B. and T.J. Howells.
Volney, M. (1826), *The Ruins: or, a Survey of the Revolutions of Empires*, Thomas Tegg.
The Trial of James Watson for High Treason . . . *taken in short hand by W.B. Gurney* (1817), 2 vols, M. Gurney.
Watson, James (1818), *More Plots, More Treason, More Green Bags: A Letter to Viscount Sidmouth*.
The Trial of the Rev. Robt. Wedderburn . . . *For Blasphemy* . . . *containing a verbatim report of the defence* (1820), ed. Erasmus Perkins [i.e. George Cannon].
The White Hat (1819).
Wilkinson, G.T. (1820), *The Cato-Street Conspiracy*, T. Kelly.

SECONDARY PRINTED SOURCES

Ashraf, P.M. (1983), *The Life and Times of Thomas Spence*, Newcastle: Frank Graham.
Beames, M.R. (1987), 'The Ribbon Societies: Lower-Class Nationalism in Pre-Famine Ireland', *Nationalism and Popular Protest in Ireland*, ed. C.H.E. Philpin, Cambridge: Cambridge University Press.
Bentley, G.E., Jnr (1977), *Blake Records*, Oxford: Clarendon Press.
Bentley, G.E., Jnr (1988), *Blake Records Supplement*, Oxford: Clarendon Press.
Bindman, David (1989), *The Shadow of the Guillotine: Britain and the French Revolution*, British Museum Publications.
Blake, William (1982), *The Complete Poetry and Prose of William Blake*, ed. David V. Erdman, New York: Anchor Press/Doubleday.
Brunel, Christopher and Jackson, Peter M. (1966), 'Notes on Tokens as a Source of Information on the History of the Labour and Radical Movement, Part I', *Bulletin of the Society for the Study of Labour History*, 13, pp. 26–40.
Burke, Peter (1983), 'The Virgin of the Carmine and the Revolt of Masaniello', *Past and Present*, 99, pp. 3–21.
Chase, Malcolm (1988), *'The People's Farm': English Radical Agrarianism, 1775–1840*, Oxford: Clarendon Press.
Connolly, S.J. (1982), *Priests and People in Pre-Famine Ireland, 1780–1845*, Dublin: Gill and Macmillan.
Cookson, J.E. (1989), 'The English Volunteer Movement of the French Wars, 1793–1815', *The Historical Journal*, 32, 4, pp. 867–91.
Corfield, Penelope J. (1991), 'Class by name and number in eighteenth-century Britain', *Language, History, Class*, ed. Penelope J. Corfield, Oxford: Basil Blackwell.
Elliott, Marianne (1977), 'The "Despard Conspiracy" Reconsidered', *Past and Present*, 75, pp. 46–61.

Bibliography

Elliott, Marianne (1989), *Wolfe Tone: Prophet of Irish Independence*, New Haven, CT: Yale University Press.

Emsley, Clive (1979) 'The Home Office and its sources of information and investigation 1791–1801', *English Historical Review*, XCIV, pp. 532–61.

Emsley, Clive (1981), 'An Aspect of Pitt's "Terror": prosecutions for sedition during the 1790s', *Social History*, 6, 2, pp. 155–84.

Emsley, Clive (1985), 'Repression, "terror" and the rule of law in England during the decade of the French Revolution', *English Historical Review*, 100, pp. 801–25.

Epstein, J. (1990), 'The Constitutional Idiom: Radical Reasoning, Rhetoric and Action in Early Nineteenth Century England', *Journal of Social History*, 23, pp. 554–74.

Erdman, David V. (1977), *Blake: Prophet Against Empire*, 1954, 3rd edn, Princeton: Princeton University Press.

Erdman, David V. (1986), *Commerce des Lumières: John Oswald and the British in Paris, 1790–1793*, Columbia: University of Missouri Press.

Essick, Robert N. (1991), *William Blake's Commercial Book Illustrations: A Catalogue and Study of the Plates Engraved by Blake after Designs by Other Artists*, Oxford: Clarendon Press.

Garvin, Tom (1987), 'Defenders, Ribbonmen and Others: Underground Political Networks in Pre-Famine Ireland', *Nationalism and Popular Protest in Ireland*, ed. C.H.E. Philpin, Cambridge: Cambridge University Press.

George, Dorothy, *Catalogue of Political and Personal Satires Preserved in the Department of Prints and Drawings in the British Museum* (1935–54), vols v–xi.

Goodwin, Albert (1979), *The Friends of Liberty: the English Democratic Movement in the Age of the French Revolution*, Hutchinson.

Holmes, Richard (1976), *Shelley: The Pursuit*, Quartet.

Hone, J. Ann (1982), *For the Cause of Truth: Radicalism in London, 1796–1821*, Oxford: Clarendon Press.

Hopkins, Robert (1978), 'General Tilney and Affairs of State: The Political Gothic of *Northanger Abbey*', *Philological Quarterly*, 57, pp. 213–24.

Keats, John (1990), *The Oxford Authors: John Keats*, Oxford: Oxford University Press.

McCalman, Iain (1987), 'Ultra-radicalism and Convivial Debating-clubs in London, 1795–1838', *English Historical Review*, 102, pp. 309–33.

McCalman, Iain (1988), *Radical Underworld: Prophets, Revolutionaries and Pornographers in London, 1795–1840*, Cambridge: Cambridge University Press.

McDowell, Robert Brendan (1979), *Ireland in the Age of Imperialism and Revolution, 1760–1801*, Oxford: Oxford University Press.

Mitchell, Austin (1961), 'The Association Movement of 1792–3', *The Historical Journal*, IV, I, pp. 56–77.

Olson, Alison G. *The Radical Duke: The Career and Correspondence of Charles Lennox, Third Duke of Richmond*, Oxford, 1961.

o Tuahaigh, Gearoid (1990), *Ireland Before the Famine, 1798–1848*, Dublin: Gill and Macmillan.

Pakenham, Thomas (1969), *The year of Liberty: The Story of the Great Irish Rebellion of 1798*, Hodder and Stoughton.

Prothero, Iowerth (1979), *Artisans and Politics in Early Nineteenth Century London: John Gast and his Times*, Folkestone: Dawson.

Roe, Nicholas (1988), *Wordsworth and Coleridge: The Radical Years*, Oxford: Oxford University Press.

Saussure, Ferdinand de, *Course in General Linguistics* (1915/1983), trans. Roy Harris, Duckworth.

Southey, Robert (1984), *Letters from England: by Don Manuel Alvarez Espriella, Translated from the Spanish*, ed. Jack Simmons (1951), Gloucester: Alan Sutton.

Stevens, John (1977), *England's Last Revolution: Pentrich 1817*, Buxton: Moorland Publishing.

Stevenson, John (1979), *Popular Disturbances in England, 1700–1870*, Longmans.

Storch, Robert D. (1982), '"Please to Remember the Fifth of November": Conflict, Solidarity and Public Order in Southern England, 1815–1900', *Popular Culture and Custom in Nineteenth-Century England*, ed. Robert D. Storch, Croom Helm.

Thale, Mary (1989), 'London Debating Societies in the 1790s', *The Historical Journal*, 31, 1, pp. 57–86.

Thompson, E.P. (1963/1980), *The Making of the English Working Class*, Harmondsworth: Penguin.

Thompson, R.H. (1969–70), 'The Dies of Thomas Spence (1750–1814)', *British Numismatic Journal*, XXXVIII, pp. 126–62.

Villari, Rosario (1985), 'Masaniello: Contemporary and Recent Interpretations', *Past and Present*, 108, pp. 117–32.

Wells, Roger (1983), *Insurrection: The British Experience 1795–1803*, Gloucester: Alan Sutton.

Williams, Gwyn A. (1989), *Artisans and Sans-Culottes: Popular Movements in France and Britain during the French Revolution*, London: Libris (1968), 2nd edn.

Youngquist, Paul (1989) *Madness and Blake's Myth*, Pennsylvania: Pennsylvania State University Press.

Unpublished Thesis

McCalman, Iain (1975), 'Popular Radicalism and Freethought in Early Nineteenth-Century England: A Study of Richard Carlile and his Followers, 1815–32', MA thesis, Australian National University.

Index

References to Thomas Spence and to Spenceans are too numerous to have been indexed.

Margarot, Maurice, sedition
transportee and returnee,
ultra, 13–15, 17, 31
McCabe, William Putnam, United
Irishman, 97
McCalman, Iain, historian, ix, 89,
129, 131, 144, 151, 165–6
Mcnamara, John, Despard executee,
53, 57, 66
McQueen, Robert, Lord Justice,
13–14
Masaniello, Neapolitan
insurrectionist, 23
Massey, ultra, 93
Mathewson, Matthew, informer,
141, 178
Medusa: or Penny Politician, 146–7,
151, 155–6, 159
Merlin's Cave, tavern, 97, 108
Miell, Charles, Bow Street runner,
106
Moggridge, Robert, ultra, tailor,
106, 161
Monteath, Rev. J., 176–7
Monument, Cato Street transportee,
196
Moody, John, alias 'Notary', spy,
ix, 18, 54, 58, 64, 111, 119
More, Hannah, author, 20
More, Sir Thomas, 10
Morning Post, 22–3
Mortimer, C.F., author, poet, 65–7
Muir, Thomas, sedition transportee,
15
Mulberry Tree, Long Alley,
Moorfields, tavern, (*see*
Johnsons), 95–6, 160, 167–8

Nag's Head, Carnaby Market,
tavern, 2, 104, 129–30
'Nature', Spencean meaning of,
151–4
Nepean, Sir Evan, under-secretary,
113
Nicolson, John, silversmith,
informer, 71

Nodder, Frederick Pollydore,
painter, engraver, spy,
(?gaoler), 19, 20–1, 29, 72–3,
111
Norcliffe, David, sedition
defendant, 70
'Notary', see Moody, John

Oakley Arms, Lambeth, tavern,
54–5
oaths, 6, 30, 58–9, 161, 187, 190–1
Observer, 98, 103
O'Coigley, Rev. James, United Irish
executee, 30
O'Connor, soldier, sedition accuser,
67
Oliver-the-Spy (W.J. Richards), 60
Owen, Robert, reformer, 130

Paine, Tom, author, 9–12, 23, 32,
71, 101, 131, 150, 173, 196
Palmer, Rev. Thomas Fysshe,
sedition transportee, 15
Panther, Jonathan, ultra,
coachmaker, 17–18
Parker, Richard, Nore mutiny
executee, 121–2
Pastorini prophecies, 50–1
Peachey, John, magistrate, 74
Pendrill, Charles, ultra, 121–2
Peterloo, Massacre of, 7, 29, 44, 88,
138, 141, 143–5, 159–63, 174
Pike, John, Despard witness, 59
pikes, 21, 116, 119, 143, 145, 147–8,
154–5, 161, 167, 175, 186
Pitts Place, Drury Lane, ?tavern/
coffee house, 169
Pitt, William, 20–1, 36, 45, 87
Place, Francis, reformer, 12, 25
Plush, William, Bow Street runner,
134–5, 140, 178
poetry and verse, 20, 23–7, 29, 43,
45–7, 65–7, 69, 78, 81–3,
85–6, 88, 95, 149–59, 165–6,
188–9, 195–6, 202
Pope, Alexander, 10, 82, 101